The Middle East Supply Centre

Commander Robert Jackson (1948 photo)
Director General, Middle East Supply Centre
1941–1945

The Middle East Supply Centre

By Martin W. Wilmington

Edited by Laurence Evans

Foreword by
Commander Sir Robert Jackson

Albany · State University of New York Press
London · University of London Press Ltd
1971

The Middle East Supply Centre

First Edition

Published by State University of New York Press
Thurlow Terrace, Albany, New York 12201
Copyright © 1961, 1971 by State University of New York
All rights reserved
ISBN *0-87395-081-X (clothbound)*
ISBN *0-87395-181-6 (microfiche)*
Library of Congress Catalog Card Number 70-136278
Printed in the United States of America

Contents

Foreword   ix

Preface   xvii

Acknowledgments   xxi

1. The Meaning of M.E.S.C.   1

2. The Shipping Crisis After the Fall of France   8

3. The Middle East Supply Problem in World War II   20

4. The Establishment of M.E.S.C.   32

5. America Joins M.E.S.C.   51

6. The Anglo-American Phase   64

7. The Control of Imports   84

8. Economic Mobilization of a Region   103

9. From Regional Coordination to Postwar Planning   140

10. Conclusion   163

Notes   169

M.E.S.C. Plan of Organization   204

Appendix A   206

Appendix B   211

Bibliography and Other Sources   219

Index   243

Foreword

ALTHOUGH this book discusses events that took place more than twenty-five years ago, there are at least three compelling reasons for publishing it, and I am happy to have been invited to contribute these prefatory comments.

The first reason for publishing the book is its historical value from the military, political, and economic points of view. Although the achievements of the Middle East Supply Centre were generously acknowledged at the time by those responsible for the great issues of military strategy and operations, little reference to its work will be found in the official histories of World War II; the explanation for this probably arises from the fact that those most directly concerned were quickly swept into the vast problems of postwar rehabilitation and reconstruction and had no time to write about their experiences. As I shall make clear later on, a great debt is owed to the late Professor Martin Wilmington for his most scholarly and comprehensive research, without which historical material of great value would almost certainly have been lost.

In terms of military history, the success of M.E.S.C.'s work has been officially recognized as "an indispensable condition both to achieving the necessary flow of supplies to Soviet Russia and to winning the battle of El Alamein." During a visit to Moscow in May 1970, it was interesting to observe, during the celebrations of the twenty-fifth anniversary of V-E Day, that the Soviet authorities still refer to this work and appreciate its contribution to the victory of the Allies.

In terms of political history, there is no doubt that the Centre materially contributed to the preservation of stability by ensuring, at all times—even during the most severe military crises—that the inhabitants of the region (there were more than 100,000,000 of them) were properly fed and clothed, and that essential medical supplies were available. Great changes were made in agricultural production in order to reduce imports; industrial facilities were directed to the needs of the Armed Services; the entire transport system was mobilized for the movement of munitions, yet at no time was there any breakdown in meeting the essential needs of the civilian population.

In an even more direct political sense, it is generally agreed that this great regional operation stimulated the imagination of political leaders in the Middle East, and directly influenced the establishment of the Arab League.

As the tide of war started to recede from this most sensitive strategic area, a unique opportunity was presented to the British and American governments to formulate constructive policies for the postwar phase. A few individual officials in London and Washington saw this opportunity, but, at the highest levels, the necessary vision, imagination, and statesmanship were lacking and what could well have been a turning point in history was lost. It is not too much to say that had this opportunity been seized, the tragedy of the Middle East—which has already brought untold agony and suffering to millions of people for nearly a quarter of a century—might well have been averted.

From a politico-economic point of view, several influential leaders advocated at this time (1943) that M.E.S.C.'s wartime organization should be transformed into a permanent peacetime institution, with a fundamental objective of stimulating economic and social development throughout the region. One of the great advantages of this development, so they argued, was that the large number of Jewish refugees who would certainly wish to migrate to Palestine as soon as the war ended would be absorbed much more easily. While I was convinced that some sort of organization—primarily staffed from the Middle Eastern countries themselves—should continue in peacetime, I never believed that any economic measures could resolve the basic difficulties inherent in the Palestine problem. It has always seemed to me that basic political agreement between the leaders of the Arab and Jewish people was, and remains, an essential prerequisite to any effective economic cooperation, and I feel that many of the most ardent advocates of regional action seriously underestimated the extent to which our wartime achievements were made possible by political agreements that existed solely because of the dominance of foreign military power. This is not to argue against the advantages of regional cooperation, for they are obvious, but such cooperation must be genuine and reflect direct political support, and not depend on the temporary and artificial pressure of a military presence.

I hope the reader will forgive me for introducing these reflections of a personal nature, for my own life was to remain related both to the Middle East and to the United Nations, in greater or less degree, for many years to come.

During the life of the United Nations Relief and Rehabilitation Administration (UNRRA) from 1945 to 1948, we dealt with some 8,500,000 displaced persons—primarily in Europe, but also in the Middle East and Asia. Large numbers of these people had endured unbelievable treatment in the concentration camps, and many of them were Jews. No one could fail to understand their passionate desire to go to Palestine and there to recreate new lives for themselves, but those who knew something of the Middle East realized the supreme political skill that would need to be exercised if yet another tragedy were not to occur.

Once more, by chance, I found myself at the heart of affairs in the United Nations, when its headquarters were at Lake Success, in May 1948. The cataclysmic political developments at that time are well known—the declaration of the establishment of the state of Israel, the recognition of the new state by the Great Powers, and the inevitable reaction of the Arab States. In those days and weeks as (so I believed) I saw the seeds of endless conflict and suffering being sown, I naturally reflected on that unique political opportunity which had existed only five years before and which might well have avoided one of the great political disasters of this century. Predicting political unrest and war in the Middle East for possibly fifty years (a generation and more) I was unable to arrive at an agreed position with the Secretary-General on this critical issue, and because of this and other reasons, my appointment was terminated. About the same time, my friend Count Folke Bernadotte went to his death in full knowledge of what must almost inevitably happen to him—a man of supreme courage and complete dedication. That was the tragedy of one man, but immeasurably worse was to follow when hundreds of thousands of Arabs became refugees with, apparently, very little hope of ever knowing a normal life again. Many of us have thus witnessed one of the most terrible tragedies and cruellest ironies of history: First the endless suffering of the Jewish people and now the endless tragedy of the Arabs.

If the political opportunities created by M.E.S.C.'s operations were lost, a considerable number of lasting economic dividends remained. In subsequent years, they have become so important that by themselves they provide the second justification for publishing this book. Within the region itself there was an impressive transfer of scientific and technological knowledge and experience. M.E.S.C. was fortunate in having a most talented staff, and to a large extent this was made possible by the enlightened use of manpower by the military leaders who encouraged us, at all times, to analyze the professional qualifications of any of the men and women serving in the theatre—there were well over a million of them—and let us have our pick. As a result, everyone was better off: The individuals' talents were put to the best use, the military effort was increased (in relative terms) and, ultimately, the people of the Middle East profited. Agricultural production and productivity were both improved significantly; the infrastructure was immeasurably strengthened; the national resources of oil were used to much greater advantage; the beginnings of industrialization were set in train; and direct support was given to those struggling with the great problems of health and sanitation. The first technical conferences ever held on a regional basis in the Middle East were initiated; some excellent books dealing with specific problems were produced, and many nationals living in the area were given special training.

It is not surprising, therefore, that those responsible for formulating the initial policies of the various organs of the United Nations system in the field of economic cooperation should have studied carefully the experience of the Middle East Supply Centre. As this book points out, the concept and formation of the four United Nations Economic Commissions in Europe, Latin America, the Far East and Africa were much influenced by M.E.S.C.'s achievements, and, as time went by, these Commissions adopted many of the Centre's techniques. The Commissions, however, have had an immeasurably more difficult task in securing regional cooperation for, as I have emphasized, many of M.E.S.C.'s results were made possible by the existence in the background of decisive military power. In the narrower, but profoundly important Middle Eastern region, the United Nations later on established (in 1963) an office in Beirut to deal with economic and social problems (U.N.E.S.O.B.) and that organization has already provided valuable services to the area, very much on the lines of some of M.E.S.C.'s operations. So, too, has the British Middle East Office (also based in Beirut) and now forming part of the British Embassy there. This office is a direct successor, in a very modest way, to M.E.S.C.'s pioneering efforts. The mere existence of these two offices, particularly U.N.E.S.O.B., is convincing evidence that the demand for the technical cooperation and services provided in time of war by M.E.S.C. has carried on—and, indeed, increased dramatically—in the succeeding years, despite all the political and economic changes that have continued to characterize the history of this part of the world.

It must be a matter of profound satisfaction to all concerned to know that many of the operations initiated by M.E.S.C. continued into the postwar years. Several of the most important of them are still active. The construction of the Owen Falls scheme at the headwaters of the Nile, the development of the Litani River in the Lebanon, and the surveys of several other rivers, such as the Awash, are lasting memorials. I am no lover of committees, but I understand that the joint committee established in Addis Ababa in 1942 to facilitate cooperation in dealing with problems of health and sanitation in Ethiopia, has done much valuable work and is still meeting regularly. Many of the projects advocated by the Centre's scientific adviser, Dr. E. Barton Worthington, have carried on steadily during the last quarter of a century; so, too, have many of the changes in the field of agriculture advanced by Dr. Keith A. H. (now Lord) Murray, Dr. Dunstan Skilbeck, and Sir Bernard Keen. The work initiated by the late Sir Norman Wright in the field of animal husbandry has developed into an active scientific and economic element in the area, and the whole complex of animal disease diagnostic centers, which have now developed with United Nations Development Programme support and the active participation of nine Governments and the Food and Agriculture Organization of the United Nations (F.A.O.), is now coordinated by an international unit in Beirut—the Near East Animal Health Institute.

Of all these continuing activities, probably none has achieved so much, nor commanded so much attention, as the Anti-Locust campaign. This operation, initiated in 1942, with the support of every government concerned, and ably assisted in the field by tens of thousands of men (including soldiers enjoying "rest" periods!) and aircraft from the United States, Great Britain, Iran, and Iraq, was of critical importance in that particular year. The great onslaughts by locusts appear to conform to a cycle of 16 years. In 1926 there had been an extraordinary devastation of crops, and all the breeding reports indicated that the threat in 1942 would be no less. If the great campaign against them had not succeeded, the Commanders-in-Chief undoubtedly would have been faced either with civil unrest, through the lack of bread, with all its implications for internal security, or with the reduction of the vital flow of munitions through the Red Sea (for El Alamein) and the Persian Gulf (for the U.S.S.R.), in order to import grain. Once more, the military commanders demonstrated an enlightened understanding of the disconcerting fact that locusts had to be fought as well as the forces of the Axis, and made available men and vehicles by the thousands, together with all the necessary supplies. Now, twenty-eight years later, as I write this in Rome, I have just noticed (in a conference room of F.A.O.) a large meeting of international experts still busy with their never-ending battle against an extremely tough and persevering enemy. I am naturally glad, through my association with the United Nations Development Programme, to have joined in the support given to forty-four governments and to F.A.O. in a major ten-year project to bring the desert locust under control. It is encouraging to learn that no swarms of the desert locust have been reported for several years and the success of this work has affected the well-being of tens of millions of people across the globe from Afghanistan to the Atlantic.

The book illustrates clearly what has now become a basic principle in the process of achieving successful development—the exercise of infinite skill and care in securing the maximum efficiency in the utilization of available resources. By 1940 this principle had already been dramatically demonstrated in utilizing the resources required for the defense of Malta—all waste and nonessential consumption had been eliminated, and local resources were being used in such a way that imports could be reduced by 90 per cent. (This achievement by the people of Malta was a decisive factor in the success of the naval convoys that supplied the fortress, and made history at the same time.) It was the application of this fundamental principle throughout the Middle East which determined the success of M.E.S.C.'s operations. Gradually, the same lesson has been learned as a result of the enormous efforts made during the last twenty years in endeavoring to mobilize the resources of the Third World, and it is fascinating, against the background of our experience during World War II to study today a recent resolution of the General Assembly of the United Nations which elaborates this principle admirably. I am convinced that the successful implementation of that resolution would do more than anything else—apart from massive disarmament—to bring peace and a reasonable degree of social justice to this world.

And so I come to the third reason for publishing this book. Each reader can make his own balance sheet of the profits and losses which were derived from the experience of a unique organization. It is difficult to disagree with the conclusion that a historic opportunity was lost in the political sense, but there are consolations in the important economic dividends which have been derived for so many years. But whatever the reader's conclusions, there will be general agreement that this book should be considered as a tribute to all the men and women from many countries who contributed to M.E.S.C.'s achievement. More specifically, however, I hope that it will be regarded as a lasting memorial to the scholarship of Professor Wilmington. Twenty years have passed since he first came to me with his proposal that the history of M.E.S.C. should be subjected to a thorough and objective analysis. For the best part of the next ten years, when he could absent himself from his other professional work, he devoted himself to a process of painstaking and precise research which took him to all parts of the world which had been concerned with the Centre's work. His sudden death, just at the end of his research and initial drafting of his manuscript, was sheer tragedy.

Through the efforts of his widow, Mrs. Paulette B. Wilmington, the manuscript was brought to the attention of the State University of New York Press, which subsequently agreed to publish the work. The manuscript was prepared for publication by Professor Laurence Evans of the State University of New York at Binghamton, who added new material to the study following examination of official documents in the archives of the U.S. Department of State and other material which had not yet been made public at the time of Professor Wilmington's research. Both Mrs. Wilmington and Professor Evans deserve our highest appreciation for helping preserve this record of the Middle East Supply Centre.

R. G. A. JACKSON

Preface

THE topic of the dissertation upon which this book is based was selected in 1951 in the belief that its discussion would contribute to the work and objectives of what was then the United Nations and World Affairs Program of New York University. In those days, the regional economic commissions of the United Nations attracted relatively little attention. Inasmuch as the Middle East Supply Centre must be considered as a historic episode that did much to project the concept of economic regionalism into the processes of international organization after World War II, a detailed history of this agency was believed to be of value for an understanding of the concept itself. In the intervening years, economic regionalism inside and outside the United Nations has grown ceaselessly in stature and status as an international formula; the number of regional economic commissions of the United Nations has doubled and regional meetings and working sessions are held with increasing frequency by the organization and its affiliated agencies.

The necessity of leaving the text as unencumbered as possible has forced upon the writer the practice of using the term "Middle East" in a somewhat volatile manner. Definitions of this term abound. In general, this writer has followed a method suggested by Dr. Keith A. H. Murray, who was Director of the Food and Agriculture Division of the Middle East Supply Centre. According to Dr. Murray's plan, the Centre, for its own operational purposes, distinguished two regions in the Middle East which were defined as follows:

> The *Inner Circle* consisted of (a) the Fertile Crescent, containing Iraq, Syria and Lebanon, Palestine and Transjordan; (b) the Lower Nile Valley, Egypt, Northern Sudan, and ultimately, when annexed by the Eighth Army, Cyrenaica and Tripolitania; and (c) the Arabian Peninsula, including the Persian

Gulf Sheikdoms, the responsibility for certain food of which was transferred to the Centre when the Indian food position became serious at the beginning of 1943. The *Outer Circle* consisted of (*a*) a northern zone, comprising Cyprus, Turkey and Iran; and (*b*) a southern zone, consisting of southern Sudan, Ethiopia, Eritrea and the Somalias.[1]

Generally, when discussing the Middle East in historic perspective, this study refers to the area comprised by the *Inner Circle* plus Iran; when the term is used in connection with operations and projects of the Middle East Supply Centre both the Inner and the Outer Circle are encompassed.

The list of persons that have given more than perfunctory assistance is too large to be reproduced here in detail. Just to acknowledge the kindness of the many who consented to lengthy interviews in the middle of their important current preoccupations would require pages. But the following cannot be left unmentioned without exposing the writer to the charge of ingratitude and undue usurpation of credit:

Sir Robert Jackson, George Woodbridge, and Ambassador Avraham Harman of Israel, in addition to granting interviews, paved the way with many valuable introductions. Marshall Macduffie and Ambassador William S. Culbertson opened their private papers and offered many helpful comments and analyses. During a study tour of the Middle East in 1954 the Governments of the Sudan and Israel, and the British Middle East Office granted access to important state papers; the Sudanese authorities also provided free transportation to places outside Khartoum. Valuable documentary help was given during visits to the Eliezer Kaplan Institute for Economic Research at Hebrew University in Jerusalem and the Royal Institute of International Affairs in London. Professor Thomas J. Hovet and Miss Carol C. Moor of New York University gave much needed guidance on United Nations affairs and documents. The sagacity and friendly concern of Professor John E. Flaherty, of Pace College, has cleansed the text of much surplus weight and loose thinking. My wife helped in a thousand ways.

A special tribute is due to the late Dr. Taraknath Das, a professor at New York University and founder of the Taraknath Das Foundation. As a teacher he rekindled my interest in scholarly studies and research; as a man he set an example of devotion to the cause of friendship among races; through his foundation he made possible a trip to the Middle East that was pivotal to an understanding of the forces and facts conjured in this study. To him who encouraged this project, witnessed its modest beginnings, and incessantly spurred it on to its conclusion, the finished product—for whose failings of course he does not answer—is dedicated in respectful memory and veneration.

MARTIN W. WILMINGTON
February 1960

Acknowledgments

THE editor of this volume wishes to express his appreciation to Commander Sir Robert Jackson of the United Nations, Professor John P. Dawson of the Law School of Harvard University, Professors John S. Badeau and Charles Issawi of the Middle East Institute, Columbia University, Professor Richard H. Dekmejian of the State University of New York at Binghamton, and Professor Harold F. Peterson of the State University College at Buffalo for reading the manuscript and making many useful suggestions.

LAURENCE EVANS

The Middle East Supply Centre

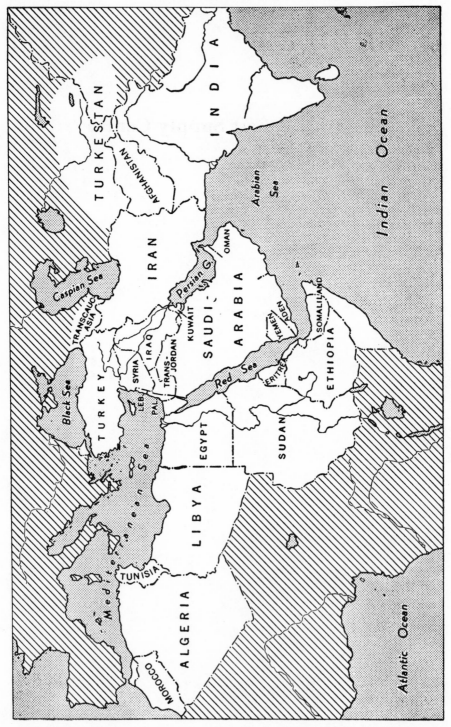

The Middle East

Map by courtesy of *The Middle East Journal*.

1

The Meaning of M.E.S.C.

THE story of the Middle East Supply Centre (M.E.S.C.) has many threads and many meanings. It is a story of how the war against the Axis brought forth bold and ingenious initiatives. It demonstrates how "under great stress, men were capable of organized efforts commensurate with the magnitude of the task with which they were confronted. They developed loyalties toward higher goals and the larger group which ordinary times do not readily foster." [1] It is a story of underdeveloped nations to whom the war and its aftermath brought a sudden bonus of foreign munificence resulting in great political and economic advances. It is a chapter in the long chronicle of Anglo-American relations, that procession of counterpoints in the comradeship of two nations irresistibly united when one is in jeopardy and promptly diverging when the danger is passed.

M.E.S.C. is a milestone in the effort to achieve unity in the Middle East. Throughout history violence and conquest have joined the peoples and races of this subcontinent in political union only to tear them asunder again and again. World War II once more set into motion the forces of union and M.E.S.C. was a major though now almost forgotten instrument.

The Centre was a monument to the soldiers of supply. In the twentieth century, more than at any time before, victory in war follows upon superiority in industry and logistics. But only the historian's labor can commit to lasting memory the great deeds of deskbound men who won crucial battles by the priming and prompting of unused or unready resources.

M.E.S.C. was one of several wartime organizations which greatly influenced the evolution of a new form of international cooperation. Historically it demands attention as an outstanding example of economic regionalism—a formula of government-sponsored international economic relationships which has gained wide theoretical and practical acceptance since World War II and has given the world a network of new interstate arrangements. The regional formula has assumed great stature in the orientation and organization of the United Nations, particularly because of the activities of the four regional economic commissions.

Before World War II, the "Middle East" as spoken of today had been in practically nobody's lexicon or map of political geography. Political control over most of the area then was directly or indirectly in the hands of two strongly antagonistic European powers which, with varying degrees of success, had tried to integrate the economics and politics of their ward lands into empires beyond the seas. As a result, for instance, the economy of Syria had closer relations with France than with neighboring Turkey. Among some members of the indigenous intelligentsia there had been a feebly sustained movement of Arab nationalism of World War I vintage, but in 1939 divisions among Arabs were just as strong as unity impulses; national independence then was a far more potent rallying point of anti-colonial elements in each country than Arab or regional unity, and of all the Arab countries, Egypt seemed to be the least interested in a close partnership with other Arabs. The very term "Middle East" was not in general use until somebody in London contrived the term in 1939 as a convenient geographic reference for a military command to be set up in Cairo with a small staff under General Wavell having formal jurisdiction over the Eastern Mediterranean and parts of East Africa. Before then the term had been employed infrequently and inconsistently to designate either the Levant States or the area made up by Iran, Iraq, and Afghanistan.

With the advent and spread of hostilities, countries and whole continents were gradually isolated from their principal sources of seaborne supplies, either because of a blockade and submarine warfare or because of the general dearth of shipping. In consequence, they had to find substitute suppliers in nearby areas, within the reach of land transport or shorter sea routes of small exposure to the enemy. The regional reorientation of trade that followed this search led in due course to schemes attempting a regional pooling of resources, talent, and policies, all aimed at effecting the needed readjustments with a minimum of waste and duplication.

In the Anglo-American sphere logistics and supply never reached the centralization observable in either the European or the Asian compound of the Axis. The armies of the Commonwealth and the United States fought on the periphery of the two vast fortress areas, without the benefit of interior lines of communications, under highly autonomous local commanders, with liaison that was faulty, and with communications links that were often precarious. While a measure of coordination existed in the making of high Anglo-American strategy and in the allocations of munitions, civilian goods and shipping, there was no single comprehensive organization directly representing all the Allies (with or without the Soviet Union and China) for mobilizing and utilizing to the utmost their aggregate resources. This encouraged the creation of smaller, geographically limited systems of economic mobilization oriented primarily toward specific theaters of operations. Often these systems were under joint Anglo-American direction and the executory agencies staffed by binational personnel.[2]

The trend toward economic integration set into motion by these agencies was in some cases reinforced by the emergence of the Regional Ambassador. The first appointment of this kind occurred in 1941 when Mr. Churchill sent Capt. Oliver Lyttleton to Cairo as his personal representative with the rank of Minister of State for the Middle East. There he acted simultaneously as the political arm and civilian supervisor of the British forces arrayed in the Middle East. His instructions gave him authority to "coordinate the policy of British representatives" in Egypt, the Sudan, Palestine, Transjordan, Iraq, Ethiopia, British Somaliland, Eritrea and ex-Italian Somaliland, Cyprus, the Levant States (when occupied) and, later, Malta, Aden, and Yemen; this meant in practice that Britain had in the Middle East a high-ranking diplomat of cabinet rank who could settle promptly matters which jointly involved several political authorities or territories. Financial and economic warfare as well as the economic health of the nations and territories included in the jurisdiction of the Middle East Command were high on the list of his coordinating duties and active preoccupations.[3]

Following the example set in the Middle East, Ministers of State were later appointed for West Africa, Southeast Asia, North Africa, and the United States. With the exception of the appointee in Washington, these regional ambassadors substantially functioned like Captain Lyttleton and his successors in Cairo.[4] The activities of their economic staffs set a new pattern for the performance of British representations abroad, not only because of their departure from the habitual country-by-country approach, but because of their breach with the service objectives of commercial attachés and consular officials. The latter traditionally had been the principal economic representatives of Britain in foreign lands. Their main function had been the promotion of trade. The economic attachés in the service of the Ministers of State, however, placed major emphasis on a grasp of the economic and social factors which shaped the political behavior of the nations they observed; they could therefore brief their government more competently on a wide range of economic policy tools—aid as well as trade—useful in the pursuit of political and military objectives.[5]

The British example was emulated by the United States with the appointment in 1943 of James M. Landis as Director of American Economic Operations in the Middle East with the rank of Minister; of John M. Hauser as the American counterpart to Lord Swinton, British Minister of State in West Africa; and of Robert D. Murphy as co-chairman of the North African Economic Board. As head of the American Economic Mission to the Middle East, Dean Landis and his office offered a regional focus for a host of U.S. economic representations in Cairo and other Middle Eastern centers, including the local lend-lease, economic warfare, and war shipping missions. As chief U.S. representative on the Middle East Supply Centre he threw the weight of American support behind the policy of regional economic integration pursued by that agency.[6]

The claim of the Middle East Supply Centre to a special place in the history of economic regionalism since 1939 rests on the scope, the success, and the resonance of its deeds.

From 1941 to 1945, the Middle East Supply Centre developed and administered a program of centralized overseas trade control and economic mobilization in the vast area defended by the British Middle East Command with two basic purposes: (1) to reduce the use of Allied shipping for ocean-borne imports of civilian goods in the Middle East, freeing shipping space needed for military supplies, and (2) to minimize the inevitable civilian hardships caused by the sharp reduction of overseas imports. The region serviced by the Centre was larger than the continental United States (see map facing p. 1). It included Malta, Cyprus, Lebanon, Syria, Palestine, Transjordan, Iraq, Iran, Saudi Arabia, Aden, Yemen, the sheikhdoms of the Arabian Peninsula, the Somalilands, Eritrea, Ethiopia, the Sudan, Egypt, Cyrenaica, Tripolitania, and Turkey.[7] Its jurisdiction comprised a complex mosaic of countries and territories of varied political status—sovereign states, colonies, protectorates, League of Nations mandates, a condominium, and former enemy lands under Allied military administration. The population living in this domain numbered nearly 100 million.

The success of the M.E.S.C. scheme is attested by statistics as well as official testimony. From a peacetime level of five million tons per year, civilian imports from overseas to the Middle East Command sector were reduced to little more than one million tons without causing any serious hardships to the civilian population or breeding dangerous civilian unrest.[8] This saving in shipping space made possible an acceleration and expansion of military shipments to the Middle East and other theaters at crucial junctures of the war. The governments of the United States and Great Britain officially acknowledged this with the declaration that

> It is believed that the success of the Supply Centre was an indispensable condition both to achieving the necessary flow of supplies to Soviet Russia and to winning the battle of El Alamein.[9]

The services rendered directly and indirectly to the civilian population were praised both by Allied and independent Middle Eastern spokesmen; [10] one of the many eulogies credited the Centre for having saved "millions of human beings" from starvation.[11]

M.E.S.C. left a notable impact not only on regionalist thinking and self-identification in the Middle East (see chap. 8) but was frequently cited as a model for economic cooperation in other regions of the world. Typical of the influence of the M.E.S.C. record was an extraordinary tribute paid by the London *Economist*. In the fall of 1943, this great and respected publication celebrated its 100th anniversary with twelve special essays on the theme "Towards the Second Century." From the lofty perspective of one hundred years of history, the *Economist* presented its choice of those policies and institutions which, it believed, could bring hope and progress to Britain and the world in the long decades to follow the most violent war in the annals of man. The Middle East Supply Centre was given the signal honor of being the subject of an entire essay, under the title "An International Example." [12]

Three years after the conclusion of the war, Barbara Ward, in her book *The West At Bay*,[13] recalled the operations of M.E.S.C. to the minds of those who were seeking a solution for the reconstruction and hard currency problems of Western Europe. She wrote:

> The Middle East Supply Center dealt with problems not altogether dissimilar from those which will face Western Europe. The basic problem of unavailable imports is common to both;

the fact that the chief limiting factor in the Middle East was shipping, while in Western Europe it is dollars, does not entirely alter the principles upon which any program of conservation, allocation and alternative supply should be based. The Middle East faced, in its modest way, the problem of increasing local production to replace supplies no longer available from overseas, and this is a problem which the central body of Western Europe must tackle on a vastly enlarged scale if some 2 billion dollars are to be cut out of its import programs by 1951. The Supply Center showed that governments as relatively backward and as technically ill-equipped as those, say, of Saudi Arabia or Iraq, could be coaxed and cajoled into using their allotted supplies to good advantage and improving local distribution in an area in which, even in peacetime, the blackest of markets found their natural habitat. In an area as much more developed, civilized, and sophisticated as Western Europe, a similar achievement should not be impossible. For the chief lesson of the Middle East Supply Center is both a simple and a very encouraging one. The organization worked. It fulfilled its aims, it maintained reasonable prosperity and considerable stability behind the Allied lines and, had it been developed on the basis of genuine Anglo-American understanding, it might still be an instrument of cooperation in the Middle East. And if under such relatively unpromising conditions, rationing, allocating, cutting back, developing local resources, relating needs to availabilities could be achieved, there is surely hope for a similar success with an infinitely stronger, better backed and better equipped organization in Western Europe.

The Middle East Supply Centre was the companion piece of two historic initiatives of the United Kingdom, both of which left an enduring imprint on the evolution of political regionalism in the Middle East: The creation of a Middle East Command (which among other things gave the region a rallying name) and the public support of the cause of Arab Unity, dramatized by the long remembered speech of Foreign Secretary Anthony Eden at Mansion House in London, on 29 May 1941.[14] If judged by political consequences, the resonance of this speech was not dissimilar to that of the Balfour Declaration. It revived various suggestions and schemes for Arab federation, among them the "Greater Syria" project of Nuri al-Said; and it was a reference mark for British aid and encouragement to the formation of the Arab League. Within this design the avenues of economic cooperation blazed by the Middle East Supply Centre had a prominent place and its contribution was recognized by Arab delegates attending the founding conference of the Arab League in Alexandria in 1944.[15] Even though in the postwar surge of anti-Westernism Britain's political contribution has received only sneering acknowledgment by Arab writers, the accomplishments of the Middle East Supply Centre have received their grudging due nevertheless. According to one Arab writer, the establishment of M.E.S.C. was "a concrete indication to people living in that area of the advantages of organizing their economy on a regional basis." [16] The same point is made by another Arab essayist who adds parenthetically that "from economic to political regionalism was a short step." [17] Official Israeli opinion, from the perspective of the postwar years, praises the work of M.E.S.C. as of "great benefit to Jewish Palestine in that it aided considerably its advance in industrial developments." [18] During the war, when the die of Arab-Jewish relations was not yet cast, Judah L. Magnes, president of Hebrew University of Jerusalem, was hopeful that in the days of postwar reconstruction the Middle East Supply Centre would bring to realization a formula of regional cooperation restoring amity to the two races.[19]

More than a quarter of a century has passed since the Middle East Supply Centre was disbanded and the countries so intimately involved in its work decided to go their separate ways in the Middle East. The intervening years of dissension, war, and hatred have denied the promise of M.E.S.C., and the hopes of those who created it and whose labors made it, for a few short years at least, a working model of Middle East cooperation. But certainly it was not in vain. The role of M.E.S.C. in the victory over the Axis powers is reason enough for those who built it from the ground up out of nothing more tangible than hope and determination to feel pride in their work. Though the past has no guarantees for the future, it can show, if not what will happen, what might happen. The history of M.E.S.C. shows what has been done and what could be done in the Middle East, and, more important perhaps for our present problems, by recording the reasons for the successes and for the ultimate abandonment of M.E.S.C. it might throw some light on what must be done to solve the present problems of the Middle East.

2

The Shipping Crisis
after the Fall of France

The Legacy of Laggard Mobilization

"The expulsion of the last Nazis from Stalingrad, completed by 2 February 1943, removed the enemy threat to the Middle East from the north as El Alamein had done from the west. Supply tipped the scales in both battles that saved the Middle East." So states the official United States Army history of the Middle East Theater, referring to the decisive impact of the supplies shipped from Britain and the United States across the seas to the armies of Zhukov and Montgomery.[1] In order for supply to sway the battle, factories must produce it and ships must carry it; a vast Anglo-American logistic effort brought this about in time to decide the fate of the Middle East. In the success of this effort the operations of the Middle East Supply Centre were "an indispensable aid." [2]

It was the British who created the Middle East Supply Centre, in Cairo in April 1941. In the British Isles, the period between the declaration of war and the French surrender at Compiègne had been a *sitzkrieg* not only in the military sense but in terms of economic preparation as well. Logistic mobilization had proceeded slowly. It is true that the refusal to be hurried was in part inspired by the commendable determination not to emulate the calamitous haste with which France had manhandled her economy for the sake of raising the numerical strength of her battalions.[3] Nevertheless there is no denying the overwhelming evidence that at the same time there was a failure to assess in earnest the full implications of the battle strength and militarized economic potential of the Axis.[4]

There seems to be an Iron Law of Strategic Behavior which makes Western democracies always one war late in preparing for their defense. Only late in World War I did England finally learn that modern war was total war. Again, it was only late in World War II that Britain and her Western Allies began to understand that total mobilization meant global mobilization.

By mid-1940, Germany and her allies had under their control a population of nearly 225 million; at the height of their penetration in Russia the number was 355 million.[5] In sheer weight of numbers, the British Empire alone could more than match this count, but while the Axis worked to draw on every wellspring of power in the men and resources under its flag, the British made only timid claims on the huge overseas lands and populations arrayed in their camp.[6]

It was true of course that one could not compare Africans and Asians with Europeans in terms of immediate usefulness for war production; certainly British dependencies could not on a par with Axis satellites "sustain a ponderous mobilization." [7] But as later developments were to prove, the capacity for military and productive contributions of the Empire was grossly underrated. A British critic recalls how in 1942 the Indian government thought the maximum force which India could equip was 100,000; an air force of nine planes with Indian pilots was considered "ambitious"; and the production of ships, automobiles, and aircraft was considered "impossible." All this was thoroughly revised later, under the pressure of unforeseen events, and India ultimately equipped and maintained a fighting force of 2.5 million.[8]

The whole question of Empire-wide defense production and levies had been seriously examined at the Imperial Defense Conference following the watershed year of 1936 and the reoccupation of the Rhineland. It is interesting to review the excuses given then for rejecting the notion of a large military buildup outside the British Isles. It was argued that to create substantial war production capacity in the dominions and colonies—most of which were only modestly industrialized and dependent on technical and capital assistance—would entail the commitment of British manpower and equipment. Since the rearmament decided upon after Hitler's march into the Rhineland would tax all of Britain's skills and resources, an Empire buildup could, it was felt, be accomplished only by subtractions from the buildup in Britain. The planners in London strongly held to the view that this would greatly diminish the effective military strength of the Empire and harm the economy of Britain, for the following reasons:

1. Time would be lost because of the need to ship machinery

and specialists to the overseas places where new plants were to be set up.

2. Getting such plants into production in semi-industrialized countries would require far longer break-in periods than in highly industrialized Great Britain, not to speak of superior efficiency which was expected to prevail in comparable British plants for a long time to come.

3. Still more time would be lost in shipping armaments produced overseas back to Britain and allied France where the brunt of any warfare with Germany was likely to be borne.

4. Since the output of war material in the dominions and colonies—just as in Britain—would be the job of private industry, and since considerable retooling and possibly reduction or even abandonment of normal production would be required, a program of military output could only be carried by the private companies involved if they were presented with long-term contracts of considerable volume—and this the meager defense budgets of the United Kingdom did not permit.

5. Unemployment in the semi-skilled and unskilled trades still was high in Britain at the start of the defense program, and the diversion of munitions orders to other lands could have aroused popular resentment which in turn would have strengthened the position of the pacifist labor opposition.

6. The new industrial capacity created in other Commonwealth countries would certainly not be dismantled after their use for armament production had ceased; a pressure for protectionist measures might ensue that would endanger the export markets so vital to the mother country. Thus, without causing any net increase in war-making capacity in the short run—and in the critical world situation prevailing after 1936 short-run results were perhaps the only ones that would matter to the defense of Britain—the decentralization of war production could mortgage the long-term economic future of the mother country.[9]

These were weighty and eminently plausible arguments. But they slighted one crucial factor: shipping. In a global war, the effectiveness of munitions output concentrated in Britain would only be as great as the ability of her merchant fleet to carry the arms to the fronts. When the weirs were down in that grim summer of 1940, with the Mediterranean closed and Hitler's submarines and planes operating from French and Italian bases, this task was clearly beyond the capabilities of the fleet.

Criticism of the excessive metropolitan orientation of British economic mobilization erupted after the fall of France. The most vocal spokesman was a distinguished scion of the older generation of Empire builders whose service had taken him through the wide expanses of British rule in all corners of the world. In a series of impassioned statements in Parliament, public meetings, and news organs in 1940 and 1941, Earl Winterton, former Under Secretary of State for India and a prominent figure in several Conservative cabinets, cried out against those who would rein the war effort of the Empire because of considerations other than the demands of all-out war. England, he said, could sustain an ever-growing war effort only by "developing all the resources and manpower and material of the Empire . . . . Let us not be afraid of supporting openly and wholeheartedly the principle of the mobilization of the human and material resources of one-fifth of the world's population." [10]

Protests against failure to achieve economic—and moral—mobilization on a truly imperial scale fell on familiar and long-trodden ground. During World War I the accepted policy had been for outlying Empire countries to concentrate very largely on manpower contribution and the output of simple forms of equipment, while relying on the highly organized industries of the United Kingdom and her Allies to do the rest.[11] Veteran leaders in Britain remembered how in time a Royal Commission had castigated the smug complacency of the Indian administration during the war and had blamed its failure to mobilize local resources and transportation for many of the deficiencies which brought about the British defeat at Kut-al-Imara, Mesopotamia, in 1917.[12] Yet, untaught by the lesson of one of her major battle reverses, Britain after World War I had continued to underplay the military role of the resources on the periphery of her orbit. The recommendation of the 1937 Imperial Conference, calling for greater decentralization of Empire defense supplies, was heard but not heeded, and as war darkened once more the horizon of the Commonwealth, a situation existed along its periphery epitomized by the following report:

> The defense of Malaya was looked upon primarily as the responsibility of the United Kingdom and Malaya's part was mainly to make financial contributions towards the cost. . . . Although monetary contributions to defense were considerable Malaya's manpower in 1939 was not organized for war.[13]

Another colonial power, France, had yielded to the same mercantilist design, and had paid the heaviest of all penalties; for it seems certain now that the lack of industry and other developed defense potential in North Africa was one of the determinants of Marshal Pétain's decision to capitulate in 1940.[14]

It was not written that Britain should suffer similar ignominy, although even after the surrender consummated at Vichy, it took months before the lesson of France (and Kut-al-Imara) had finally been learned: A global war means global mobilization and a global strategy of shipping and supply.

Nowhere was the mistake of overconfidence and underdefense more stubbornly repeated than in the early phases of the war in the Middle East. Early in 1940 the Anglo-French authorities in the Levant were seriously planning for an attack on Russia through the Caucasus, and an expedition to the Balkans,[15] yet gave little thought to the stimulation of local productivity in support of the enormous task of defending the area while mounting an attack to the north. Even where the local population was anxious to serve as armies or bases of supply, as in the case of Palestine, hopes were dashed that encouragement and assistance would be given to a large native build-up in military and economic strength.[16] In March 1941, for example, the Director of the Palestine War Supply Board warned against excessive optimism regarding the role of local industry in the war. Although he admitted that at the Eastern Group Supply Conference in New Delhi in December 1940 British representatives from all Empire points east of Suez had drawn a long list of articles that Palestine could produce for the common war effort, he cautioned his listeners that the military commanders would make full use of Palestine's potential only if costs were held down! [17]

In Egypt the prevailing mood of complacency was mirrored by the Governor of the National Bank of Egypt, a British subject, in his address at the bank's annual meeting in February 1940: He congratulated his listeners on the fact that conditions in Egypt were "not far removed from normal," extolled the advantages of Egypt's position in the first six months of the war, and rejoiced in the fact that the prospect of an Italian invasion had disappeared. Initial economic dislocations had been shortlived; he took pride in noting the absence of rationing in Egypt and the increase in the rate of cotton exports in comparison with 1939; he then proceeded to devote the core of his remarks to the postwar prospects of Egypt's economy.[18] Symbolically, it was not until 1942 that it occurred to the predominantly British management of the bank—and presumably to British censorship in Egypt—that the publication of foreign trade statistics was deemed a source of aid and comfort to the enemy throughout the belligerent world and that in consequence the traditional disclosure of Egypt's foreign trade movements in the bank's annual reports had better be discontinued!

Insufficient appreciation of the military outlook in general and the supply and shipping problem in particular also permeated the military echelons in the Middle East. The record here speaks through Mr. Churchill's constant remonstrances against the inefficiency and wastefulness of rearward services in the command and through the repeated complaints in a similar vein of various United States emissaries visiting the area in 1940 and 1941.[19]

The Shipping Crisis and the Middle East

The neglect of the economic potential at the Empire periphery not only placed an oppressive burden on the productive capacity of the British Isles, but brought to a crescendo the shipping crisis which began to envelop the Commonwealth after the fall of France and the Italian declaration of war. A sharp rise in submarine sinkings, a slowdown in the rate of merchant ship construction, the need for a reduction in vessel speed to accommodate convoys, the congestion of British ports due to bomb damage and the closing of the Mediterranean route, now confronted the British and Free Europe merchant marines. Now also deprived of French naval and port assistance, they had to assume responsibilities for the supply of armies and civilians in various overseas theaters which, under more far-sighted preparations, could have devolved in part on local theater resources. Shipping became, in the words of Churchill, the "stranglehold and sole foundation" of British war strategy. Now, another incriminating fact emerged in bold relief: available cargo space, precious as it was, was wastefully employed. Cargoes of goods obviously unrelated to the war effort were sailing overseas; cargoes of non-essential or surplus character were arriving in Britain—where rationing and allocation controls were still shy of full effectiveness—tying up port facilities already strained by the lack of streamlined handling procedures. Waste of shipping space was sufficiently flagrant to arouse loud American complaints with the Prime Minister when he appealed for United States help.[20]

The effective control of vessel space in the face of mounting claims immediately became a major issue in the Middle East Theater of Operations. The English language has few superlatives which could adequately portray the place of the Middle East in the scheming and toiling of wartime Britain. Since the expulsion of Napoleon, "the protection of her interests in the Middle East has been a fundamental obligation on Britain's armed forces second in importance only to the defense of the British Isles themselves."[21] Mr. Churchill had inherited and faithfully carried forward this tradition. In 1921 he had called the Middle East the center of the British Empire to be defended at all costs; in World War II he was to describe it as the "hinge of fate on which our ultimate victory turned."[22] As he stood at the helm in 1940 and 1941, the defense of the Middle East, next to that of England, dominated all claims and calls on British resources. His determination to hold Egypt at all costs never faltered despite the gloom of advisers on both sides of the Atlantic, despite the indignant demands of other commands, despite the insistent plea of Allies for "Second Fronts" and despite the mortal danger to England herself.[23] Few episodes in the pageant of world empires have equalled or ever will equal the sense of duty and determination which prompted the government in London to dispatch in the fall of 1940, from an island seemingly defenseless against an invader, nearly half of its available tank force to the banks of the Nile.[24]

The stakes played there were high indeed. They went beyond the possession of the Suez Canal and the oil wells of Iraq and Iran. A British defeat in 1941 would have severed the most important link with the Soviet Union, doomed India, foreshadowed the confluence of German and Japanese armies, and paved the way for the occupation of North and Northwest Africa; the latter in turn would have endangered shipping in the South Atlantic and communications between the United States and Latin America.[25] On the other hand, the Middle East, for a long time, offered the only arena in which British forces could heed their Prime Minister's warning against a "defensive atmosphere," and his constant exhortation to attack wherever the enemy was in contact.[26]

In the crucial years of 1940 and 1941, these stakes were entrusted to the care of an army of about 300,000 men (mostly British and Australian) out of which 183,000 were fighting troops, facing numerical odds that at times reached proportions of 4 to 1.[27] The generalship of Wavell repelled the initial Italian onslaught on Egypt and scored the first military victories to cheer the Western world.

But the riposte of the Afrika Korps clearly showed the frailty of the forces guarding the Nile Delta. On their shoulders lay the conduct of multiple operations from the Libyan desert to the highlands of Ethiopia; the dash to the defense of Greece; the ejection of pro-Axis régimes in Iran, Iraq, and the Levant; and the administration of occupied lands. They also had to police communications in an alien area larger than Europe among all the stresses and strains resulting from nationalism, Axis propaganda, and the hardships of war. In relation to its task, this force was Liliputian, and still it was plagued by demands for releases to other fronts, in particular when the Canberra government began to press for the return of the Australian division to stem the Japanese advance.[28] But its greatest handicap was not its size; the defeat of Marshal Rodolfo Graziani had proven that large numbers of troops are not always an advantage in a theater where communications and water supply forbid the deployment of large forces. The great dilemma was supply.

The Middle East Supply Problem

The supply troubles of the Middle East Command too had begun to boil in June 1940 with the twin blows of French capitulation and Italy's declaration of war. Overnight the link between the Desert Army and the arsenals of Britain and the United States had been lengthened from 5,000 to 12,000 miles and more. The Mediterranean was closed, much more so than during World War I, when even with France unbowed and Italy an ally, the British still had encountered great difficulties in keeping the Mediterranean route open against the U-boat threat.[29] Now mortal danger lurked not only in Hitler's modern and more numerous submarines, but in the Axis air forces and the guns of the Italian fleet; later another unprecedented peril arose from the Japanese advance in the Indian Ocean with ominous implications for Red Sea and Persian Gulf shipping.[30]

Thus, the struggle for supplies in the Middle East Theater was not merely one of wrestling with the quartermasters of other Allied fronts; it was also one of finding the ships, sending them safely around the Cape to Middle East ports, unloading them with dispatch and forwarding their cargoes to Army depots. Delays and deficiencies at all these points of passage were at the heart of the shipping emergency which reigned in the area until 1943 and never fully subsided until the end of the war; for the expanding campaigns of the Anglo-American (and Soviet) forces in North Africa, Europe, and the Pacific decreed again and again sudden cargo subtractions from the Middle East quota just when more bountiful sailings were in sight.[31]

Added to the shipping problem was that of port facilities and of efficiency in cargo use. Unfortunately, the ports of the Middle East, although considerably expanded during and after World War I, were still limited in number and capacity.[32] Alexandria, the most important harbor, was many times reduced in capacity by bombing raids and by occasional obstruction of the Suez Canal.[33] Ports on the other maritime approaches of the Middle East, with the exception of Basra and Haifa, were of small assistance not only because of size, but because of lack of inland transport links as well as their specialization in one type of cargo such as oil or minerals, particularly the Red Sea ports.[34] Political conditions, such as the neutrality of Turkey, the revolt in Iraq, and "collaboration" in the French Levant permanently or temporarily removed valuable harbors from strategic use by the British. The scarcity of loading equipment as well as the shortage of skilled loaders further strained the capacity for handling the urgent cargoes floating in for the support of armies and civilians.

In 1940, the total annual accommodation in Middle East ports was estimated to be about 5.5 million tons; by the time of El Alamein, the military program alone required more than 5 million tons.[35] Thus it happened that in 1940 and 1941, and to some extent later, piers became hopelessly clogged, with ships and their precious cargoes waiting endlessly for unloading space while unloaded goods piled up in huge warehouses with little chance of onward movement; a shipment of tanks arriving in 1941 took twelve days to disembark while the battle for Suez hung in the balance.[36]

It was in those days that strange changes could be observed in the terrain surrounding the Suez Canal: the sudden appearance of odd-looking hills quite unfamiliar to the travellers who since the Canal was opened in 1869 had looked upon the impassively flat desert on either side as they floated through the isthmus. Upon closer inspection they proved to be modern pyramids consisting of garish piles of unopened crates of beer, stockings, cosmetics, men's shirts, lingerie, refrigerators, and tinned delicacies for which shopkeepers and consumers were waiting impatiently in the bazaars of the Eastern

Mediterranean. The tempers of men from the Eighth Army and from the Cairo headquarters would rise when they passed the "Suez Dump," for these were some of the goods which had contested shipping and unloading space with the tanks, the planes, the ammunition, and the guns promised to them yet preposterously delayed.[37]

Civilian goods had been arriving in Middle Eastern ports without apparent restraint, and the confusion and congestion therefore had been to a large extent caused by cargoes obviously unrelated to the needs of battle.[38] At times the inflow of goods of no war value had run as high as 30 per cent of the arrivals.[39] To add further insult, it was discovered that some of these goods later found their way through Turkey, Iraq, and Iran into the Axis camp.[40] It was hardly surprising then that, unable to stop the arrival of such goods, the military authorities had in despair ordered the civilian "stuff" to be thrown into the sea or dumped on the silent desert, so that the piers would be free. But what about future shipments? It was hardly defensible that British and Allied seamen should continue to bring in, at the risk of their lives, bountiful cargoes only to see them rot on the banks of the Suez Canal. Should London be advised and Washington be urged to halt all "non-essential" shipments by summarily barring all civilian goods from Middle Eastbound flotillas?

Military hotheads might have been tempted along this course, but it was obvious that one could not simply equate *all* civilian imports with non-essential shipments. Since the days of Munich the regions of the Eastern Mediterranean had been obsessed by one fearful prospect: that war would conjure up a repetition of the martyrdom which had been their lot in World War I. Then, the Allied blockade of the Syrian coast and the harshness of local military and civilian administrations in the Ottoman and Persian states had brought famine and pestilence which, together with the massacre of suspect minorities, had wiped out up to half of the population in various *vilayets* east of Suez;[41] Egypt alone had escaped disaster under British occupation. The memory of those years was still fresh when the new war took shape and throughout the towns and villages a furious wave of stockpiling began. On the farms and landed estates the watchword was hoarding of grain; in the towns the run was on manufactured items likely to be short if imports ceased. Meanwhile, cables and airmail went out to overseas destinations to initiate one of the most spirited import sprees the region had known; because of the slow progress of local and foreign controls over foreign trade and shipping this went on unabated in 1940 and 1941.[42]

A portion of this trade was essential for the sustenance of the Middle East population. In peace time as much as 5 million tons of goods were imported from outside the region each year, including foodstuffs needed to offset the fluctuations of its agricultural production.[43] Statistically speaking, the Middle East is nearly self-sufficient in cereals in normal years, but prices, inflexible local habits, defective communications, feeble trade liaison within the region, a propensity to hoard, and recurring crop failures lead to considerable overseas purchases of grain in normal as well as abnormal years. Palestine, Cyprus, and the Arabian peninsula depend upon Australian and Canadian wheat; the Persian Gulf areas buy their main staple food, rice, in Burma; Egypt must import from 500,000 to 600,000 tons of Chilean fertilizer annually to sustain her cereal output. The area has important deficiencies in tea, sugar, coffee, hard fats, spices, and processed foods made up by imports from the Balkans, Southeast Asia, and the Western Hemisphere. Agricultural and transport equipment plus parts and accessories such as tires are vital aids to food production and distribution; they come over the seas as does the coal that fuels factories, utilities, and the railroads. The low stage of industrialization demands purchases in Europe and America of most manufactured goods desired, not only to give the Middle East a veneer of modern comforts and conveniences but also to provide the towns with a means of exchange for the produce of the country; foremost is the need for textiles, in the furnishing of which many overseas countries, including Japan, had a share. Also not to be forgotten are "morale" items such as newspapers and cigarettes, the former relying on newsprint from England, the latter, increasingly before the war, on cheap Japanese tobacco imports.[44]

In short, the Middle East could not do without a modicum of imports from the Allied world beyond the seas, and this fact was far more compelling now than in peacetime because Continental Europe, an important customer and supplier in normal days, was fenced off by the iron rules of war, and Anglo-American sources had to take their place. A brusque embargo would mean economic paralysis, even famine; political tremors might ensue in the rear of the Desert Army with consequences that might cancel out the gain from extra shipments of men and materiel.

The British too had vivid recollections of the tribulations they had grappled with during World War I in this theater and of the significance then of nonmilitary factors in the battle for the Middle East. In 1914, the Allies' Asian and African possessions stood peril- ously close to a cataclysmic insurrection which could have come had Islam's children everywhere spoken the fateful word in response to the Ottoman Sultan's call for a Holy War. In World War II, the potential catalysts of trouble were the twin fires of nationalism and Axis propaganda; a combination of Allied reverses and local fam- ines could easily fuel these flames into raging holocausts beyond the control of the Middle East Command.

Shipments of nonmilitary cargo to the Middle East could not be suppressed; they had to be compressed. A balance had to be found between the claims of the military and the civilian population, so as to free ships to serve General Wavell's rapidly expanding commit- ments, soon to include the feeding of hundreds of thousands of Italian and German prisoners, without causing potentially explosive dislocations in the civilian hinterland.

3

The Middle East Supply Problem
in World War II

Infirmities of Middle East Economy

THE closest approximation to a program of ship space rationing in the Allied world in the early stages of the war was the "navycert" system instituted to control shipments to neutral countries over international seas. It had been an answer to the question of how to sustain the goodwill and the stamina of such nations while making certain that goods carried to them across the oceans would not directly or indirectly contribute to increased trade between them and the Axis. For this purpose all ships venturing on the high seas had to carry a certification from the Royal Navy lest their cargo be seized as contraband by the Fleet.[1]

This procedure led to rather unusual arrangements between Britain and various neutral nations. The latter in effect were compelled to adopt foreign trade controls at British insistence, as well as rationing schemes, and an elaborate system of statistics which would yield at regular intervals a clear statement of the minimal import requirements of each neutral nation along with justifications based on reports of production, consumption, availability of substitutes, and other relevant data. On the British side, corresponding facilities were set up for auditing these statements. On this basis shiploads bound for neutral countries were certified by British consulates in the loading areas. Failure to prove conclusively the need for a particular shipment meant denial of a navycert with all its consequences should the ship go out anyway.

While the navycert system achieved satisfactory results in the control of trade with European neutrals, which had the government machinery and social organization required for handling its meticulous detail, this was not the case in the Middle East where the existing administrative and social conditions were ill adapted to such a system.

All the normal grievances of a society that has limped behind the trends of the twentieth century yet must constantly cope with modern challenges, were magnified by the urgency and extent of the demands thrust upon the Middle East at the outbreak of hostilities: a civil service inadequate in numbers, deficient in training and short in reserves; widespread illiteracy and a tradition of defiance to established authority—the latter a legacy of prolonged foreign dominion—which thwart the enforcement of the best-meant of ordinances; awkward and sketchy networks of distribution and transportation; a shortage of skilled workers and foremen coupled with aversion to industrial discipline; undeveloped public and private financial institutions with resultant inhibitions to the raising of revenues and the operation of strict fiscal and credit controls; powerful resistance to economic change from foreign and native groups interested in the perpetuation of prevailing patterns; scarcity of specialists in economic matters capable of grasping the full national impact of sudden external developments; fatalism in face of recurring natural disasters such as crop failures, infestations of the locust and the senn pest,[2] the spread of deadly or deadening diseases; dearth of statistics and of facilities to collect them, aggravated by deliberate or unwitting census sabotage by the people to be counted; corruption and an appalling absence of civic spirit—only feebly compensated by religious charity and a generous sense of responsibility toward family and clan. A background, in short, more akin to England in the days of the Tudors than to modern industrial societies, a social climate that makes "the hoarder, the profiteer, the regrader and forestaller . . . dominant types in the economic history of the East."[3]

So grimly stated, this generalized pathology of course does not apply uniformly to all sectors—for islands of progress and the prehistoric mingle freely in the Middle East—but it emerged as the dominant response to the many special stresses laid upon the region by several specific complications arising during and because of the war:

1. *The presence of foreign armies.* Foreign troops appeared in considerable numbers in Egypt, Italian Africa (including Ethiopia), Palestine, Syria, Lebanon, Iraq, and Iran at various stages of the war. The first important concentrations under Allied control were the French Army of the Levant (until 1941) and the British forces

in Egypt; later Iran became the base for large bodies of British and Soviet occupation troops, and in the latter stages small air detachments and a considerable force of supply personnel came from the United States to work in the area from Eritrea to the Persian Gulf and beyond.

The troops brought with them both the horn of plenty and the box of Pandora. Through army contracts and work in army installations, paid at generous rates, as well as through compensation paid for the use of local facilities, munificent employment was afforded to untold thousands, new life was breathed into faltering enterprises, and fat revenues poured into state treasuries or their sterling exchange accounts; the total disbursements of Allied armies in the area were upward of $2,000,000,000 by the end of 1944.[4] Other windfalls came from French, British, and American grants and loans or both (including advance royalties paid by the oil companies) to Saudi Arabia, Turkey, Palestine, Hadhramaut, Cyprus, Ethiopia, Iran, Syria, and Lebanon.[5] Moreover, the British Army made emergency loans and gifts of food and other scarce goods to local governments, built roads, airfields and port installations of permanent civilian value, created new rail links, expanded irrigation works, participated in flood control, helped with harvesting and civilian grain collections; in this they were assisted by the American forces whose lasting contributions included the extension and modernization of the Trans-Iranian Railway, the construction of the new Cairo airport, the creation of the port of Khorramshahr in Iran and the expansion of the port of Massaua in Eritrea.[6]

But the same expenditures which brought the trappings of war prosperity to portions of the Middle East also contributed to inflation and the disarray of the civilian market. Many army purchases were urgent or were thought imperative and were therefore placed without much attention to cost and the effect on the civilian economy; wages and prices paid under such contracts immediately contaminated the remainder of the market, as did the purchases of food and other civilian items bought by the forces in competition with the civilian consumer.[7] Also, the prosperous condition of the individual soldiers, particularly the Americans, and their free spending habits aroused dreams and desires of higher living precisely at a time when the watchword should have been austerity and frugality.[8]

2. *Economic warfare.* Alongside and behind the armies marched the agents of "economic warfare," buying commodities in order to thwart the Germans or to help friendly governments. Representa-

tives of the British government made pre-emptive purchases in Turkey often at exorbitant prices, but it worked to the detriment of the Turkish public as it paid for these trade bonanzas with a rising internal price spiral; [9] British bulk purchases of cotton, flax, onions, dates, tobacco, wheat, barley and other products in Egypt, Iraq, and Turkey buttressed the sagging structure of local economies at critical moments of the early phase of the war but they also raised prices and slowed down the switch to food crops as demanded by the mounting danger of famine.[10]

Generally, the Allied armies strove hard to spare the local economies the more disruptive effects of their presence by pursuing a policy of maximum supply autonomy for food and other items essential for the civilian population. Thus, in spite of the stringent shipping situation, the armies imported many requirements from overseas and endeavored to limit local purchases to goods in surplus, with the approval of the local government.[11] But in the stress and confusion of the war it was not always possible to avoid instances of competition between army purchasing agents and the local population in the markets for civilian essentials; even less avoidable was the military preemption of land transportation—a matter of most serious import in an area of underdeveloped communications. Moreover, there were two important exceptions to the rule of supply autonomy. The French Army of the Levant, after passing into the Vichy orbit, was cut off entirely from France and Middle Eastern sources as a result of the British blockade and had to be fed and paid from the reserves of Syria and Lebanon until the Gaullist liberation.[12] In Northern Iran, Soviet occupation forces throughout the war requisitioned food crops and local supplies without paying attention to neighboring Azerbaijan's function as breadbasket of the nation; they in fact deliberately withheld shipments to the British-occupied South of Iran despite surpluses in their zone.[13]

3. *The departure of foreign technicians.* On the outbreak of the war many European and American technicians packed up to return to their own countries, and industry found itself suddenly deprived of key employees at a time when the shortage of parts demanded doubly careful handling and maintenance of machinery.[14] In some cases this was merely a case of foreigners being drawn home either by the call of safety or at the urging of their own governments; in other cases they resulted from the expulsion (or internment) of Axis nationals from countries passing under Allied control. A special problem in this respect were the Italian colonies after the defeat of

the Duce's troops, for the massive flight or expulsion of Italian civilians left the territories bare of hard-to-replace administrators, technicians, and skilled workers. Here the situation became so serious that, for instance, in Ethiopia the Emperor, just returned from exile, after first insisting on the complete evacuation of all and everything Italian, had to give reluctant stays to 4,000 out of the 34,-000 Italians slated for banishment.[15]

The urge to move toward safer shores reached as far south as Aden where several thousand urban dwellers took ships for India and East Africa after war was declared.[16] In the same category were the multiplying expulsions of badly needed talent and capital following widening campaigns against minority groups and foreign residents who, within the pattern of racial division of labor so frequently found in the East, had dominated certain trades and professions. In Egypt, under the guise of wartime necessity, the government attempted with some success to dislodge foreigners and minority Egyptians from positions in trade and industry by the creation of government monopolies; in Turkey the notorious *varlık vergisi*, a capital levy on minority groups, led to the mass liquidation of long-established firms.[17] From the viewpoint of efficient import controls this development was highly undesirable since many importers belonging to minority groups such as Armenians, Greeks, and Jews had special personal reasons to be cooperative and comprehending in regard to trade restrictions that would contribute to the defeat of Hitler and Mussolini.[18]

4. *Turkish mobilization.* Turkey's full-scale mobilization, maintained for almost the entire length of the war, removed large numbers of workers from the farms of Anatolia and reduced cereal output to a point where instead of being nearly self-sufficient in grains the country became an importer and had to look for suppliers in the Middle East, Europe, and overseas.[19]

5. *Political uncertainties.* Hovering over all policy-making in the Middle East was the uncertainty confronting most wellsprings of leadership in the area, as the result of Anglo-French misfortunes in Europe. In Britain a wave of military setbacks would bring forth a resurgence of national spirit and a multiplication of national energy; for she knew only one road before her, the road of resistance, and in that she was sustained by her allies as well. But in the Middle East the ominous rumblings of Italian belligerency and, later, of Rommel's advance brought forth a halting hiatus of weeks and months as friends and foes of the Allies alike were in doubt as to

what the next step would be. The supporters of the Axis would want to mark time in anticipation of the entry of Italy's and Germany's forces; then, for instance it might not be necessary to do as the British demanded and curtail cotton output since the Axis Europe was starved for the fiber.[20] Those who bet on the Allies, and their number at times melted like butter, were in agonizing suspense awaiting the verdict of London on whether the Middle East was to be forsaken or to be held. The record shows that there were in London and Washington on various occasions persistent and powerful advocates of withdrawal from the "untenable" Nile front and of concentration of all military resources in the British Isles. The loss of Egypt, they argued, would be disastrous but not yet conclusive, while the loss of England would surely seal the fate of Western civilization.[21] After each setback, in Western Europe, in the Balkans, in Libya, in the Caucasus, and in the Pacific, the doubts arose anew. Would London abandon the Nile to insure the defense of the Thames? Awaiting this answer, working and planning in the Middle East slackened as people there weighed the alternatives.[22]

6. *Natural disasters.* Nature made her own contribution to Middle Eastern woes with the old and inexorable curses which seldom miss their turn in the cycle of adversities germane to the area. Floods and the senn pest were visited upon Iraq in 1940; an exceptionally severe winter in 1941–42 took a heavy toll among Iraq's livestock, particularly her sheep herds. Iran suffered a wheat failure in 1940, while in Egypt the reign of perennial diseases which holds 90 per cent of the population in its grip produced a malaria epidemic reaching its climax in 1943. A new locust breeding cycle was approaching completion in 1943. And in 1941 one of the worst crop failures in recent memory befell the larger part of the Middle East with most countries unprepared for it. Indeed, in 1942, bread crises followed by food riots occurred in Cairo, Teheran, Beirut, and Damascus; children, both European and native, died in the shiekhdoms of the Persian Gulf for lack of milk; near-famine conditions stalked five of the Iranian provinces; workers in British camp installations went on strike for lack of adequate food allocations; emergency appeals for wheat came from the governments of Turkey and Egypt. "Bread, carrots, potatoes, beans, radishes and rice became the politics of the Levant." [23]

7. *Neutralism and opportunism.* A spirit of identification with the Allied cause was on the whole conspicuously absent in the region. The Middle East had become a primary theater of war not of

its own volition but because of its unwilling membership in the Franco-British orbit. With the exception of pro-Allied foreign residents, the kings of Saudi Arabia, Iraq, and Transjordan, the Jews, and other minority groups with foreign ties, the area not only recognized no important stake in the war against Hitler and Mussolini but on the contrary burst into open sympathy with the Axis on a number of occasions, notably in Iran and Iraq. Through centuries of capitulations and foreign occupation, the habit of watching the antics and aggravations of alien compounds in their midst, with little concern for the stranger's hazards, had become an ingrown trait of the Middle East population. The proprietary way with which the Western nations had brought World War II into their lands and fought battles on their soil fortified the resentful conviction that this was merely a foreigner's war from which one should suffer as little as possible and profit as much as possible. Even the anti-German zeal of Jews in Palestine could not be fully translated into all-out support of the Western cause either because of Zionist resentment against the British White Paper of 1939 restricting Jewish immigration or because of British reluctance to encourage such support for fear of damaging repercussion on the delicate structure of Anglo-Arab relations.

German propaganda was feverishly at work and consummately effective when it could play on British reverses in Libya, Greece, and elsewhere, or on food shortages blamed on Allied requisitions, or on the inevitable incidents arising from cases of misconduct and open arrogance displayed by Allied soldiers on leave.[24] Very powerful was the effect of promises of emancipation lavished on the area through Axis radio messages and official proclamations; they gained emphasis by the disintegration of French power and prestige in the Levant, the pro-Axis Rashid Ali revolt in Iraq and the brusque imposition of a new government on King Faruq by the British ambassador and his historic tank escort.[25]

There was, therefore, beneath a thin veneer of uneasy cooperation, the flighty mood of opportunism breaking into defeatism, and loyalty switches when the enemy rode the crest, or crass profiteering when Allied fortunes surged high. Always there was readiness to decry controls recommended by the Allied command and to misconstrue their intent. Always there was the inclination of local leaders to blame all war-born difficulties on British malevolence as an easy way to escape the duty of protecting the public welfare by stringent —and unpopular—measures. Always there was a penchant for subtle blackmail to extract supply concessions from the Allies coupled with the secret hope that assistance from them might make a tightening of belts and intensification of effort unnecessary.[26]

And always there was the lusty and pervasive habit of merchants, producers, and service purveyors to charge the Allies for all they were worth, for this was a foreigners' war and its cost did not burden the treasury of local governments but only that of the rich potentates in the West.[27]

The intensive kingmaking in which the British had to engage to secure their hold in the critical years of the Middle East war also weakened self-control and self-discipline in key sectors of the area. New regimes rode into power in Syria, Lebanon, Egypt, Iraq, and Iran on the coattails of British tank commanders, Anglo-French liberation armies, and Anglo-Soviet occupation troops; they exhibited understandable reluctance to mortgage their shaky beginnings and their compromised standing with unpopular restrictions; nor were their equally embarrassed British godfathers overanxious to push them or reject pleas for special favors. The Wafd leaders in Egypt who, during their days of opposition, had sent peremptory messages to the British ambassador demanding an end to burdensome emergency measures, promptly abrogated the requisition of grains, controls on food distribution, and penalization of hoarders as soon as, by the grace of the British Ambassador, they had retrieved the seals of office from their King. And throughout the war some British officials were ready to plead Prime Minister Mustafa al-Nahhas Pasha's case when he and his ministers vied for special favors and special exemptions from Allied supply restrictions.[28]

It was part of the story of the "foreigners' war" when angry charges of "blackmail" and usurpation were heard in reply to urgent British requests for more efficient consumer controls in Iran or Egypt—the almost inevitable consequence of the difference of outlook which divided the belligerent and the sheltered non-belligerent, unable to comprehend the sense of urgency of the other.[29]

The whole peculiarity of the relationship between the nations of the Middle East and the Western powers and its paralyzing effect on local economic initiative during the war is illustrated by two incidents. In the second half of 1940, the Egyptian state railroad decided upon expanding its equipment and made inquiries concerning a purchase in the United States. Although they received quotations and delivery dates, the purchase was postponed because of the belief that Britain would buy the equipment to strengthen the defense of Suez and therefore make Egyptian disbursements for this purpose unnecessary.[30] Close toward the end of the war in Europe, the Egyptian government addressed a request to the Allied authorities to leave as much of their military establishment as possible in Cairo, during the shift of operations to the Pacific, in order to avert the economic repercussions of a sudden withdrawal of the large headquarters and installations set up in the country.[31] And the oratorial campaign for the "evacuation of Suez" already was in full swing!

Curiosa such as these point to one of the perennial dilemmas of the Middle Eastern states in their recent history, described by one writer as the choice between the dictates of fervent nationalism and the need of small powers to lean on stronger ones.[32] For Middle Eastern society in World War II it was a dilemma between indifference to the call for sacrifice for the Allied cause on the one hand, and the tacit reliance on Allied initiatives and help on the other hand.

8. *The impress of colonialism.* Much of what has been said to describe the inadequacy of public administration in these pages of course referred to governments and echelons manned by *indigenous* leaders and officials. The surprising fact is however, that, at least in the initial stages of the war, *colonial* officials,—members of the British administrations in Palestine, Transjordan, Cyprus, Aden, and the Sudan—were unequal to the task of instituting austere wartime controls in their ward areas. Partly, this was a reflection of the leisurely pace of mobilization at home; in some degree it was a natural disinclination to take unpopular measures which might upset the delicate political balance through which Britain could rule her possessions with mere handfuls of troops. But unquestionably two aspects of colonial rule were major sources of obstruction: (1) The innate disposition of colonial officials to underrate the capacities of their subjects; [33] (2) the innate orthodoxy of economic policy in colonial administrations. As an example, one could cite the pride with which colonial governors would report the absence of budget deficits through many years of tenure, at the very time when in London and other Western countries deficit financing as a means of financing full employment, economic growth, or rearmament was in full vogue. Such an attitude naturally interfered with any intention to place colonial economies on a full war footing. Even in the later stages of the war, there were frequent clashes between Allied officials bent on full economic mobilization and representatives of colonial administrations pleading for caution and orthodoxy.[34]

Towards a Solution of the Shipping Problem

No one surveying the needs and frustrations of the Middle Eastern economy in the early months of 1941 could view with less than great pessimism the prospects for a rational, politically tolerable scheme of shipping space control for civilian imports from overseas. But, by 1943 almost four-fifths of the civilian tonnage floating towards the Middle East had been eliminated, by edict—and yet the people of the region were fed, the industries were humming, and the economy was able to pour out large quantities of munitions and quartermaster items for the armies fighting in the Middle East and beyond. In all its creakiness the economic structure of the Middle East ultimately withstood the test of World War II and contributed in its own ways to the achievement of victory. Once more it became clear that the stages of success in modern war never are and never can be an unbroken tale of heroics and perfection. On the contrary, every modern conflict if viewed microscopically presents, as it unfolds, a boiling brew of error, larceny, and petty pursuits riding the wave of achievement and high endeavor. Whether one studies the Civil War in the United States or the behind-the-scenes details of the two world wars, the impression is unavoidable that the great impulse to conquer must laboriously wade through a marsh of blunder and shabbiness.

In the Middle East, economic mobilization and self-control were still in the stage of blunder and shabbiness as the second year of the war rolled on. Except for Syria and Lebanon, which in their Vichyite isolation had to cope with problems of exceptional harshness, no comprehensive emergency controls were in evidence anywhere. Nowhere was there a master plan of war economics, nowhere a central agency endowed with power and plenipotentiaries to set the pace for a regional alignment of consumption and production. There was no general scheme of rationing, only isolated instances of restrictions. There was not even a remotely adequate scheme of commodity allocation to industry anywhere. Few price controls and no schemes for the allocation of labor were in effect. No drastic measures for the stretching of supplies, whether the adulteration of bread or the conservation of paper, had been enacted. Few steps had been taken to convert land to food production. No important campaigns against inflation had been launched. Only feeble warnings and deterrents had been addressed to the hoarder and the profiteer. And no drastically effective regimes of import control had appeared.[35]

The issue of foreign trade curbs, central to any solution of the shipping crisis, was complicated by the need to consider powerful interests outside the region. In 1940, the major trading nations outside the Axis ring were still tempting Middle Eastern importers with eager offers. To thwart these endeavors with harsh efficiency could alienate friends and run into strong opposition even in Britain. There the traders were among the loudest hawkers, encouraged by their government's drive to earn the dollar and sterling credits so badly needed to pay for purchases of arms, food, raw materials, and local services required by armies operating in foreign lands; the ministries cheering them on in good faith thus were obstructing the very purpose of others concerned with shipping. This had its counterpart in British dependencies in the Middle East where in 1939 and 1940 the prime object of trade regulations was not to save shipping space but to save dollars.[36]

Parallel with the British effort were the intense activities of American, Japanese, and Russian traders or trade envoys. United States exporters worked feverishly to cash in on the elimination of their German, French, and Italian competitors from the Middle East market; the Japanese and Russians on the other hand were after the cotton of Egypt and Iraq for which they offered such desirable baits as textiles, tobacco, and fertilizers.[37]

Relations at this stage between Britain and these three nations were delicate. Interference with the flow of trade to the Middle East therefore would not only raise problems within the region but might corrode the goodwill of neutral nations which held the balance of power for the final outcome of the war. This was confirmed by the sharp and noisy reaction of private and public spokesmen in the United States to the trade restrictions installed in Britain in 1940 and 1941.[38]

All the time, meanwhile, intolerable pressure was building up around the leadership of the Middle East Command in view of their inability to cope with the shipping difficulty. Shortage of transport and delays in unloading at port were ever-recurring subjects in acrimonious exchanges between Cairo and London. Questions of supply and logistics, the Prime Minister noted, seemed to overshadow if not completely smother the spirit of "offensiveness" for which he consistently clamored.[39] New commitments and fronts bestrode the command with every new month; at one time nine campaigns were being conducted simultaneously.[40] The evidence was mounting that the accumulation of military tasks and civilian problems within the jurisdiction of the Middle East Command were overtaxing the capacities of the Commander-in-Chief, his lieutenants, and his opposite numbers in the British embassies and legations in various Middle Eastern capitals.[41]

But as the shipping crisis inexorably moved toward a climax in the spring of 1941 the reins of the Middle East supply challenge were at last picked up in London. The new sense of urgency which had begun to pulse through Britain's war organization with the advent of the Churchill cabinet and the spur of Dunkirk at last reached into the outposts of the Empire and quickened the search for a new global supply policy. Even as Earl Winterton spoke in Parliament, delegates from the dominions, the colonies, the mandates, and the commands East of Suez were preparing to meet at a conference in New Delhi in December 1940 to consider the greater use of local resources for the supply of British armies in Asia and Africa and for the relief of British shipping and arsenals. Out of this grew the Eastern Group Supply Council, one of the first of several Commonwealth and inter-Allied organizations through which the stimulation of local production and the resource pooling of land-connected commands was raised to the status of official policy.[42] At the same time, in response to urgent inquiries from Cairo, a scheme was slowly maturing in the inner recesses of the British Ministry of Shipping which was destined to execute with signal success the task of "rationalizing" the problem of Middle East supply. The birth of this scheme coincided both with new directives of the Prime Minister ordering a "more efficient use of our shipping," [43] and a major reorganization of the Middle East Command designed to remove a long list of shortcomings that had given unending irritation to the watchful war leader of Britain.

4

The Establishment of M.E.S.C.

A Plan for Regional Mobilization and Supply

THE plan to regulate civilian supply and shipping in the Middle
East emerged late in 1940 from the deliberations and proposals of
three British establishments: An interministerial committee set up
in London in the fall, under the chairmanship of Lord Hankey, the
Paymaster General; the Middle East Command; and the British
Embassy in Cairo.

Lord Hankey's committee was formed following the Italian invasion of Greece on 28 October 1940.

> The first task of the committee was to settle policy issues aris-
> ing out of the new demands of Greece [for assistance]; but in
> addition it had to co-ordinate procurement and shipping pro-
> grams for the whole eastern Mediterranean and the Middle
> East. Coordination of plans and their execution were secured
> by meetings at the Ministry of Shipping of officials drawn from
> the service departments, and from the Ministries of Supply,
> Food, and Economic Warfare.[1]

At about the same time, a series of staff conferences was sum-
moned in Cairo by General Wavell for the specific purpose of discussing the complications arising out of the contest for shipping
space and supplies between the Middle East Command and the civilian population of the Command area. In these deliberations support was developed for the policies formulated by Brigadier B. A.
Hutchinson, Deputy Quartermaster of the Command, which embodied the following principles:

> a. local production of essential civilian and military goods
> should be encouraged to the utmost;
> b. all Middle Eastern countries should adopt the practice of

calling on each other for help from local surpluses before turning to overseas sources;

c. civilian demands for overseas goods should be scrutinized by a British authority in Cairo to determine their relative urgency, having in mind the availability of alternate sources or substitutes in the Middle East.[2]

These proposals found a most eager echo at the British Embassy in Cairo, particularly with the Commercial Counsellor, Charles Empson. For some time, the Embassy had received complaints from other countries of the Eastern Mediterranean, particularly Greece, Palestine, Malta, and Turkey, that Egyptian restrictions on the exports of wheat and other commodities were throttling their economies. The Egyptian Government, on the other hand, was voicing its rising alarm over serious shortages developing in the country. It blamed them on the withholding of shipping space and local purchases by the British Army, and rejected a plea to release stocks to her neighbors. As a result, Empson had made a study of the civilian import problem, and in his conclusions he had urged the Ambassador to demand the establishment of machinery through which the production and imports of the region could be adjudicated among the countries of the region according to need.[3]

Against this background, the Ambassador to Egypt, Sir Miles Lampson (later Lord Killearn), joined General Wavell in an urgent appeal to London, proposing that a strong central organization be established in the Middle East to collect, on the spot, all pertinent information required to advise London intelligently on the allocation of shipping space and supplies from the United Kingdom and other sources to all countries of the Middle East.[4] The communication added that the only "regional" body in the Middle East—the Middle East Command—could not undertake such an assignment but that a new civilian agency headquartered in the Middle East should assume the task. It was further suggested that ultimately such an agency should institute and manage vigorous import controls for every country and territory in the region.[5]

The proposals reached London in the wake of the first series of *blitz* attacks and amid the furious labors of the Churchill government to make Great Britain battle ready for the supreme test. Nevertheless, the ministries represented on Lord Hankey's committee and the Foreign Office examined the matter at length. In January 1941 an interim reply was sent from London, indicating that as an emergency step, the Middle East office of the United Kingdom Commercial Corporation (U.K.C.C.) would be authorized to undertake a program of local purchases and sales designed to balance surpluses and shortages in the area.[6] This was welcomed in Cairo but both the Embassy and Wavell insisted on more comprehensive measures.[7]

Nothing further happened until the matter landed on the desk of one of the economic advisers in the Ministry of Shipping, E. M. Nicholson.[8] This marked the first of a series of largely fortuitous events through which a whole chain of brilliant and imaginative officials became directly associated with the business of steering the Middle East economy safely through the maelstrom of World War II.

Nicholson had made his peacetime mark as an economist during the Great Depression when he had founded and guided the famed Political and Economic Planning committee (P.E.P.) as an assembly of original and highly influential social science thinkers in Britain. The Middle East proposals attracted his attention because he had only recently been called upon to deal with the problem of coal exports to Egypt and the proposed conversion of Egypt's state railroads from coal to oil operation for the sake of shipping economies.[9] A closer study of the Wavell-Lampson plan convinced Nicholson that of all the civilian cabinet offices, the Ministry of Shipping had the most immediate stake in a scheme of this nature. Delays and wastage of shipping space on the vital London-Capetown-Suez lane were enormous, and his Ministry received much of the blame without having any authority to deal with the root of the problem, namely the continuance of nonessential trade and the resistance of the military to civilian interference in their theater. Now, the Commanding General of the Middle East front, of his own volition, offered to a civilian ministry, on a platter as it were, the opportunity to take allocational command over the important civilian component of supplies to be loaded on ships bound for the Middle East.[10] His Ministry, Nicholson reasoned, could control this allocation by refusing shipping space to supplies considered non-essential and applying a graduated system of shipping priorities to "approved" supplies. Here indeed was a great opportunity for what Mr. Churchill had called "a brilliant administrative exertion which might produce results in war economy equal to those gained by a considerable victory in the field." [11]

So far, there had been no source of regular, reliable information which would enable the Ministry to ration the Middle East effectively without starving it. Nicholson and his immediate superior, Sir Arthur Salter, Parliamentary Secretary of the Ministry and as Secretary of the Allied Maritime Transport Council one of the masterminds of inter-Allied shipping controls during World War I, agreed that in most aspects the proposals sent from Cairo could be the basis for reasonably informed guidance for rationing of both shipping and supplies for the Middle East. They rejected, however, any arrangement that would force local governments in the area, particularly those actually or nominally sovereign, to turn over the control of their foreign trade to a regional super-agency under British management. A blueprint which Nicholson prepared for consideration by the Minister of Shipping reflected the strong opinions which he and Salter held on the necessity to accommodate as far as possible the sensibilities of an area swimming in nationalism and constantly stirred up by enemy propaganda. What they visualized was a planning and consultative body, analogous in some ways to the Program Committees of the Allied Maritime Transport Council in World War I, capable of dispensing data and guidance to the shipping authorities at home. This organization would function in Cairo, nominally a part of the Middle East Command's supply structure but in fact an outpost of the Ministry of Shipping; this ambiguity might further preclude the impression that the British government was usurping governmental powers in the capital of a foreign country where its troops were quartered as allies, not occupiers. The new organization would solicit the voluntary cooperation of all countries and territories in the Middle East in its task of collecting data on their essential overseas import requirements. After scrutinizing the information for evidence of extravagance and overstatement of needs, the office would, periodically, make its recommendations on the allocation of shipping space and supplies for Middle Eastern civilian use to the Ministry of Shipping, which would subject them to the audit of an inter-ministerial committee on Middle East supplies. In framing its recommendations, the agency would be guided by broad policy outlines established in London in the light of current political and military conditions; these directives would, for example, determine the degree of liberality with which the agency would frame its own analysis of regional needs. It would also be the task of the agency to explore the present or potential availability of stocks and production facilities within the region which could serve as substitute sources for goods normally imported from overseas. And, in order to mobilize hoarded surplus stocks for the benefit of the region as a whole, it would advise the British government of cases where guarantees of shipping and supply were needed to obtain a country's consent to the release of reserve stocks.[12]

This plan was approved by the Minister of Shipping, the Cabinet and the British authorities in Cairo.[13] On 1 April 1941, what was guardedly described as a "small supply section" installed itself in a one-room office of G.H.Q. (M.E.) in Cairo, under the chairmanship of General Hutchinson. Sir Alexander Keown-Boyd, a director of U.K.C.C. with long business and government experience in the area, assumed the post of executive vice chairman.[14] A few weeks later, the new section officially assumed the name which Nicholson had chosen for it: Middle East Supply Centre.[15]

The term "Centre" occurs rarely in the nomenclature of British governmental organization. Its choice was deliberate and reflected once more Nicholson's extreme sensitivity to political complications. He has stated his reasons as follows:

a. to emphasize the consultative character of the agency.
b. to demonstrate the regional scope of its activities.
c. to reduce possible antagonism from public opinion and governments in the Middle East. The use of conventional terms like "Board" or "Commission" might have suggested more vividly than was desirable that control over vital economic interests in their area was exercised by a British bureau in which the people directly affected had no say.[16]

Changes in the Middle East Command

Urgent as had been the supplications from Cairo that had led to the establishment of the Centre, its opening and the first meetings called by its chairman received scant notice, despite the fact that they were attended by a bevy of officials from all over the theater.[17] Far greater changes held the attention of the British leadership in the Egyptian capital, among them a thorough overhaul of the Middle East Command's rear echelon.

Following the New Delhi Conference in December 1940 and the adoption of a new economic and logistic policy for the Empire east of Suez, the Eastern Group Supply Council (E.G.S.C.) had drawn up a rough inventory of military and paramilitary stocks believed to be procurable in the territories represented by the Council, including the Middle East.[18] To coordinate such procurement and provide for resource pooling between the individual areas, a Central Provisions Office was created in New Delhi, and the opening of local offices in the principal centers of E.G.S.C. jurisdiction suggested.[19] Promptly, General Wavell set up in Cairo a "Middle East Provisions Office" to oversee and stimulate the procurement of Army supplies from local sources in the Middle East theater on a more active scale than heretofore.[20]

But London had become impatient with the management of supply in the Middle East and the general conduct of military operations there. In February 1941, Prime Minister Churchill sent Anthony Eden and General (later Field Marshal) Sir John Dill, Chief of the Imperial General Staff, to Egypt with the mission to survey the manifold diplomatic and military issues arising or bound to arise from military campaigns in progress in Ethiopia and Libya and from future actions now slowly maturing on the planning boards, such as aid to Greece.[21] The Prime Minister wanted a critical appraisal of General Wavell's leadership and his capacity to transact the multifarious business of the Command—in the desert, in the chancellories, and in the domain of logistics—in the light of mounting complaints of wastefulness and sluggishness received in London.[22]

Also in the Middle East at this particular moment was Churchill's son Randolph, who sent his father detailed reports of what he saw as shortcomings in the structure and management of the Middle East Command. Primarily as the result of the recommendations submitted by Eden, Dill, and Randolph Churchill, but hastened by the unexpected reverses in Libya following the advance of Rommel during April and the German invasion of Greece, a series of peremptory commands reached Cairo between April and July 1941, in which the Prime Minister gave the Middle East theater a new leader, in the person of General Sir Claude Auchinleck, and a thorough overhaul in organization.[23]

The object of the administrative reorganization, as given in Churchill's military directive of 4 April 1941, was to lighten the burden of the new Commander-in-Chief by providing him with a civilian apparatus somewhat similar to that enjoyed by military commanders in Britain.

> Here at home General Brooke [commanding the troops based
> in Britain] has a very large army to handle and train, but he
> has behind him the departments of the War Office and of the
> Ministry of Supply. Something like this separation of functions
> must be established in the Middle East.[24]

Churchill proposed to achieve this by the appointment, in April, of
General Sir Robert Haining as "Intendant General of the Army
of the Middle East" and, in July, of Oliver Lyttleton as "Minister of
State for the Middle East." Into their hands was placed the urgent
mandate to clear out the weeds and underbrush which faulty logistics, improvident economics, and lack of political coordination had
allowed to luxuriate in the supply depots of the Eighth Army.[25]

Haining, a former Deputy Chief of the Imperial General Staff,
was expected to take full charge of all matters connected with procurement, shipping, transportation, repair, and maintenance behind
the army lines, including the all-important processing of shipments
from North America; he assumed the direction of the Middle East
Provisions Office and the chairmanship of the Middle East Supply
Centre. He was told to set up a system which would integrate the
supply functions of the three Services (Army, Navy, and Air Force),
and "external" agencies such as the Ministry of Aircraft Production,
the Ministry of War Transport, the Egyptian Government, and
other civil authorities in the Middle East and London. Most important, he would report not to General Auchinleck or the naval and
air commanders in chief but directly to the War Office for whatever
powers he needed to complete his task.[26]

This was a unique and ambitious assignment, but it was short-
lived. While the military in Cairo had been most willing to relin-
quish the handling of civilian supply questions to a civilian authority like M.E.S.C. or the Minister of State, they were most unwilling to
conform with the extraordinary idea of abdicating their control
over military supplies to an officer not subject to their command.
Logistic problems had been the limiting factors in all of Wavell's
campaigns and it was unthinkable to turn their management over
to a parallel "intendancy" reporting directly to London.[27] On the
other hand, Haining's dealings with civilian authorities on matters
of mobilization and supply inevitably collided with the roving activities of the Minister of State, particularly in the matter of American supplies. Captain Lyttleton was a strong man [28] fortified by the

personal friendship of Churchill and his status as member of the War Cabinet. He brooked no intervention.[29]

With little or no staff, sabotaged by the three armed services which he was supposed to serve as well as depend upon, snubbed by the civilian authorities, and deserted by London, "the Intendant General thus found himself somewhat of a fifth wheel to the Middle East coach." [30] He resigned in November, and the Intendancy disappeared. In its stead, General Auchinleck created a new staff function in his command, the "Lieutenant General (Administration)." This officer, fully subordinate to the Commander-in-Chief, in addition to acting as Quartermaster General for the Command, became the chief coordinator of the military supply and procurement arms of the ground, naval and air forces; he assumed the direction of the Middle East Provisions Office; and he became the chief liaison agent of the armed services vis-à-vis British civilian agencies concerned with supply in the Middle East theater.[31] Thus ended the brief tenure of the second chairman of the Middle East Supply Centre and one unorthodox attempt to solve the thorny quartermaster problems of the Middle East Command with Napoleonic methods.[32]

A quite different fate was reserved to the other prong of Churchill's reform drive, the dispatch of a Resident Minister of State. The talents and energy which Captain Lyttleton demonstrated in all his wartime assignments (and which made him a stalwart of Conservative cabinets after the war), as well as his close friendship with Churchill and his membership in the War Cabinet, gave him a firm footing in a slippery and precedent-making assignment.[33]

Lyttleton stayed but seven months in Cairo, thereafter to return to London as Minister of Production. In this short time he made his office a fulcrum of cooperation and orientation for a series of enterprises serving both the armies and the civilian population. These ranged from relations with governments in exile (Greece, Yugoslavia, Ethiopia, Free France) to famine relief, from occupation policy and espionage to censorship, from the acceptance of volunteer armies (Free Poles, Palestine Jews) to propaganda. In due course a coral reef of theater and regional organizations formed around the Minister, some of them centers of consultation for the three services and agencies of parallel interests, others specialized operational or advisory units. They ultimately included the Middle East War Council, the Middle East Supply Council, the Middle East Intelligence Centre, the Middle East Economic Advisory Committee, the Petroleum Subcommittee, the Middle East Medical Unit, the Middle East Anti-Locust Unit, the "Special Operations Executive—Middle East and Balkans" (subversive operations), the Occupied Enemy Territories' Administration, the Office of the Censorship Adviser, the Department of Propaganda, the Middle East office of the Ministry of War Transport, the Middle East Relief and Refugee Administration, the Middle East Board of the United Kingdom Commercial Corporation, and others.

Among the possessions of the short-lived Intendancy inherited by the Minister of State was the chairmanship of the Middle East Supply Centre. In the waning weeks of 1941, the Centre was still a small, indistinct niche within the administrative sprawl of the Middle East Command, operating with a minuscule staff. It had shown its potential usefulness during several of the year's great supply emergencies. M.E.S.C.'s assessment of needs and stocks in the Middle East had greatly eased the work of the Minister of State when he had to answer a Turkish appeal for 50,000 tons of wheat to overcome a crop deficit, meet a little later a dangerous food shortage in Syria and Lebanon, and allocate a sudden regional surplus of goods when a large number of ships sent to the aid of Greece returned to Middle Eastern ports with all their loads because Greece had fallen to the Germans while they were sailing.[34]

The Centre also had made its first impact on the misuse of shipping from British and Atlantic ports—as American exporters had noted. But it was far from having achieved the measure of authority and organization that would have enabled it to cope effectively with the massive flood of nonmilitary goods following the opening of Red Sea ports to American merchant vessels.[35]

Centre officials ascribed their sluggish progress to two major causes. One was very obvious: The absence of any coordinating arrangement with the United States. The second was the strictures placed on them by their parent agency. In fact, no sooner was the Centre constituted in Cairo when its chief executive officer, Keown-Boyd, had remonstrated with the Ministry of War Transport that in order to operate effectively he would need special powers with which to impose certain rules on the governments of the area and on British military authorities as well. M.E.S.C. would have to be in a position, he said, to dictate most of the imports of the region and to compel each country to surrender its surplus; to make mandatory the reporting of accurate information on production, foreign trade, stocks and productive capacity in the territories; to disburse funds for the purchase of reserve stocks, the financing of industrial expansion, and price supports for local grain producers.[36] In reply, the Ministry had categorically insisted that M.E.S.C. remain an advisory agency, relying exclusively on persuasion and voluntary cooperation in its drive for reduced imports and increased local production.

Under this stricture Keown-Boyd apparently had been unable to galvanize his agency; M.E.S.C. had languished, had failed to expand its staff materially, and had progressed slowly in creating foreign trade controls in the Middle East.[37] Now Lyttleton took up the cudgels. His proposals to London went further than those of Keown-Boyd: He wanted no less than a new strong supply council covering not only the Middle East but South and East Africa, with an executive organization to deal with both civil and military supplies; this body would absorb M.E.S.C. as well as the Middle East Provisions Office. Again, London demurred, rejecting an expanded geographical scope and ruling out pooling of military and civilian supply controls; while it was agreed that M.E.S.C. might need strengthening, there was an emphatic restatement of the belief that for political reasons the Centre must remain an advisory agency with no powers to compel.[38]

Lyttleton yielded but did not abandon his purpose to put teeth into the management of civilian supply. His own experience in the Middle East had taught him that vague instructions and loosely defined authority can become powerful tools of administrative action if manipulated with strength, adeptness, and a driving ambition to succeed on the largest possible scale. M.E.S.C. had not enjoyed this type of leadership in the first months of its existence. Lyttleton now set out in search for a man who could provide such direction. His choice fell on a young officer of the Royal Australian Navy, Commander Robert Jackson.

Jackson Becomes Director General of M.E.S.C.

Jackson had turned up in Cairo as representative of Malta during a session of the Middle East Supply Council—one of Lyttleton's more ephemeral creations. An aura of heroic accomplishment and unrivalled experience surrounded the young Australian naval officer for he "had been at Malta" during the massive air and submarine offensive against the small fortress island and had distinguished himself in planning its defense and rearmament; at the Council meeting he caught general attention because of his success in organizing military and civilian supply lines in an area under severe attack. So great was the impression he made that Captain Lyttleton asked him to study M.E.S.C. and make suggestions on raising its effectiveness. In a report which carried all the marks of the harrowing experience at Malta behind him, Jackson called for a bold and incisive program that made short shrift of all the diplomatic, mercantile, and colonial excogitations which had inhibited a full-scale economic mobilization of the Middle Eastern economy. Victory in the Middle East, he said, required strict licensing of imports everywhere in the area; ruthless schemes of cereal collection and distribution to eliminate hoarding and profiteering and promote the regional distribution of local surpluses; maximum stimulation of local production regardless of cost factors as long as shipping could be saved; and intensive forward planning of national and regional imports from overseas. The most striking aspect of Jackson's statement, however, was his belief that this could be achieved without changing the advisory character of M.E.S.C. itself; he agreed that direct control over the region's imports would be politically unwise. If the British government could be persuaded to back up M.E.S.C.'s import recommendations to the fullest, then M.E.S.C. could obtain region-wide compliance with its policies through the mere threat of recommending the denial of shipping space for the imports of any country or territory refusing to cooperate; these "supply sanctions" could be as effective as direct controls but would be less harsh on national or bureaucratic sensibilities.[39]

The Minister of State fully concurred with these conclusions. He indicated this in a report to London along with the suggestion to make Jackson the executive head of a Supply Centre revitalized through the policies outlined by him. The Ministry of War Transport (Shipping) agreed with the policy outline, but it strenuously objected to the designation of a man barely thirty years old, with little experience in economic and political affairs, unknown to both the public and the business community in the Middle East, to a post as exacting and important as the directorship of the "new" M.E.S.C.[40]

Lyttleton now took a step of great consequence for the future of the Centre: he appealed directly to the War Cabinet to sustain him in his selection of Jackson. He won his point. Early in December

1941, Keown-Boyd resigned as chief executive officer of M.E.S.C. to be succeeded by Jackson bearing the new title of Director General. At the same time, the Centre was declared "associated" with the Office of the Minister of State and, symbolically, moved from General Headquarters to 10 Tolumbat Street, the seat of the Ministry.[41]

This decision of the War Cabinet brought the Middle East Supply Centre to the watershed of its history. What so far had been an existence of struggling obscurity became in the passage of a few months a life of commanding influence in the affairs of the Middle East. As an arm of Britain's most powerful political representative in the Middle East, it enjoyed the direct support of a minister who could successfully plead for more funds, more personnel, and for the support by all relevant agencies in London and the Middle East for the policies and measures the Centre would recommend to ease the shipping situation.

This new dimension in M.E.S.C.'s sphere of influence was put to dramatic and astonishingly effective use by the new Director General. Commander Jackson turned out to be a prize find, unquestionably one of the outstanding administrators of the war. As M.E.S.C. expanded in scope and size to take on responsibilities equal to that of a super-ministry of economics for a vast and variegated region, Jackson became almost overnight a key figure of enormous prestige and influence in Middle Eastern and Allied affairs. Belying his youth and his recent emergence from a modest and unspectacular career in one of the smallest navies in the world, he seemed quite at home and thoroughly in command whether he argued with generals about grain for Teheran or with the United States Department of State about postwar plans; whether he addressed the Middle East War Council on truck and railroad conditions in the Levant or lectured, without notes, before a spellbound meeting of the faculty of the Hebrew University of Jerusalem on the theory and practice of economic regionalism for war and peace in the Middle East; whether he answered detailed questions on the world shipping situation or checked off statistics on army boot output in Khartoum; whether he chatted over cocktails with Anthony Eden or, over a dish of *pilaf,* tangled with the old warrior King of Saudi Arabia, Ibn Saud; whether he welcomed a large regional conference on agricultural development or persuaded a group of Persian Gulf sheikhs to help him proselytize their subjects from wheat to rice consumption; whether he pleaded with the War Cabinet for *more* shipping space for the Middle East civilian or with King Faruq's ministers for the acceptance of Palestine-made medicines and toothbrushes to *save* shipping space. Only a few months after assuming his post a diplomatic challenge of the first order came his way when the United States became a cosponsor of M.E.S.C. and the first Americans arrived to assume codirection of a fully organized purely British organization. Tension and friction seemed inevitable. But most of the American arrivals took to "Jacko," as he was known to his associates, and what might have been an act of painful grafting surgery developed into a most amiable merger and ultimately into a major example of dedicated Anglo-American teamwork.[42]

Jackson directed the affairs of the Centre until February 1945. His subsequent career gave further proof of the exceptional talents shown by his record at M.E.S.C. He became Senior Deputy Director General of the United Nations Relief and Reconstruction Agency (UNRRA)—the chief executive officer under Director General Herbert Lehman—and thereafter Assistant Secretary-General of the United Nations, all before reaching the age of thirty-seven. At UNRRA too he became a legend for his extraordinary ability to cut through the Gordian knots of bottlenecks and bureaucracy.[43]

The Middle East Supply Centre Reaches Maturity

For a hiatus of several weeks the new Director General faced uncertainties and inhibitions. His take-off into activity in a new job under unfamiliar circumstances required close consultations and communion with his new chief, Lyttleton. But this was December 1941. The British government, the Middle East, indeed the whole anti-Axis world was in trepidation as the consequences of Pearl Harbor were weighed and assayed. As one of Churchill's closest advisers and a man "very well esteemed at Washington," [44] Lyttleton kept his attention riveted on London and Washington where the bylaws of a new Grand Alliance were under urgent debate. A cabinet reshuffle was in process at Whitehall and a new, more responsible, post was mapped out for him. There was no time to continue the close watch he had kept over the tiny supply center in his vast stable of subaltern organizations. So, instead of carrying a new mandate from the Minister of State to the far corners of M.E.S.C. jurisdiction, Jackson was found pacing like a caged lion in the two small offices constituting his headquarters, impatiently waiting for a call to action; at one time he announced his intent to resign and volunteer for the Far East front.[45] Then opportunity struck.

In February, Lyttleton was named Minister of Production in Churchill's cabinet and returned to London. His successor, Richard G. (now Lord) Casey, former Australian Minister in Washington, did not arrive until the middle of May. This long interregnum plunged the Office of the Minister of State into temporary inactivity, with little to sustain its influence except reflex of the nimbus which Lyttleton had imparted to it. For many men this would have been an invitation to sit back and wait for the handshake of the new boss. Jackson's reaction was characteristically different.

He knew that the departing minister had shared his plans and ideas. As long as his successor was still far away, Jackson concluded he could carry out his former chief's policy in his name without consulting on details. He packed his bags and armed with the "nimbus" of the Minister of State, speaking boldly in his name, he embarked on a series of tours that took him to most Middle Eastern capitals. His mission was one of dispensing blunt warnings and urgent counsel for cooperation. When he returned there was a new awareness in ministries and embassies throughout the area that Britain meant business.[46]

To listen to some accounts of Jackson's grand tour, he must have swirled through Government Houses, embassies, cabinet chancelleries, local military headquarters, and royal palaces, in person and by telegram, like a circuit rider on a spirited steed. Depending on circumstances, he would plead, cajole, persuade, or threaten, always making full use of Lyttleton's magic name and speaking as his emissary; here and there he might drop a hint on his Malta experience to shame the smug. But he did not merely demand; in exchange for cooperation he promised the full measure of his assistance to any legitimate demand for civilian goods and shipping space from overseas. And as his hosts scanned the latest headlines on ship sinkings in the Atlantic and the Japanese advance, they knew their countries were in for a period of drastic austerity during which they could ill afford to lose the goodwill of the Minister of State and his lieutenants in charge of supply matters. Moreover, the scheme proposed by Jackson seemed eminently sensible.[47]

There were immediate and concrete results. Jackson received firm promises from local authorities that they would institute stricter licensing of imports and share their exportable surpluses with the rest of the region. Agreement had been reached to submit all licenses for overseas imports to periodic M.E.S.C. scrutiny. The principle of maximum local production of civilian and military goods had been accepted. Favorable consideration had been indicated for regional sources of supply that M.E.S.C. might recommend in lieu of an overseas source. And all governments had subscribed to a more energetic pursuit of policies that would place their areas on an austerity footing in keeping with the gravity of the war situation. In return, Jackson had convinced his interlocutors that he would use all the influence at his command to obtain for cooperating territories their legitimate share in supplies and shipping space allocated in Britain. He also had secured from the Ministry of War Transport in London a strong reconfirmation of the commitment to respect as far as possible in its allocations of shipping space the recommendations, negative and positive, which M.E.S.C. would submit on all import orders for overseas goods licensed by the governments of the Middle East. In addition, he had been granted authority to recruit more staff.[48] Fortified by this assurance, he had made it clear to all and sundry in the Middle East that he could, if forced, "blockade" a country that reneged on its pledge of cooperation.

By the middle of May when the new Minister of State arrived, the Middle East Supply Centre had grown almost beyond recognition from the lowly condition of winter days. The staff had increased from 28 to 94, and London had already agreed to a total establishment of 158, including 66 executives; M.E.S.C. men were swarming all over the stately villa at 10 Tolumbat Street and crowding in on the space reserved for Casey's own small staff. Floods of telegrams and emissaries from all corners of the Middle East were streaming in, evidence of the existence of a network of regular communications and consultations which linked M.E.S.C. to the nerve centers of its ward area. Intensive negotiations were in process to cope with cereal crises in Egypt and Syria and to effect the long-sought conversion of railroad operations from coal to the use of oil; the last step alone promised to shave more than 300,000 tons annually from the civilian shipping allocation of the Middle East. A drastic reduction of fertilizer imports, made possible in part by a regional distribution of stocks hoarded in Egypt, had already been accomplished. And Casey's ears were ringing with the praise heaped on his fellow countryman by the Commander-in-Chief and his supply services for the contribution he had made in just a few weeks to the clearance of ports and ship hulls for an accelerated flow of munitions.[49]

The Centre, at long last, had reached maturity. It had organization, status, and a functioning scheme.

First Stock-Taking

During the summer of 1942 the first comprehensive audit of the organization and activities of the Middle East Supply Centre was submitted by the Treasury to the British government. Its purpose was to examine the justification for a demand presented by Commander Jackson for a second major expansion of his staff and for a substantial increase in operating funds. The author was N. Baliol-Scott, a Treasury official.[50]

Baliol-Scott paid tribute to the efficiency with which M.E.S.C. had organized control of imports and the meeting of civilian requirements in the Middle East. At the same time, he gave a graphic picture of the enormous complexity and scope of the task the Centre had shouldered. Its jurisdiction stretched over an area larger than Continental Europe, with a population of almost 100 million, encompassing six sovereign states, four British colonies, four League of Nations mandates (including two wrested from Vichy and governed by a temperamental Gaullist regime), one Anglo-Egyptian condominium, former Italian colonies, and others.[51] While there were in this vast expanse certain unifying factors of religion, culture, language, history, and race, there were also deep divisions, resulting from differences in form of government and stage of economic development, from deficient transportation and communication links, from dynastic jealousies and historic grudges, and from the intrusion of colonial powers which had bound individual Middle Eastern lands to far away centers of policy and had contaminated the region with power rivalries and ambitions.[52] While London and the Middle East Command tended to be aware only of the needs and emergencies of those parts of the area where important military or political developments were in progress, M.E.S.C. had to look after the needs of all the territories at all times. The differences in political status and relationship to the British government of the various territories had to be constantly borne in mind. Programs and policies had to be constantly adapted to the impact on Allied shipping and supplies of new battle fronts opened in other theaters and new campaigns in preparation; the landings in North Africa, for example, had a drastic effect on the shipping that could be made available to the Middle East. Consultation with, and the cooperation of, the military authorities were needed at every stage; at the same time M.E.S.C. had to meet the wishes and carry out the policies of several Cabinet ministries.[53]

Summing up, the report described in impressive terms the unique character of the Centre. Within a single organization, said Baliol-Scott, were comprised what might be regarded as regional offices of the Ministries of Food, of Supply, and War Transport, as well as the Board of Trade and other agencies.[54]

The report was circulated to all the ministries concerned, including, of course, the Ministry of War Transport. For many government officials dealing with some aspect of the war in the Middle East, it was the first opportunity to grasp the magnitude and intricacy of M.E.S.C.'s assignment. Not only was the request for additional personnel and facilities promptly approved and implemented, but henceforth the Centre was to receive the most punctilious attention in its dealings with London.[55]

At this juncture, the government also decided to remove some of the wraps of secrecy and acquaint public opinion in Britain and the Middle East with the work and objectives of the Middle East Supply Centre, as an example of the contrast between Allied and Axis treatment of foreign populations.[56] Among those who took note were the news organs of the enemy. Quoting a British announcement, *Il Messagero* of Rome ridiculed the "pretentious" nature of the new organism and called it simply a mask for the "total failure of the British authorities" in face of the grave economic difficulties their presence and their "plunder" had brought upon the people of the Middle East.[57] Yet, at the very time these lines appeared before the eyes of Italian readers, the Middle East Supply Centre had already met its first crucial tests and in doing so had played its part in the victory of El Alamein.

Let us look back to 1941. The watchword then was *"Rommel Ante Portas."* Hammer blows had shaken the British cause in the Middle East: the reverses in Libya, the fall of Greece and all the Balkans, the Rashid Ali revolt, the German advance toward the Caucasus, the terrible toll of submarines and air marauders in the Mediterranean.[58]

There are a few successes, but even they mean further strain on Allied supply lines. Conquests and liberations brought new pensioners to be fed and rehabilitated. The new alliance with the Soviet Union brings but temporary military relief and no improvement at all to the pressure of supply: The Middle East's shipping ration now has to be shared with the demands of the Persian Gulf supply route to the Russians. The winter auguries point to one of the worst harvests in recent memory. There seems to be but one mitigating blessing: the growing assistance from the United States, expressed in emergency sailings of ships with tanks, munitions and other lend-lease goods carried now on both American and British vessels. Then, on 7 December 1941, this too appears to vanish into thin air. Large cargoes awaiting departure for the Middle East in America's East Coast harbors are summarily cancelled in the first impact of the Pearl Harbor panic.[59] Worse than that, Japan now threatens the only open sea link with the West, the Cape Route.

The year of 1942 looms bleak and foreboding. Indeed the peak of the shipping crises is yet to come—in the dark days when the Afrika Korps stands at the gates of Egypt, when state papers are burned in G.H.Q. backyards at Cairo, when moving vans begin the temporary transfer of M.E.S.C. to Palestine, when outbound trains and planes are besieged by panic-stricken Western civilians and when in many secret alleys mob leaders practice for the reception of the German conqueror.[60]

The year 1942 comes and passes. As if by a miracle, the tide of disaster is stemmed before the summer is over. Much of the miracle is due to the constantly accelerating ability of workshops, factories, and farms of the Middle East to deliver quickly munitions and other supplies at a time when their delivery across the Atlantic would have taken weeks, even months. Much is due to the long-delayed but massive arrival of reinforcements and materiel from overseas, particularly America, quickly unloaded at decongested ports and forwarded to eagerly waiting defenders. Much of it is due also to the absence of riots and open rebellion in all parts of the theater, because there is no famine or economic chaos to stir passion beyond reason.

For the weighty contribution of local production to the British potential at El Alamein, the energetic procurement of the Lieutenant General (Administration) of the Middle East Command, acting through the Middle East Provisions Office takes the credit. The high military proportion of incoming shiploads, the increased efficiency of the ports, the relative tranquillity of the hinterlands and the responsiveness of local industry and agriculture to Allied military procurements, redounds largely to the credit of the Middle East Supply Centre.

How the Centre earned its reputation will be detailed in the following chapters. Before this, however, a digression is needed to relate an important phase in the formative stage of the Centre: how the United States of America helped win the battle of Middle East supply and became a partner in the M.E.S.C. scheme.

5

America Joins M.E.S.C.

First Anglo-American Contacts [1]

IN the fall of 1941 an urgent communication from the Imperial Government of Iran arrived in Washington requesting the assistance of the United States Government in the procurement of large quantities of pharmaceutical supplies. Delivering the message, the Iranian Minister informed the Department of State that epidemics were threatening his country against which his government would be helpless unless medical supplies were dispatched without delay.

Only a few weeks earlier Iran, much against her will, had become a participant in the war as a result of a joint Anglo-Soviet invasion and mass sentiment in the country was known to be anything but friendly to the anti-Axis cause.[2] The State Department readily agreed with the envoy that an explosive outbreak of disease so shortly after this event would embarrass the two occupying powers in their anti-Axis mission besides endangering the health of their troops. Frederick G. Winant, the recently appointed Chief of the U.S. Export Control Office, was asked to expedite the Iranian request. He complied, assisting with procurement and granting the required export clearance with dispatch.[3]

To his amazement Winant learned shortly thereafter that the medical shipment after having been assembled for the account of the Teheran government was stranded in a New York warehouse. The only available ships sailing for Persian Gulf waters at this time were under the control of the British Ministry of War Transport, Winant learned, and the agent of the Ministry at the Port of New York had categorically refused to accommodate the Iranian consignment.

This made no sense whatsoever, since the security of British troops in Iran had been a prime consideration for expediting the shipment on the American side. A somewhat caustic inquiry was addressed to the British Supply Council in Washington. The reply stated that the Iranian demand for cargo accommodation on a British vessel had been referred to a recently established advisory committee attached to the Middle East Command in Cairo and had been returned with the comment that there was no shortage of pharmaceuticals in Iran which would justify the allocation of scarce shipping space to such supplies during the current naval crisis in the Atlantic and Mediterranean. Thereupon the Ministry of War Transport agent in New York had blocked the loading of the shipment. This, Winant later recalled, was his first encounter with the Middle East Supply Centre.

What on earth was this "committee" in Cairo? How could a group in Egypt know better than the Shah in Teheran whether serums were needed there or not? How was it that a British agency operating in the Middle East apparently had veto power over the allocation of shipping space in the Port of New York? An immediate answer to these questions seemed imperative to Winant and an investigation was started. The trail led through the State Department, the Office of Lend-Lease Administration, the British Embassy, several American export houses, and the New York Office of a "United Kingdom Commercial Corporation" to Maj. Gen. Russell L. Maxwell, Winant's predecessor, who had just gone to Cairo as head of the U.S. Military Mission to North Africa and the Middle East. Also consulted were the American ministers in Cairo and Teheran.

It turned out that the Department of State and foreign traders in New York had some acquaintance with the new Cairo agency. Alexander Kirk, the U.S. minister to Egypt, had advised the Department in April of the appearance of M.E.S.C. and had later commented favorably on its purpose after attending, as observer, several executive meetings at the Centre. At the same time vehement complaints had been reaching Washington from export houses along the Eastern Seaboard against the activities of the United Kingdom Commercial Corporation in New York; this organization, it was claimed, acting on behalf of the British Ministry of War Transport, since April had been blatantly interfering in all American trade with the Middle East by refusing British controlled shipping space to American consignments to that area. Costly delays had been experienced and a great many of the highly lucrative orders received from Middle Eastern merchants had been nullified. The U.K.C.C. had explained its actions with references to the shortage of shipping space and specifically to recommendations of a "Middle East Supply Control," as one exporter put it.

The British Embassy could not contribute much detail but confirmed that the new "Centre" in Cairo appeared indeed to have a great deal to say about the quantity and type of nonmilitary cargo which British vessels were allowed to carry to Middle Eastern destinations. On the other hand, spokesmen of the British Supply Council gave a graphic picture of how a flood of civilian "luxuries" had overwhelmed the limited port facilities in Alexandria and Suez and thereby gravely compromised the supply of the hard-pressed Middle East Command; a report from General Maxwell confirmed this emphatically.

The most impressive statement, however, came from Teheran: it was indeed true that no serious shortage of pharmaceuticals existed in the country. The government had simply found it more convenient to order new supplies in the United States than to start a running fight with the politically powerful merchants who were hoarding most of the available stock.

Winant also learned that the British Government had on several occasions extended a cordial invitation to the United States to join in the sponsorship and direction of the Middle East Supply Centre. Just as he was concluding a detailed study of the organization and procedures of the Centre, the news from Pearl Harbor struck the nation, and then America herself was at war and in a shipping crisis of her own. Like Britain in 1940, the United States now, too, made a heroic and historic decision: after a short panicky hiatus during which all lend-lease sailings were summarily halted in American ports, Washington, despite the denuded state of American defenses and the possible imminence of a Japanese invasion, issued the orders which meant that American supplies would continue to flow to the Middle East.[4]

But there was no more room for openhandedness in civilian exports. American merchant ships were decimated by the fury of the German submarine attack and every shipload that pierced the torpedo curtain was as important a prize to the Allies as the capture of a strategic dune or hill in Libya or the Caucasus. The temptation to terminate summarily all nonmilitary shipments to foreign non-belligerents was great, at least as long as the United States lacked the facilities and experts to effect a judicious screening of them. In this general atmosphere Winant circulated his report on the operations of the Middle East Supply Centre. He stressed the political and military implications of an embargo of civilian shipments to the Middle East. He described as "eminently sound" the system of screening and scrutiny based on voluntary cooperation of the various Middle Eastern countries which M.E.S.C. had begun to establish, echoing the favorable reports which Kirk and General Maxwell had rendered on the initial efforts of the Centre. He pointed out the benefits which U.S. agencies would derive from aligning their activities in the Middle East with those of a government which had long experience in the area and had a considerable head start in building and testing economic controls at home and in foreign theaters of operations, in contrast to the dearth of qualified American personnel and the infancy of U.S. control schemes. He concluded with a strong recommendation that the United States associate itself with Britain in sponsorship of the Middle East Supply Centre.

Winant's arguments were favorably received and negotiations started in Cairo during February 1942 with a view to transforming M.E.S.C. into a combined Anglo-American project. In July Winant flew to Egypt as the first U.S. representative on the Executive Committee of the Centre.

United States Policy in the Middle East

It is doubtful that many persons in Washington envied Frederick Winant his new assignment. He was headed for a front which many of his country's military and political leaders viewed as distinctly secondary.[5] Behind this front he was to join hands in a combined agency with the representatives of a nation committed to a last-ditch defense of their position in the Middle East whereas the Chiefs of Staff of his own country had on several occasions termed this very position as untenable and an unjustifiable drain on American aid.[6] He was to speak the mind of America in the only major theater of military operations where, except for the brief presence of the Ninth Air Force, no American combat forces of any significance were committed to battle; it was also the only major Allied command which until the end of the war remained exclusively under British direction.[7] And he was to practice the diplomacy of supply in the only part of the Allied world which Anglo-American consultations from "Arcadia" (the Churchill-Roosevelt Conference of December 1941 and January 1942) to Quebec had readily acknowledged as a British sphere of influence.[8]

Moreover, the pessimism of the U.S. Chiefs of Staff appeared to be thoroughly vindicated by the situation Winant found on his arrival. British military fortunes were at their nadir. Tobruk had fallen.[9] The Eighth Army had lost a large portion of its armor and air strength and was now preparing for the loss of the Nile Delta in face of the swift advance of the Afrika Korps. The evacuation of Cairo had started; Winant was not even certain where he would set up shop since the staff and most of the records of M.E.S.C. had been removed to Jerusalem.[10] The airfield receiving his plane was beleaguered by panicky foreigners struggling and screaming for room on outbound airliners while Arab bystanders looked with contempt on what seemed like the last undignified flappings of a long and arrogant regency now finally departing.[11]

Driving from the airport into the tense city he saw more of the "bystanders." Unlike the men at the terminal, the teeming population of Egyptians, Sudanese, and Levantines on the streets seemed neither scornful nor hostile; they merely looked unconcerned. It was obvious that a march-in of the Afrika Korps would not prompt them to the barricades. This was not a land of determined Allies, out to welcome the emissaries of the United States as helpmates in an hour of desperation. Nor was this occupation territory where Allied officials could rule by simple decree. This was a region of sullen landlords forced to quarter troops in their lodgings and to make the best of the rental lease but who expected no worse from other tenants whether they wore *feldgrau* or khaki.

Winant knew that with the Atlantic Charter written into the code of Anglo-American conduct, these landlords and their co-nationals in Egypt and all over the Middle East, 100 million of them, had to be treated with dignity and care. Yet, to help ration their claims on American goods and shipping, which would be his particular job, there would have to be skilful interference with their ways and changes in their rules. For such a job there were few Americans with appropriate experience. In this Middle Eastern region the United States had never been an overlord nor a combatant nor a very active political maneuverer nor business investor. Except for World War I and occasional impulses of activity connected with Philanthropy, Petroleum, and Palestine, the history of relations between America and the Middle East had been one of slight interest on both sides.[12]

At the bar of Shepheard's Hotel, the traditional rendezvous of the foreign colony, Winant encountered a few American war correspondents, still holding forth with views that typified the traditional righteous detachment of the United States in this area. Their refrain still was the biting indictment of British inadequacies and follies which had made such good reading back home, undiluted as it was in general by soul searching questions on why in this important bastion of the free world Britain was represented by soldiers marching daily to their deaths while America only held forth with some munitions, technicians, and carloads of preceptorial advice.[13]

A few random but typical incidents are worthwhile recalling in this context as evidence of the spasmodic and restrained nature of political and economic traffic between America and this region before World War II.

1. In 1933, Washington accepted without commotion an announcement by the Egyptian government banning from consideration all non-British tenders for a Nile Dam construction project; both the American Minister in Cairo and the Secretary of State agreed after a brief exchange that a protest was not warranted since Egypt should be considered a "legitimate sphere of British interest." [14]

2. At the outbreak of the war, the diplomatic relations of the United States with Egypt and Saudi Arabia both were conducted by one minister accredited simultaneously to the two countries.

3. As late as the middle of 1941 the War Department was found so ill-equipped for assignments in the Middle East that no reliable maps could be found in its intelligence department for planning a program of military aid shipments to Russia through the "Persian Corridor." They had to turn for information on highways and transport routes in Iran to the Consultant on Islamic Archaeology at the Library of Congress.[15]

4. During the first phases of the lend-lease program, allocations for Middle Eastern countries were made through the intermediary of the British government. One of the reasons (besides certain restrictive stipulations of the Lend-Lease Act) was the unavailability of American personnel and facilities for the screening of applications and supervision of the final use made of lend-lease material. The White House then notified King Ibn Saud in 1941 that grants to his country would be made through British channels since Saudi Arabia was "remote" from the United States.[16]

5. When an American destroyer sailed to Jidda in 1945 to fetch King Ibn Saud for his rendezvous with Roosevelt, it had the distinction of being the first United States man-of-war to steam through the Suez Canal in more than twenty-two years.[17]

Against this background, the position of the United States at the start of World War II in the Middle East was once aptly described by a War Department historian: "The second war found the United States unprovided with a long-range policy. None had been needed up to 1939 save general friendliness." [18]

As if to remind him of this historical perspective, Winant had received a piece of discouraging news from his chiefs before leaving Washington. Although the Middle East Supply Centre at this point had a staff of nearly one hundred persons and was rapidly expanding, he was told that he would have to carry the U.S. share with only three other American officials for the time being. The State Department had persuaded the Board of Economic Warfare, the Office of Lend-Lease Administration, and the Department of Agriculture to deputize William A. Rountree, Marshall Macduffie, and Ben Thibodeaux, respectively, for service on the Middle East Supply Centre—the latter two on a part-time basis. Winant himself was asked to take on the additional duties of lend-lease representative in Cairo.[19] This was all the United States of America could spare at this point for service in an agency which was to bear important Allied responsibilities for logistic success and political stability in a vast region of strategic primacy.

This augured badly for the success of Anglo-American cooperation within the Supply Centre. Without a thorough American impregnation of the Centre it was hard to visualize how its recommendations could be effective in Washington. Unlike the economic mobilization of Britain, the system of wartime controls in the United States was still in the disarray of experimentation. Confusion and suspicion, owing to inexperience, might well predispose the controllers of civilian allocations against the views of an agency ostensibly Anglo-American but completely dominated by British personnel.

From the very start of the war, the issue of civilian trade controls had been a frequent source of friction and suspicion between the two countries. There had been a furious uproar in the United States in the months before Dunkirk when London, anxious to save dollars for munitions purchases, had curtailed or embargoed certain costly but not essential imports from America, primarily tobacco and cotton products and motion pictures. Spurred by Congressional and newspaper attacks the State Department had protested on 4 May 1940—a few weeks after the German occupation of Denmark and Norway and only days before the invasion of France—that the restrictions violated the Anglo-American trade agreement of 1938.[20]

Particularly violent had been the American reaction in the notorious "Turkish tobacco" case. This concerned the purchase by Britain of large portions of Turkey's tobacco crop for the purpose of (a) replacing dollar-consuming purchases from America, (b) denying the tobacco to the Germans, and (c) bolstering the economy of Turkey then assiduously courted by both belligerents. Following outraged representations by tobacco growers, a blistering note over the signature of Cordell Hull was delivered to the Foreign Office. To assuage the Americans, the British government had ordered the destruction of most of the tobacco purchased.[21] The tempest abated after that, but the anticipation of British trade conspiracies and wile never quite vanished from the American wartime scene.[22] M.E.S.C. itself, during its all-British phase, had been a cause of American protests. With only four Americans serving part-time alongside a hundred experienced Britishers, the Centre would seem to stand little chance of overcoming adverse attitudes in Washington.

True, the problem now was not one of eager American exports straining at the leash of British currency and shipping curbs. At least for a while the major preoccupation would be, on the contrary, not to let Britain dump all her economic problems into the lap of the American economy while the latter was mobilizing for war production. But intergovernmental suspicion, once kindled, gladly grasps for new straws.

Much of course depended on how respectfully the British would accept the "American slant" which the Winant embassy of four was to implant in M.E.S.C. policy. Here too, the circumstances were hardly auspicious. If the middle of 1942 marked a dismal low in Britain's military posture in the Middle East and elsewhere, it was even less a period in which the United States of America could appear with pride and assurance before the judgment of the world. Her baptism of fire had been a macabre succession of defeats and humiliations; her fleets were crippled, her defensive outposts unthinkably bare, and her flag in retreat in the large expanses of the Pacific. Only recently, the naval battles of Coral Sea (7–8 May) and Midway Island (4–7 June) had for the first time slowed down the Japanese. In the Atlantic, the United States was making little progress against the submarine menace. And whatever brave battle plans the American Chiefs of Staff were formulating for the immediate future hinged all on a large preponderance of British troops in the forefront of action, since American soldiers could not be trained, equipped and brought across the oceans soon enough to bear their equitable share.[23] This was a political and psychological handicap likely to militate against a commanding position for the American standard bearers in the Centre.

Under these inauspicious circumstances Winant made his inaugural call at 10 Tolumbat Street, seat of the office of the British Minister of State and the half-evacuated headquarters of the now Anglo-American Middle East Supply Centre.

The American Role in the Middle East

When he returned to Washington almost exactly a year later, the political and military constellation in the Middle East had changed beyond recognition. The bid of the Axis for mastery of the Middle East had gone down to final defeat in North Africa and north of the Caucasus at Stalingrad. American troops had had their baptism of fire in North Africa and were now leading and outnumbering the armies of Britain in the Allied assault on Italy. The Indian Ocean was safe from Japanese intrusion and the amphibious march of the United States toward Japan was past its first island markers. Nearly 30,000 U.S. servicemen were toiling in the Persian Corridor, hauling cargo to Russia at an annual rate of more than 1.25 million tons, over incredible terrain; they were manning or directing assembly plants with an output of almost 4,000 transport vehicles and 80 aircraft per month; and they were in the process of building port installations, highways, rail and road transport facilities, factories, workshops, and the like, at a cost to the American taxpayer of $61,000,000.[24] This American contingent now was not only larger than either the British or Russian occupation forces in Iran, but the largest military unit maintained by any Allied nation in any sector of the Middle East theater outside North Africa.

Supply depots, service installations, and air transport bases flying the Stars and Stripes were strewn from Massaua to the Elburz Mountains, and American aid and equipment had built a trans-African air route connecting Egypt with the Gold Coast via Khartoum and ferrying men and materiel across the continent in impressive numbers and quantities.[25] The machinery of lend-lease was in full gear, ultimately pouring into the area, on credit or "cash-reimbursable" terms, more than $75,000,000 worth of goods and services for both military and civilian consumption.[26] In Cairo, a full-fledged

American theater command, United States Armed Forces in the Middle East (U.S.A.F.I.M.E.), held forth, comprising among its elements the Eritrea Base Command, the Middle East Service Command, the Levant Service Command and the Persian Gulf Service Command.[27] Numerous U.S. civilian missions in Iran were at work dispensing technical assistance to local governments on matters of finance, agriculture, food controls, internal security, public health, the management of pharmaceutical imports, petroleum economics, and rural education. In Iran alone there were more than ten such deputations (sometimes with overlapping assignments), among them the missions headed, respectively, by Col. H. Norman Schwarzkopf (gendarmerie), and Dr. Arthur C. Millspaugh (grain collection, price control, fiscal policy, transportation, and consumer goods distribution); all of them had come at the special request of the Teheran government.[28] In Iran also were several military missions and at one time the government proposed the designation of an American officer as "Intendant General of the Iranian Army" to take logistics and paymaster problems under his wing.[29]

Another testimony to American expansion in the region was the proliferation of U.S. plenipotentiaries, roving reporters and visiting Senators (including the Truman Committee); Washington doled out travel orders to the Middle East with far less parsimony than before. The United States now had a resident minister in Saudi Arabia—instead of collateral accreditation of the U.S. Minister of Egypt—as well as new diplomatic missions in the fledgling republics of Syria and Lebanon.[30] The embassies, legations and consulates were coming alive with the bustle of representations speaking for a growing assortment of federal departments and bureaus, such as the Departments of Commerce, Agriculture, Labor, Justice, and the Treasury, the Offices of War Information, Lend-Lease Administration, Censorship, Strategic Services, Economic Warfare, Agricultural War Relations, and the Petroleum Coordinator for War, the War Shipping Administration, the War Food Administration, the Board of War Communications, the Bureau of the Budget, and others.[31]

A year before the giant beyond the Atlantic had only been stirring. But now, in the days of August and September 1942, the continuous disembarkation of tanks, artillery, and dismantled planes had marked at last the "full stride" phase of American succor, and a few weeks later these same tanks, guns and planes, fully mounted, assembled and serviced with the help of U.S. quartermasters and mechanics on the spot, had set the stage on which General Montgomery and his Eighth Army commenced their march to Tunis.[32]

The only American enclave that appeared to be untouched by the historic invasion of American manpower in the Middle East was the U.S. contingent at M.E.S.C. headquarters. Its size was still microscopic. But the opposite was true of its impact on the stature and status of the Centre. Though grossly outnumbered, Winant and his companions had not been buried. M.E.S.C. was an Anglo-American team, and it had been a matter of blending, not grafting. In London and Washington, M.E.S.C. recommendations were respected regardless of the nationality of the official who happened to have signed them.[33] The London *Economist* referred to the Centre as a remarkable and successful piece of *international* machinery.[34] In the United States it was cited even in popular literature as an example of how the *United Nations* were organizing themselves to meet the problem of civilian supply in Allied countries.[35] And the Centre was enjoying a growing reputation as the "best example" of how the United States and Britain, despite trade rivalries in peacetime, succeeded in planning and executing together a joint program of exports and aid to the civilian sector of a region.[36]

Evolution of Anglo-American Supply Coordination

Anglo-American integration in the Centre was part of a larger evolution which by the end of 1942 had, according to some observers, made the Grand Alliance an "economic even more than a political and military fact." [37] Through the instrumentality of numerous boards, committees, combined agencies and less formal arrangements, the resources of America and the Commonwealth were allocated for overseas use, in ever larger measure, according to the dictates of war needs, not national trade interest. Both nations closed out entire production lines in favor of concentrated production and procurement in the partner country. If tires for overseas could be more efficiently procured in the United States even though British tire factories had been the traditional suppliers then so be it; if oils and fats needed somewhere could be shipped over a shorter distance from a Commonwealth source, bypassing normal U.S. suppliers, then make way for the Commonwealth.[38] "Economic rationalization on an international scale had existed in earlier times, but never to anything like the same degree." [39]

That this cooperation could evolve so rapidly was attributable to a great extent to the foundations laid months before the United States had actually entered the war. The same was true of the fruitful amalgamation achieved in the Middle East Supply Centre.

Long before El Alamein there were a number of notable instances when U.S. assistance had come just in time to avert a serious deterioration of the British position in the Middle East.[40] The story of American aid in the Middle East actually began in the first days of 1941 when General William B. Donovan toured the area as personal representative of the White House to make an assessment of the political and military outlook.[41] Several technical survey missions were now dispatched. By May 1941, shortly after the enactment of lend-lease and the opening of the Red Sea to U.S. merchant shipping (from which the Neutrality Act of 1939 had barred them heretofore), Churchill could already report that the President was "pushing U.S. supplies toward Suez to the utmost," [42] and that one could look forward to making the port of Basra in Iraq, "a real American assembly point." [43]

Now lend-lease equipment was starting to arrive. The Middle East front was one of its earliest beneficiaries, receiving, for example, more than half of the first lot of General Grant tanks produced, almost before the ink had dried on the Lend-Lease Act.[44] With lend-lease came new swarms of special emissaries to report on whether the British authorities receiving the goods faced up to strategic requirements, quartermaster efficiency, combat effectiveness and other performance standards demanded by stern Congressional auditors of aid programs at home.[45] Leading the host was W. Averell Harriman, the President's personal representative and troubleshooter for aid to Britain. His report not only included a sympathetic statement of Britain's far-flung needs and desperation, but echoed the general censure of British arrangements for the reception, processing and combat validation of American equipment.[46] The rivulets of all these findings brought forth in Washington, on 13 September 1941 a presidential prescript known as the "Middle East Directive." In it President Roosevelt outlined a program of substantially increased American aid and personnel for the Middle East coupled with provisions for more direct participation of the United States in the local decisions affecting the utilization of American equipment in the area. Measures were also authorized for the creation of U.S. facilities for servicing this equipment on the spot.[47]

The very issuance of a separate presidential directive for lend-lease aid to a whole region was unusual. It emphasized the importance the Middle East was gradually attaining in American eyes; so did the specific enterprises stipulated by it.

Two military missions were to go to the Middle East, one to Iran to be stationed in the port of Basra in Iraq and a "North African Mission" to be headquartered in Cairo. Furthermore, the President ordered the establishment forthwith of a string of American supply depots from Central Africa to Northern Iran for the assembly, testing, and repair of lend-lease materiel. Provisions were made for the instruction and training of British and Russian personnel in the use and proper handling of materiel delivered into their hands. Finally, technical advisers were to be assigned to the British forces to assist in the elimination of supply bottlenecks and the general overhaul of the logistic apparatus of the Middle East Command then in progress.[48]

Bearing in content and phrasing the personal imprint of President Roosevelt and some of his closest advisers,[49] the Middle East directive was quickly implemented. General Raymond A. Wheeler commanding the United States Military Mission to Iran, and General Maxwell heading the United States Military Mission to North Africa, arrived in Basra and Cairo respectively during the latter part of November;[50] work on the first American supply depot was started in Gura, Eritrea, during the same month. In Iran, U.S. activities were focused on accelerating the organization of an overland supply route to Russia first started by the British Persia and Iraq Command (Paiforce). In Cairo, American attention was riveted on the urgent needs of the Eighth Army.

Out of the Iranian and North African Missions grew the Persian Gulf Command and U.S.A.F.I.M.E., fattening slowly but steadily on larger assignments and consignments under the impulse of America's own belligerency and mobilization. It took months after the arrivals of Generals Wheeler and Maxwell before the lend-lease aid they were to administer was more than a trickle.

In preparing for the day of reckoning with General Rommel, the Britons and the growing number of Americans in the Middle East concluded the numerous formal and casual arrangements which made Anglo-American cooperation in the theater an operational fact.[51] This precedent of comradeship was the first foundation for the successful "scrambling" of British and American elements in the Middle East Supply Centre. The other was the formula under which rank and responsibility was allocated to the new American arrivals and the spirit in which they were accommodated as they reported for duty.

6

The Anglo-American Phase

The American Contingent

In May 1942, General Maxwell and the Minister to Egypt, Alexander Kirk, officially took their places as American spokesmen in the Middle East War Council.[1] As soon as Winant arrived he was installed as chairman of the Executive Committee of the Middle East Supply Centre. The agreement between the two governments provided that the Executive (or Working) Committee of the Centre be composed of four members, two each from the United States and the British Commonwealth. The second American seat was given to Rountree who also acted as Secretary of the Committee. The British members were Commander Jackson and a representative of the Minister of State.[2]

In principle, complete numerical parity was to prevail between the two nationalities. Positions were vacated or created to seat the Americans as they arrived. Macduffie, after first serving as Winant's assistant and stand-in, was placed at the head of a new Division of Materials and Industrial Production which ultimately directed the industrial mobilization effort of M.E.S.C., while Thibodeaux became assistant director for agriculture of the Food Division and joined the first M.E.S.C. Agricultural Mission on a tour of Middle Eastern countries. (Late in 1942, Thibodeaux was replaced by R. S. Kifer.) [3]

No more shuffling of places was needed. For some months to come, no additional Americans came to bolster the team of Winant, Rountree, Macduffie, and Kifer. By themselves they carried the full load of U.S. participation through the climactic events which ended with the expulsion of the Germans from North Africa and their decisive defeat in Southern Russia. Only then did change occur. In mid-1943, Winant returned to Washington for medical treatment. His place was taken temporarily by Douglas M. Moffat, a New York corporation lawyer and personal friend of Secretary of War Stimson.[4] Meanwhile, Winant labored in Washington to ensure an accentuation of the "American slant" in M.E.S.C. through the dispatch of additional personnel. He also urged the appointment as his successor of a man of high rank and international standing to counterbalance the political and military *haut monde* representing the United Kingdom in Cairo.[5]

His counsel was heard. In September 1943, the United States resolved to establish in the Middle East a new diplomatic post, a regional ambassador with primary concern for economic affairs. His title was to be Director of American Economic Operations in the Middle East, his headquarters a new "American Economic Mission to the Middle East (A.E.M.M.E.)." He was awarded the *personal* rank of Minister, as a badge of protocolary equality with the British Minister of State. He was to "coordinate" (in fact, to assume) most of those responsibilities which, in a large integrated regionwide theater of military activities could not be adequately administered by localized diplomacy, particularly in the economic field; he was given the additional title of "Special Assistant" to all American legation and embassy heads as a placating gesture toward the regular chiefs of missions in the Middle East. His primary function was to serve as Principal Representative of the United States on the Executive Committee of M.E.S.C. and its chairman, just as Winant had.[6]

Several candidates were considered for the job, among them William C. Bullitt, former U.S. ambassador in Moscow and Paris, Maj. Gen. Patrick J. Hurley, and Winant himself. Bullitt proved unavailable, Hurley declined, and Winant protested that somebody of more conspicuous standing in national and international affairs than himself was needed.[7] Finally on 10 September, a White House release announced the designation of James M. Landis.[8]

Although the new regional ambassador had little diplomatic or Middle Eastern experience, his qualifications were nonetheless impressive in terms of what was needed for M.E.S.C.—a flair for administrative creativity and prestige in the world of American officialdom. He had been a professor of law and Dean of the Law School of Harvard University, and Washington abounded with former students and associates of the Dean. He had served in high and at the same time pioneering offices of state—as a member of the Federal Trade Commission, a member and later Chairman of the Securities and Exchange Commission, and as Director of the Office of Civil Defense. He had been closely associated with the "brain trust" of the early Roosevelt Administration and was believed to have the ear of the President and some of his closest advisers. He also had had at least some live acquaintance with the Asian milieu, having spent part of his younger life with his missionary parents in Japan and China and serving later as Trustee of The American University in Cairo.

Dean Landis arrived in Cairo in December 1943 after stopping for consultations with American and British officials in London. Within a short time he gathered various contrifugal and highly individualistic missions representing the U.S. government in matters of lend-lease, economic warfare, shipping, relief, monetary, and other nonmilitary responsibilities, under the coordination of his American Economic Mission to the Middle East. He also began to campaign vigorously for an intensification of U.S. economic diplomacy in the Middle East and persuaded Washington to send him a modest number of assistants to serve in Egypt and points East. With their help American aid and counsel was brought to bear on the wartime problems of many Middle Eastern countries where before U.S. officials had worked rather unobtrusively in the shadow of opulently staffed and mandated British agencies.[9] Many formal and informal Anglo-American arrangements hastily concluded in past days under the pressure of emergencies were now subjected to a more leisurely review and revision. This also applied to understandings relative to the Middle East Supply Centre.

From the crop of new U.S. arrivals in Cairo, Minister Landis seconded a number of top assistants for part or full-time duty at the Centre; almost overnight, the American contingent grew to fifty. Top echelon ranks were promptly provided for them in the rapidly expanding M.E.S.C. organization. Livingston L. Short, Landis' chief lend-lease officer, became the third U.S. member of the enlarged Executive Committee. George Woodbridge was made Director of the all-important Division of Programming. Dr. Henry Van Zile Hyde was named Director of the Medical Division and John Coneybear, after first leading the Transport Division, went to Saudi Arabia to head the now M.E.S.C. office in Jidda. Early in 1945, Woodbridge was elevated to the post of Deputy Director General. These were only the most important among many changes following the new American influx.[10]

The peak of American membership in M.E.S.C. coincided with the beginning of the end of the war. Allied shipping, and Anglo-American supply cooperation in the Middle East were subjected to one more convulsive strain during the weeks preceding the landings in Normandy and Southern France. Thereafter demobilization began hastened by the urge of all ranks to go home or transfer to more active theaters.

Mr. Landis resigned in January 1945. For a time his functions were divided. Harold B. Hoskins, formerly chief M.E.S.C. representative in Iran, was appointed by the State Department as economic counsellor for the Middle East area, accredited to each of the U.S. diplomatic missions in the countries of the M.E.S.C. area. The Foreign Economic Administration appointed, as its representative in the Middle East, Dero A. Saunders, formerly assistant chief of the Middle East Division of F.E.A. in Washington. He was succeeded as F.E.A. representative in March 1945 by John P. Dawson, who had been chief of the Middle East Division in Washington. When Harold Hoskins resigned as economic counsellor in August 1945, Dawson was appointed by the State Department as acting economic counsellor for the Middle East and similarly accredited to U.S. diplomatic missions in the area. He continued as F.E.A. regional representative at the same time. He returned to Washington in December 1945.[11]

A Successful Partnership

Dawson was in Cairo when M.E.S.C. closed its doors and attended the farewell proceedings at which Britons and Americans, prior to "unscrambling" and scattering to the corners of the earth, reviewed nostalgically the extraordinary amalgamation of two nationalities which had been practiced for more than three years of great stress, while assisting and protecting the subsistence of other nations.[12]

It had been an extraordinary partnership. World War II had presented many Americans with the necessity or opportunity of mixing with men of other nations in armies and agencies of joint endeavor. The rosters of these "combined" organizations were impressive documents of binationality and masterpieces of compromise in their ground rules and judiciously calculated division of titles, tasks and trust. Their fate as instruments of alliance varied. Some fostered unity, others accentuated disagreements. In some, various nationalities became true partners, often despite numerical disparity; in others they merely sparred as keen barterers.[13] In the Middle East Supply Centre, four Americans joined with nearly a hundred nationals of the Commonwealth coming from Britain, Australia, South Africa, and New Zealand, to reach, in the dark months of 1942, that rarely touched pinnacle of international partnership in which nationality yields to functionality. Later when the danger had passed and fissures appeared in the higher echelons of the Great Alliance this *esprit de corps* was challenged by a few American latecomers. Echoing Anglo-American divergences at the summit about such questions as colonial emancipation, the removal of trade restrictions, access to Middle Eastern oil, and relations with the Soviet Union and other problems, these men deemed the national interest endangered by an agency which was dominated numerically by the British, yet decided, for example, whether a given Middle Eastern country should import from the United States or Britain.[14] Attempts to substitute tough nation-to-nation bartering for technical decision-making ensued. They failed to undermine the integration of views of earlier days. Instead of a clash of nationalities a collision of personalities developed, as most Americans opted against the proposed concept.[15]

The men and women who witnessed and lived "Operation Scramble" are almost unanimous in attributing much of its overall success to the extraordinary dimensions of M.E.S.C.'s work. The first Americans reporting for duty found it easy to blend into Commander Jackson's hard-driving team without fuss or fanfare. For almost immediately they were caught in a high sense of purpose and a feverish quest for results that would help stem the German invader poised only a few dozen miles away. There was little room for disagreement on policy or priorities; and in terms of protocol, there was nothing higher for the Americans to ask than the chairmanship of the Executive Committee the British had already conceded to Frederick Winant.

After the battle of El Alamein the fervor and fever did not subside. The emphasis at M.E.S.C. now shifted to a mission in which Americans of the Roosevelt era and Britons of the era of the Beveridge plan and the Colonial Welfare Acts had little difficulty in finding common ground: the protection from disaster of the long neglected, often wretchedly governed, and sorely underprivileged masses of a large subcontinent. Here too the technician was not sorely tempted to yield to the politician. Threats of famine, unemployment, epidemics, floods, riots, and rabble-rousing inspired by shortages, had to be countered. Nine cases out of ten were emergencies, and ten out of ten involved human welfare and communal peace. Here was a multidimensional opportunity to do good; here also was an unusual concentration of power to do good. None of the Americans or Britishers sent to serve with M.E.S.C. had ever enjoyed such opportunity and such power.[16] The eagerness to use them for the welfare of other nations easily restrained the urge to serve the narrower interests of one's own government.

The excitement and drama of M.E.S.C. operations cast a spell on every American who came to serve, whether they came as volunteers or as "draftees," whether they stayed for years or just a few months. Macduffie, who volunteered for M.E.S.C. service and worked in the Centre for almost three years of continuous duty, longer than any other American member, related how on the very day of his arrival he found himself engulfed in a

> rush of exciting activity that never seemed to let up until it was time to go home at the end of the war. Around us was the constant reminder that the lives of millions depended on our decisions. Before we had set up our desks and filing cabinets, hundreds of letters, memoranda and telephone calls started to pile up requiring us to make decisions big enough to frighten a prime minister. So involved did one become in the problems of the Middle East that Britishers and Americans alike more often than not forgot about their nationalities and acted as if they were elected plenipotentiaries of the populations around them. Very soon we were working 18 hours a day with no letup for weekends or holidays, and only an occasional getaway for a movie. I never worked so hard in my life—and never had so much fun.[17]

Moffat, who stayed but a few months (he had been "drafted" by Secretary of War Stimson as temporary replacement for Winant and agreed to the assignment despite his sixty-odd years only on condition that he would stay no longer than six months), found M.E.S.C. such an "interesting place" that he deeply regretted having insisted on a short tour of duty. "I would have gladly stayed to the end had they asked me to." [18]

These sentiments were echoed on the British side by the Economic Adviser to the Minister of State in these comments on Anglo-American comity in the Centre:

Anyone who had experience of the friction sometimes generated in the two capitals could not fail to be struck with the cooperative spirit and single-minded interest in the job that prevailed in Cairo. The importance of the work that M.E.S.C. was doing appealed to the most crusty and disillusioned of its temporary officials, but the majority of its staff were neither. They were either experts engaged in a job which gave them greater scope than they had before or administrators with a sense of mission and a flair for getting things done. Each in his own way found that working together in M.E.S.C. yielded a satisfaction that was enhanced rather than diminished by different national backgrounds. As an experiment in joint Anglo-American administration, M.E.S.C. must be pronounced a success.[19]

The Combined Agency for Middle East Supplies (CAMES)

Nothing attests better to the accomplishment of M.E.S.C. as a focus of intergovernmental cooperation than the spillover of its spirit and techniques into the machinery for Middle East Supply in London and Washington. M.E.S.C., it should be remembered, had no executive or enforcement powers. It could only study and recommend. All the skill, competence and good fellowship practiced in Cairo would be futile if the arbiters of supply in England and America distrusted and ignored the Centre's recommendations. International cooperation in the field could be easily nullified by self-centered national review at the home base.

In sharp contrast to the procedures adopted for other foreign areas, the two governments took the unusual step of entrusting the adjudication of civilian supplies for the Middle East to mixed Anglo-American committees in Britain and the United States working closely with the Centre and geared to its operational concept.

In the United Kingdom, a Middle East Supplies Committee comprising representatives of various ministries concerned with supply, shipping, and Middle Eastern affairs, and of the U.S. Embassy, determined the allocation of British controlled supplies and shipping for the Middle East (on the basis of half-yearly programs proposed by M.E.S.C.).[20]

In the United States, a Combined Agency for Middle East Supplies (CAMES) was created in 1943 for the adjudication of supplies and shipping tonnage of American origin. CAMES undertook not

only the formulation of half-year supply programs, but also the release of export licenses and lend-lease certificates covering individual shipments. These operations were guided by committees composed of representatives of the Foreign Economic Administration,
the State Department, the Treasury, the War Production Board, the
War Shipping Administration, the War Food Administration, the
British Supply Mission, and the British Colonial Supply Council.[21]

The touchiness of U.S. authorities and the public regarding any
system that would give a foreign country a determining voice in the
allocation of U.S. production during the war is well known.[22]
Under these circumstances the toleration until October 1944 (when
CAMES was dissolved) of a procedure leaving the certification of substantial U.S. exports to the discretion of a "combined" agency was a
remarkable testimony to the influence of the experience in Cairo
where the method had first proven itself.[23]

It is worth noting that the investiture of CAMES in September
1943 came at a time when close cooperation between the two nations in Middle East supply measures was, in a strict sense, much
less opportune from the American viewpoint than early in 1942
when the creation of such an agency had first been proposed—and
bypassed.[24] Then there were only two persons in the whole machinery of the United States government working full-time on matters connected with nonmilitary supplies for the Middle East; lack
of knowhow and personnel had simply forced the Americans to
turn to British officials for advice and guidance.[25] Yet Winant's proposal in 1942 to establish a combined agency met little enthusiasm
then.[26] By 1943 the number of full-time personnel assigned to economic relations with the Middle East was nearing thirty, most of
them members of the Middle East Division of the U.S. Foreign Economic Administration; there also were numerous operatives out in
the field, including hundreds of American specialists, in mufti or in
uniform, working on supply and transport problems in the Persian
Corridor. Washington now had the machinery and manpower—
although not necessarily enough intimate knowledge of the region
—to "go it alone" in supply and other non-military rubrics of Allied activities in the Middle East; in fact, as far as petroleum was
concerned, the United States had already begun not only to move
without Great Britain but against her.[27] Nevertheless, the United
States at this juncture moved toward greater rather than less cooperation with Britain in matters concerning Middle East supplies, and
CAMES was born.

Of all the administrative additions to the original edifice of M.E.S.C., the Combined Agency was on all counts the most important. CAMES was the official channel of all communications between the Centre and American and Allied authorities in the United States. CAMES reviewed all programs, requests and vetoes of the Centre affecting procurement in America, in the light of its own assessment of Middle Eastern needs. CAMES argued the case of the Middle Eastern civilian before the controllers of American production and transportation in Washington. CAMES pressed producers and shippers for priorities and a speed-up of production and shipping schedules. CAMES issued, speedily, the release certificates without which no non-military shipment for Middle Eastern destinations could leave the country.[28] The CAMES office in New York looked after early sailing dates for goods awaiting shipment and worked closely with exporters, forwarders and warehousemen to ensure observance of official priorities and locate the source of all needless delays. It also established close relations with the Office of Cargo Clearance of the Anglo-American shipping pool in the Port of New York, seeing to it that the first ship, regardless of flag, bound for the Middle East would take a specified cargo.[29]

This constant effort to expedite individual shipments to the Middle East, once authorized, at all the levels of the complex procurement structure in the United States was almost as important as securing the original lump authorizations themselves. Many foreign diplomats and importers discovered to their chagrin that the receipt of an export license was but the first among many laborious and exhausting marches through a labyrinth of negotiations and appeals before the merchandise sailed—if at all.

> Middle East governments and traders were fortunate in having at their disposal machinery which ensured that facilities were nearly always granted for whatever imports were approved. If this had not been the case, it would have been almost out of the question for individual governments to undertake the burdensome and time-consuming task of processing their requirements through all the different bodies which might raise questions and objections.[30]

One might add, that in view of their lukewarm war records, some Middle Eastern countries would have found the going particularly toilsome.

Most agencies allocating American-controlled production and

shipping to foreign countries had to seek periodical guidance from the Combined Boards whose task it was to determine whether the proposed allocation fitted into the over-all supply situation of the Allies.[31] This work of global data corrolation, however, was anticipated by CAMES, inasmuch as the main function of its British members was to furnish information on availabilities under British control for each supply case under consideration. (A similar opportunity for "comparison shopping" was furnished by the American members of the Middle East Supplies Committee in London.) Another time-consuming phase in the allocation process was therefore foreshortened.

All this greatly fortified the position of M.E.S.C. in its own area of operations as a conduit, spigot, and pump for the waters which the parched economies craved. A serious threat to this position appeared on the horizon, however, when the United States began to authorize Middle East countries not under British control to negotiate lend-lease aid directly with Washington.[32] There were, as was to be expected, many attempts by these countries to seize the opportunity of direct negotiations to obtain favors that would circumvent M.E.S.C. controls.[33] In 1943 and 1944, the productive and transport capacity of the Allies had reached such formidable dimensions that the civilian needs of the Middle East, from the Olympian perspective of a government mustering and equipping an army of more than 10 million, loomed no bigger than the nibble of a mouse. The scrupulous screening conducted in Cairo struck some officials in Washington like the mindless automatism of an officious bureaucracy that did not know when it was time to quit.[34] U.S. exporters started to stir again and diplomats from Egypt and other Middle Eastern nations were not only persistent but furious in their conviction that United States officials were either malevolent or overly pompous in their practice of combing the infinitesimal claims of the Middle East to America's titanic resources.[35] Perhaps, it was suggested, a generous rule-of-thumb might do the trick just as well as the ponderous M.E.S.C. machinery.[36]

It was fortunate that the Centre had in Washington a powerful advocate in the Combined Agency led by the former M.E.S.C. chairman Winant. From the intimate knowledge which their experience with the Supply Centre had given them, Winant and his colleagues could demonstrate effectively to the State Department and the lend-lease administrators the economic upheaval that would follow a suspension of the controlled austerity patterns which M.E.S.C.

through its regulation of trade and shipping had created and solidi-
fied in the Middle East.[37] As a result American support of M.E.S.C.
procedures was reconfirmed; specifically, lend-lease allocations for
civilian use were only made within the scope of import quotas fixed
by CAMES and the Supply Centre.[38]

Strength Through Combination

American co-sponsorship did not change the Centre's statutory tools
of action; to the very end its influence

> rested not on any executive powers conferred on it but on the
> fact that the controllers of shipping and supplies in London
> and Washington relied on its recommendations as to the treat-
> ment to be accorded to the requests of Middle East govern-
> ments for facilities. Apart from this indirect source of authority
> it had to depend on securing the voluntary cooperation of gov-
> ernments and establishing relations of mutual confidence with
> ministers, officials and traders in the territories concerned.[39]

American co-sponsorship did not change the basic procedures of
M.E.S.C. It merely strengthened and lengthened certain branches of
the organizational tree, such as the regional offices and representa-
tion in the United States.

American co-sponsorship did not bring, as has been shown, a surplus of sorely needed personnel; Americans attached to the Centre
never exceeded a ratio of one to ten. Nor did it add new dimensions to the finances of the Centre. To the very end, M.E.S.C. remained technically a British government bureau whose overhead
expenses and salaries (except the emoluments of U.S. officials) were
"borne upon the vote of the Minister of War Transport." [40] Great
Britain also defrayed part of the overhead cost of CAMES headquarters in Washington and most of the budget of the CAMES office in
New York.[41] The only general financial contribution made by the
United States was a book credit of $500,000 to the lend-lease ac-
count of the United Kingdom (reverse lend-lease).[42]

But American co-sponsorship gave to the Centre the decisive card
to play in the situation it encountered: Almost complete control
over American commercial and lend-lease exports to the Middle
East for civilian use. This was the trumpcard Commander Jackson

played when he transformed his miniature parish from an ingatherer of statistics into an instrument of statecraft.

It is no coincidence that the British scheme for regional control of shipping and overseas trade in the Middle East languished in 1941 but sprang to sudden life almost at the very moment when the United States signified its official readiness to participate, in February 1942. When the scheme was conceived and hatched by the specialists in the Middle East Command and the British Ministry of War Transport, British shipping and trade were the principal provisioners of the Middle East; American exports, while respectable, were held in rein by the Neutrality Act which barred U.S. shipping from the Mediterranean and the Red Sea. It was expected that by closely subordinating the allocation of British shipping—and therefore shipments—to the recommendations of the Centre the latter would be in a position not only to effect a practicable reduction of non-essential imports but, through the threat of "supply sanctions," [43] promote austerity, rationing and stricter foreign trade controls throughout the area. But just when M.E.S.C. opened its doors, the British government was reaching the reluctant conclusion that its strained production facilities no longer could produce a significant surplus for Middle Eastern civilian consumption and began to advise importers to shift to American sources of supply wherever possible—despite the ominous meaning of such action for Britain's postwar trade.[44] At the same time the United States reopened the Red Sea to American merchant vessels and adopted the lend-lease Act. Very rapidly exports from the United States soared to a level more than twice the prewar record of 1938 [45] and moved into a commanding lead over British trade.

The flood of American shipments to the Middle East had substantially blunted the Centre's attack on port congestion and stolen the thunder of its austerity campaign. The Centre had to compete with the din of Axis propaganda, resurgent nationalism,[46] and popular protests against shortages, all plaguing the waking hours of kings, chancellors and colonial governors. It had neither reward to offer nor punishment to threaten, because imports from America sailing on U.S. ships were beyond its call or recall. Meanwhile the question may well have been asked in the lands of the Middle East whether it would not be downright foolish to adopt stringent and unpopular restrictions at the very time when bountiful relief from many shortages was sailing in from America on ships inviolate to German submarines. Why not take maximum advantage of the reprieve instead of quibbling on whether nylons and refrigerators were essential or not? And what guarantee could M.E.S.C. offer that the sacrificial cooperation of one country would not be abused to increase the pickings of another country?

Unable to control the now reigning sources of civilian supplies and shipping and with London being unwilling to sanction compulsive measures (which would arouse both the nationalists and the Americans),[47] M.E.S.C. stood helpless.

In February and March 1942, the new Director General of M.E.S.C. returned to the charge. But now he carried a stick as well as a carrot. The United States had placed its licensing, lend-lease and loading dispositions under the guidance of M.E.S.C. wherever civilian requirements for the Middle East were involved. With some of the Allied war production load shifted from Britain to America, the former could again assume responsibility for some import requirements of friendly or neutral countries. Given the indispensability of American and British supplies, the Supply Centre now had not just a stick but a deadly bludgeon in its hands with which to threaten any local government in the Middle East not in the mood to follow M.E.S.C. "recommendations." Once the Egyptian Prime Minister, or the Governor of Palestine, or the Regent of Iraq, or an influential Levantine merchant found out that no circumvention of M.E.S.C. by direct appeals to London and Washington or by separate, divisive approaches to either was possible, cooperation came forward without delay.

The contrast between 1941 and 1942 in the operations of the Centre—the "before" and the "after" of the Anglo-American marriage—was too sharp to be merely a coincidence or the work of better leadership, or the emergence from organizational infancy. It was the contrast between an organization that spent months of fruitless negotiations to get the government of Iraq to authorize the export of a small surplus quantity of barley to a starving neighbor [48] and an organization that initiated a gigantic cereal collection scheme in Syria, induced Persian Gulf sheikhdoms to switch from rice to wheat consumption, forced Egypt to buy drugs in Palestine rather than in the United States or Britain, caused the Lebanon to eat gray rather than white bread, administered large reserve stocks of grains and coal which it moved to critical points in the area as needed, brought a new leather industry to the Sudan, mounted a twelve-nation campaign against a locust invasion, and told a High Commissioner's aide in effect to go and hang himself when he plaintively protested against a veto of import licenses approved by his staff.[49]

The teeth which the Centre's privileged access to American resources put into "supply sanctions" as a punitive instrument represented but one side of the American contribution to M.E.S.C.'s "striking power." The bludgeon of supply sanctions could work wonders but it could not do the whole job. In the long run more than submission to blackmail was needed to maintain local responsiveness to so many initiatives emanating from the Centre in so many ramifications of Middle Eastern life. Besides, the same scruples which kept the Allies from using naked force to impose their scheme of economic discipline, also kept them from applying the bludgeon of supply sanctions too radically. It did not take much wisdom and experience to conclude that the men running the affairs of the Middle East Supply Centre would not really go to the extreme of starving or crippling a country economically in order to punish it for non-cooperation. Had this realization been consistently put to a test, the M.E.S.C. scheme might have floundered.[50]

In the long run, the ability to inspire confidence not only in their competence but in their motives was an indispensable prerequisite of effectiveness for the leaders and agents of the Centre. Here politics came into play as indeed it must in any scheme of supranational interference in matters of bread and butter. And here British agencies had to cope with the long inheritance of distrust which foreign rule in the Middle East had imbedded in the minds and attitudes of so many of the men who had to be dealt with on the local level. The Middle East Supply Centre was no exception. Why did the British press for the curtailment of Egyptian cotton acreage? To make room for more grain production, as they claimed, or to give a boost to competing cotton growers in the Sudan? Why was all this encouragement given to industry in Palestine dominated by the Jews? To increase regional self-sufficiency, as M.E.S.C. affirmed, or to bolster the drive for a Jewish state? Why impose a drastic and immensely unpopular grain collection scheme in Syria and Lebanon? To feed hungry Egyptians, Turks, and Kuwaitis, as the sponsors declared, or to discredit the new regime of independence? Why discourage the establishment of new import and export firms? To halt a proliferation that would have complicated the control of foreign trade, as the British ambassador stated on behalf of M.E.S.C., or to preserve the predominance of British traders?

That this propensity to suspect did not gain the upper hand in local attitudes is partly a debt which M.E.S.C. owed to the anti-colonial nimbus of the United States.

In the wartime years the prestige of America in the Middle East rose to new heights, not only because of the omnipresent evidence of her material prowess, but because of the image of American liberalism which the Atlantic Charter and the actions and pronouncements of Franklin Roosevelt had successfully implanted in the Arab world.[51] Arabs, Iranians, Ethiopians, Cypriots, and Jews, as well as Indians, Indonesians, and Africans had taken good note of the unabashed "anti-imperialist" views openly stated by the President and many of his principal lieutenants.[52]

How conscious Americans were of the sensibilities of nations and populations in areas subjected to colonial rule, was shown by Patrick Hurley's refusal to accept a commission from the President to serve as "American Ambassador to all the Middle East nations." He gave as his reason that this "was an imperialistic tactic and tended to humiliate the nations involved," [53] an obvious reference to the British Minister of State. Roosevelt apparently took the hint. When James Landis was chosen to be the American opposite number to the British Minister of State, his title pointedly stressed economics rather than a political scope ("Director of Economic Operations") and he was given the rank of Minister explicitly in a *personal* rather than *functional* capacity.[54]

These were the days when Wendell Willkie toured the world and reported confidently in his "One World" account on the great reservoir of goodwill toward America he had found everywhere. In the Middle East, this reservoir had been fed by conspicuous monuments of American philanthropy such as the American universities and colleges established in Beirut, Cairo, and Istanbul, the outstanding effort of Near East Relief after World War I, and in the continued benevolence of foundations and church missions.[55] The charms of these benefactions had not been scarred, like those of other countries, by conquest, plunder, and imperialist acquisition. Except for Arab resentment at the official American support of Zionist aspirations, the American slate was remarkably clean at the start of the war. When, therefore, the United States became a consort in the British drive for greater economic self-control in various countries, the old inheritance of native distrust and truculence was attenuated by a realignment that could draw liberally on America's store of goodwill in the region.[56]

The "consortium" could do so not only because of what America had done in the past but because of what was expected of her in the future. The war had given new impetus to the hope for a loosening of foreign domination in the Middle East. The emergence of the United States as an active political force in the region created a ready-made opportunity to solicit American help for the drive against this domination. Shahs and sheikhs and chiefs of governments were easily induced to follow a tactic, sometimes subtly, sometimes crudely practiced, which tried to trade deference to Allied advice and plans for the promise of help to nationalist causes after the war.[57] Americans connected with the Middle East Supply Centre were not spared from exposure to this time-honored device. The most dramatic episode of this kind involving one of them was the secret, almost conspiratorial visit which King Faruq paid Landis in 1944. Amid elaborate precautions taken at the request of the King to dissimulate his nocturnal presence in Landis' home, he expounded his grievances against the British and begged for American assistance to his country's struggle.[58]

It would be unreasonable to expect Americans to remain insensitive to such appeals. As a consequence, Allied solidarity was often breached in the Middle East, particularly where preordained or preconceived anti-British prejudices of long standing affected the vision of the men involved. Where this solidarity remained intact, the Allied cause gained enormous strength from the combination of British knowhow and the American "halo." Such was the case at M.E.S.C. The continued, and loyal willingness of the United States to lend its "good name" to the Centre unquestionably had much to do with the fact that it retained a large measure of local influence long after the political climate had become adverse. In 1944 some Arab delegates to the Middle East Agricultural Development Conference could be heard speaking of the possibility of a postwar continuation of M.E.S.C., even though the whole region, in particular Egypt, reverberated with a flare-up of demands that Britain get out of the Arab World.[59]

The full meaning of American participation in the activities of the Middle East Supply Centre became evident at the close of the war. There were many proposals and many pressures to make the Centre a permanent fixture in the Middle East as an aid to economic development and political stability,[60] perhaps as a regional ramification of the United Nations.[61] This had wide support in British circles,[62] but was doomed to failure the moment it became clear that the official United States policy did not favor the project.[63] The Centre, which had started as a purely British enterprise could not, so it seemed, endure without American collaboration.

The detailed affirmation of the American contribution to the success of the Middle East Supply Centre must not be allowed to obscure the continued indispensability of Britain's share even after the predominance of the United States as a source of supplies and the relative immaculateness of America's political record in the Middle East had cast their spell. To the end, this was a partnership enterprise not only by agreement but by necessity.

Britain's merit was not only one of progeniture and precedence, having conceived the scheme, having given it organizational flesh and blood and having borne the initial brunt as emergency supplier and shipper, when the dispatch of coal, fertilizer, and wheat, from Britain and Australia, staved off an imminent series of crises.[64] The Commonwealth, indeed, continued to furnish a respectable supply of scarce materials to the Middle East long after the United States had entered the scene, partly because the new ally relieved some of the pressure on British-controlled resources, and partly because for months after Pearl Harbor the United States, caught in the birth pangs of its own mobilization, protested against having the whole load of Allied commitments in the world thrown into its lap.[65] The British merchant fleet for its part remained prominent in the Allies' capacity to ship civilian and military goods.

Nor can there be any question that the political hegemony and military presence of Britain, in this corner of the world, while a psychological handicap to M.E.S.C. at times, nonetheless gave much-needed leverage to certain aspects of its work. It is no coincidence that trade and rationing controls proposed and prompted by M.E.S.C. progressed faster in territories under colonial and mandatory rule or under military occupation, than in sovereign lands of the region.[66] The same factor was responsible for much of the excellent data flowing into the files of the Centre and serving its examiners and decision-makers. Again and again the Americans at M.E.S.C. had to recognize the great superiority of British fact-finding in the region. It was not only a matter of having more people at the sensitive points: It was also a matter of method.[67]

As noted earlier, it was in the availability of qualified personnel that the Commonwealth dominated its partner. The 10 to 1 staffing ratio prevailing in the M.E.S.C. establishment also held true out in the field, where British specialists were frequently engaged by local authorities to man important government positions, such as that of

Director General of Cereals in Iraq or of Co-director of Syrian Wheat Commission.[68] Only in Iran did Americans render comparable services.[69] Macduffie relates the perpetual wonder with which he and his U.S. colleagues saw the British produce overnight an expert or capable administrator when needed anywhere in the Middle East. He might come from the Middle East branches of u.k.c.c., from special contingents like the Spears Mission in Beirut, from obscure assignments in England (where Max Nicholson located him), or from members of Britain's large business community in the Middle East of prewar days.[70] If need be the armed services would search their meticulous records; orders would go out to Palestine, Aden, Eritrea, or Malta, and within a few days a man of appropriate qualifications would report to the Centre or a local government.[71] By contrast, pleas for American staff would go long unheeded; [72] some of the men finally sent lacked so much in certain qualifications that top U.S. officials in Cairo constantly apologized for them; [73] and the release of U.S. Army personnel for duty in the Centre never occurred, despite the massive accumulation of logistic talent in General Brehon B. Somervell's Services of Supply in Washington.

Manpower was not the only item of assistance m.e.s.c. received from the British Army and Navy and the r.a.f. There was an exceptionally close partnership between Jackson and General Sir Wilfred Lindsell, chief supply officer for the three services in Cairo,[74] thanks to which the military could be counted upon to surrender food, equipment, and other facilities to meet civilian emergencies. Outstanding examples of the Army's cooperation were the dispatch of soldiers and trucks to save a harvest in Iran and the voluntary postponement of repatriation by a batallion of South African engineers, so that they could build a tunnel for an irrigation project in Lebanon.[75] Meanwhile a long and arduous battle was waged between the U.S. Legation in Teheran and the Commanding General of the Persian Gulf Command because of the latter's persistent refusal to use his resources to participate in measures and projects designed to bolster the shaky economy of the country.[76]

The basic difference between the attitudes of the two cosponsors —and one which enormously enhanced the British contribution to m.e.s.c.—was that London, its legations and embassies in the Middle East and the leaders of the Middle East Command were firm, even enthusiastic, in their backing of the Centre's ambition to be not only a source of restraint but a dispenser of valuable services to the civilian populations of the region.[77] On the American side this concept was shared by a number of American officials in Cairo and in CAMES in Washington, but not on the higher government echelons; there the Centre was little more than a convenient mechanism for the control of exports and shipping.[78]

Thus, the support which the British gave to the activities of M.E.S.C. as an agency of civilian welfare in the Middle East was more valuable in the long run—though not decisive—because it expressed a policy rather than a confluence of circumstances; the American contribution was decisive in the short run—but less valuable later—because of the overwhelming supply superiority of the U.S. war economy.

United States cosponsorship greatly raised the executive potential of the Director General and his staff by sheer inadvertance. Until the Americans joined up, the Director General stood at the bottom of a ramified chain of command which involved the Ministry of War Transport, the Middle East Command and the Minister of State, with the latter, in the person of Lyttleton, taking firm control over the Middle Eastern end of M.E.S.C. operations. Then, the Anglo-American consortium reduced the status of the Minister to membership in a mixed committee in which Commander Jackson had co-equal status. Also, Lyttleton departed in the middle of this reorganization and his successor, R. G. Casey, arrived only after a hiatus during which Jackson had accumulated considerable personal prestige and influence,[79] which the relatively inexperienced newcomer showed no inclination to challenge.[80]

With Lyttleton's departure, the strong supervisory hand of one man now was replaced by the uncertain gropings of a committee which the Director General as a full member could easily dominate with his grasp of detail and ceaseless initiatives. Such a loophole the Commander did not leave unexploited. He and his staff prodded the local authorities with increasing personal assurance and independence. The Minister of State ceased to be a commanding factor in M.E.S.C. operations though he remained useful as statutory coordinator providing a roundtable where "jurisdictional disputes and crossing of wires" between M.E.S.C. and military authorities could be ironed out.[81] Meanwhile, it became increasingly difficult for British diplomats or administrators in the region to bypass M.E.S.C. with an appeal to anywhere except London. And there consultation with Washington often was necessary before countermanding became possible. For the rest, Commander Jackson had powerful friends in both capitals (such as Lyttleton and Winant) to support him.

Here, undoubtedly, lies one of the explanations for the somewhat mystifying executive posture of the chief of an "advisory" agency in dealing with local authorities—an agency bestriding the Middle East economy like a giant and imposing its views and wishes on the production and consumption of nearly 100 million people toiling in a vast subcontinent.

7

The Control of Imports

Basic Procedures [1]

BY the time the first Americans arrived at 10 Tolumbat Street and took up residence in the crowded and feverish capital city of Egypt, the organizational structure and standing operating procedure of the Middle East Supply Centre were firmly anchored. Here was one of the few instances of combined operations in the Anglo-American alliance where the United States played no significant role in conceiving and developing the basic organization; her representatives walked into a "ready setup" and had to be initiated step by step into the details of work begun and now fully mastered by their British colleagues.

In the middle of 1942, the system of shipping control had settled down to a consummate routine. Macduffie relates his first attendance at a meeting of M.E.S.C.'s Licence Committee: Arrayed around a table were seven trim men in British Army uniforms.[2] Before them were sheaves of papers consisting of licenses which local governments in all parts of the Middle East had granted to importers for the purchase of overseas goods. The committee's assignment was to determine which import licenses were essential and which were not. The meeting lasted about an hour and resembled a tobacco auction held in low conversational tone. The papers were picked up and quickly passed down the line of uniforms with barely audible comments in the clipped rapid-fire speech that is characteristic for person-to-person communications among the British military. The session ended without Macduffie having understood a word of what was going on. Yet in that short hour several hundred claims on Anglo-American resources, of vital importance to millions, had been processed, most with finality, a few with referral to further study. It took some time before Macduffie and other Americans became sufficiently apprised of procedure and the facts to take their appropriate place with the prerequisite mastery of speed-up English.

The organization and procedural flow that stood behind this "routine" session in which for all practical purposes the livelihood of the Middle Eastern civilian was expeditiously yet responsibly decided was simple in concept but most intricate in conduct. Making allowance for the procedural integration and elaboration that took place in 1943 and 1944, the structure of M.E.S.C. at the height of its assignment stood as described in the following paragraphs.

First, a brief restatement of the place of M.E.S.C. in the Allied scheme for victory against the Axis. The Middle East could not live, let alone make a productive contribution to the war effort, without a modicum of supplies from England and the Western Hemisphere, and these had to be brought in by Allied merchant ships. Allied shipping as well as provisions were in short supply and had to be apportioned all over the Allied and neutral world in carefully measured amounts. Determining the size of the allocations could not be left to the market mechanism of world trade. Nor could it be left to the government of each claimant country, for demand most assuredly exceeded supply by a wide margin even on this basis. The two nations which at the same time were the prime sources of supply and the protagonists of the fighting had to make the allocation themselves. The system conceived for the allocation of nonmilitary supplies and shipping to the Middle East was based on import licenses issued by local authorities in each country or territory of the region, but these were centrally screened on the regional level by the Middle East Supply Centre in Cairo. "Screening" meant judging how essential the import being licensed was likely to be in fending off economic disaster to the country; how much of the need, if not all of it, could not be met from unused or unrevealed or misused resources in the country or in other parts of the region or neighboring regions; and which overseas source was the most suitable. Then, the appropriate agencies in the United States and Britain would consider releasing goods and shipping to the Middle Eastern countries, guided but not necessarily compelled by the recommendations of the regional screening authority, M.E.S.C.

The organization of the Middle East Supply Centre ultimately spanned the whole Middle Eastern region (see chart, pp. 204–205). Local branches or agents assisted governments in arriving at a licensing policy that would conform roughly with the standards of austerity and equity formulated in Cairo. Twice each month the governing authority in each country and territory cabled copies of the licenses issued to M.E.S.C. headquarters.

There a new perspective was added. Licenses had been awarded within the context of local resources and pressures. Now they were reviewed by men who had before their eyes a rough topography of resources and pressures in the whole region as best their research and personal knowledge could map it. The torrents of cables flowing in on the first of the month were now divided into broad functional categories regardless of territories and subjected to intensive combing by a specialized division. Raw materials and equipment for industry came under the province of the Materials Division; the Food, Medical Requirements, and Transport Divisions divided up the remaining lot. Each license was "graded" at the conclusion of the scrutiny. Four different letter grades expressed the judgments of the Centre as to the priorities the licenses rated in the Allied supply scheme: "A" stood for essential; "B" for desirable but not urgent; "C" for non-essential; "X" for undetermined, pending further investigation.

Since some import licenses pertained to commodities affecting more than one division, an inter-divisional License Committee met regularly to expose each item to cross-reference analysis. Here the grades were either finally confirmed or referred to further study or, in case of stubborn disagreement, submitted to the Executive Committee for arbitration.

Long before that, the Executive Committee and the Director General had issued general directives to prescribe the spirit and the policy framework in which licenses were to be graded. Depending thereon, the scrutiny would be lenient or harsh; the decision geared to immediate or long-term savings in shipping space; the emphasis placed on restricted consumption or the stimulation of local production.

The passage of the monthly crop of Middle Eastern import licenses (for overseas goods) reached its final M.E.S.C. station at the Program Division. This division drafted a suggested shipping program reflecting the recommendations of the License Committee and regional import requests made outside the normal commercial channels.[3] The "program" listed under various commodity headings the total tonnages which in the opinion of the Supply Centre should be allocated to the Middle East for civilian consumption and use.

Before an M.E.S.C. program could become a reality in terms of shiploads of precious commodities sailing into Middle Eastern ports, it had to pass the gamut of allocation, production shipping controls in the countries designated as the potential source of supply, or in M.E.S.C. parlance, the "loading areas." The fortunes of war, the overwhelming role of British and American merchant production and shipping and certain intergovernmental arrangements (mainly among members of the British Commonwealth) had concentrated loading area decisions in London and Washington. Following as much as possible the wishes of the importing principal, but making changes where instructions from higher instances and known shipping and supply conditions warranted it, the Program Division divided all licenses into two bundles, as it were, the contents of which were cabled to London and Washington respectively; the proposed tonnage program was split and communicated in like manner.[4]

Copies of licenses involving procurements of goods in East and South Africa, India, Ceylon, Australia, and New Zealand were sent to M.E.S.C. agents in those places. However, the release of supplies and shipping space was decided in London.

The listings which arrived in London and Washington included those graded as nonessential or deferrable by the Centre. The two governments retained their full freedom to overrule M.E.S.C. either way.

In the two capitals of the Allied war effort, the M.E.S.C. program and each license was fully exposed to the pitiless glare of a supply and shipping strategy that embodied an awareness of the urgent needs of large armies and large continents all equally avid for entitlements to the hard-pressed larders and assembly lines serving the foes of the Axis.

The receiving point in the United States was the Combined Agency for Middle East Supplies to which various agencies vested with allocational authority had delegated much of their authority. CAMES reviewed the monthly programs and each individual license, then issued export releases; a Policy Committee representing civilian and military departments and agencies concerned with various aspects of U.S. relations with the Middle East brought a coordinated American viewpoint to bear on the general frame of reference underlying each release. The export release enabled the Middle Eastern importer and his supplier to set into motion the various transactional processes that would ultimately transform an order into a shipment. The thorny road to a pier in New York harbor meandered through other government offices which were dispensing production, inland transport, and shipping priorities;

through offices of manufacturers and wholesalers scheduling output and delivery; through the antechambers of shipping companies booking passage, and through port control headquarters clearing the shipment for accommodation in an Eastbound convoy. All along this path CAMES expediters helped with advice and intercessions.

In Great Britain, the "Monthly Programme" drafted for loading areas under Commonwealth control was received at the Supply Section for the Middle East (S.S.M.E.), Max Nicholson's niche in the Ministry of War Transport, and presented to the Middle East Supplies Committee. There men knowing and speaking the minds of the Ministries of Food, Production, Supply, and Economic Warfare, the War, Foreign, Colonial and India Offices, the Treasury, the Board of Trade, and the U.S. Mission for Economic Affairs hammered out a consensus on what the Commonwealth could spare, with due regard to Britain's own irreducible wants, her political, military, and economic stakes in *all* parts of the world, and the Commonwealth's capacity to produce, release from its stores, and ship. This consensus then was taken over the final official hurdle— the inter-ministerial Shipping (Civil Requirements) Committee, which settled the question of when and at which port shipping space would be on hand to accommodate the various cargoes approved. Again, because of the demands of other continents and countries judged more pressing, or because of a rash of sinkings or delayed return voyages, or sudden new political and military constellations,[5] some of the allocations approved by the Supplies Committee could be nullified by a denial of early transport facilities.

Once a reasonable shipping schedule was obtained the Middle Eastern importer and his supplier were helped through various procurement stages by expediters, in this case men from the U.K.C.C. or, where colonial destinations were involved, Crown Agents of the Colonial Office. They in turn were prompted by frequent cables from M.E.S.C. headquarters in Cairo; their labors in each case only ceased at the docks as a crane swinging a bale or a crate marked Suez, Alexandria, Haifa, or Basra toward a waiting ship came into view. And sometimes they could be seen prowling on deck to make sure that a particularly urgent load received a berth near the top of the cargo pile; this way the consignment would be among the first to teeter ashore on the back of a sturdy Egyptian, Palestinian, or Iraqi stevedore.[6]

Like everything else the grind of this machinery in Britain, in the

United States, in the Middle East and in the many other loading and unloading areas of the Allied realm, must pay heavy ransom to the caprice of war. But one regular chore performed with growing skill by the Program Division and the Executive Committee of M.E.S.C. did much to slice the ransom: the drafting of half-year advance programs. Twice a year a bulky document classified top secret and signed by the Middle East Supply Centre arrived in the precincts of CAMES and S.S.M.E. It carried a carefully calculated and argued forecast of the Middle East's civilian supply and tonnage requirements for the next six months. The same practiced eyes and busy fingers that screened the monthly programs went through these forecasts. After intensive trans-Atlantic consultations flowing ultimately through the Combined Boards, an Anglo-American consensus of allocation was formulated in terms of tentative tonnage totals for the half-year period ahead. Its shadow not only sheltered the monthly programs from excessive arbitrariness but reduced many interdepartmental consultations to a speedy routine. It was the availability of these detailed half-year programs that made possible in the United States the issuance of a half-year "program license" for Middle East shipments to CAMES (see chap. 6) and gave the latter the opportunity to steer M.E.S.C. recommendations around many potential delays and roadblocks.

The exertions of the expediters in the "loading areas" might come to rest when the ship leaves, but not those of the M.E.S.C. staff assigned to see the shipment through to the ultimate point of consumption. Its progress on long routes exposed not only to enemy attack but bureaucratic blunder, unauthorized diversion, mechanical breakdowns (the shipping shortage required the employment of ships regardless of age, state of repair, or seaworthiness), and delays at way-station harbors was carefully charted so as to permit both a forecast of the cargo's availability in the Middle East and a scheduling of disembarkation at the port of destination. Often, as in the case of very important shipments, assistance was rendered in securing in advance overland transport priorities for the goods once unloaded. Finally, through its local representatives in the various Middle East territories, a close watch was kept on the ultimate disposal of the commodity amid the many potent pulls and speculative lures of a severely rationed economy.

Not all extra-regional imports of the Middle East during the war came from overseas. In its later stages M.E.S.C. created offices in India and East Africa to facilitate the small volume of Middle Eastern purchases there. In Nairobi, an M.E.S.C. office spoke for Middle Eastern needs on boards set up jointly by the British possessions in East Africa to determine the allocation of the area's production. In New Delhi an M.E.S.C. agent pressed for more generous textile export permits.

The "Bulk Indent," and Anatomy of a Case

Within this elaborate system of scrutiny and supervision private trade channels were allowed to handle the mercantile mechanics of most of their countries' overseas imports. An exception was made for certain commodities, among them grain, pharmaceuticals, coal, tires, sugar, fats, oils, tea, coffee, canned milk, meat, and fish. So thin was the margin between available supplies and fatal scarcity here that procurement and equitable distribution could not be left to commercial channels. Therefore the Middle East Supply Centre was authorized to purchase and import bulk goods on its own account, store them in central locations all over the Middle Eastern Area, to be released to local merchants and public institutions such as hospitals in accordance with clearly established needs, and with strict instructions as to their use. The mechanics of buying, shipping, storing, and distributing these goods were entrusted to the U.K.C.C. operating under the directions of M.E.S.C.

Under this "bulk indent" policy, M.E.S.C. became the direct importer of great quantities of pivotal commodities. At the same time the direct management of the storage and wholesale distribution of these bulk imports placed the Supply Centre in a position to intervene promptly in emergencies arising in various parts of the region from food shortages, epidemics, transport breakdowns, and similar crises.

There was a third method of M.E.S.C. control over imports from overseas: inland transport. The roads and rails of the Middle East could not serve the transport needs of the area without imported maintenance material, equipment, and spare parts. With its power to regulate imports, M.E.S.C. soon found itself in a position to influence the use of freight capacity in inland communications throughout the area. Trucking companies and railroad administrations had to adjust their scheduling of freight and their runs to the distribution plans of the Centre or would find themselves denied the right to obtain badly needed equipment and parts from the only accessible source of supply (outside the black markets where, for example, a single tire could cost hundreds of dollars).

This, in broad outline, was the machinery of advisory shipping control, the master thread in the web of trade regulation which M.E.S.C. in four years of operation spun over the economy of the Middle East in the cause of allied warfare and local welfare. No procedural description of the basic design can do justice to the three-dimensional drama that lurked behind the day-by-day routine of decision-making in Cairo, in Washington, or in London, or the fascinating symphony of circumstances intruding from all corners of a war-torn globe into the once so simple chore of placing with the workshops of the Western world as routine and unglamorous an order as, for example, two dozen replacement pistons for tractors ploughing farmlands in Palestine. Here is a hypothetical case of piston procurement as it might have happened.

Somewhere on a community farm in the hills of Galilee, let us say, a tractor breaks down in the middle of a busy day. A harried mechanic arrives, cursing the fate that compels him to spend his day patching up run-down machines, which could fall apart at any moment for lack of replacement parts. This evening he will make another trip to the city to scour the flourishing black market which gets its supplies through devious channels, mostly from broken down military vehicles stripped stealthily by experienced motor cannibals while the guards are not looking. He will pay any price, for a paralyzed tractor means less grain, while his *kibbutz*, his friends in the city, and the army fighting the Nazis are all clamoring for bread. No use trying the authorized dealer in General Motors parts; his shelves have been bare for months.

But the General Motors parts dealer is not idle. He knows the situation on the farms and he knows the good profit to be made in tractor parts. Only last month he had written the General Motors Company in the United States again, pleading for a shipment; once more he had been told that nothing can be shipped without an export license which Washington has so far refused: why not try again to get his Government's backing for the order; maybe this time Washington can be persuaded. Once again he completes the exhausting array of application forms for an import license authorizing the importation of two dozen tractor pistons Series A2345, GM catalog 1938, page 10. He carries it personally to Palestine's War Supply Board to impress his case on the agricultural machinery officer.

The Board needs no convincing that the importation of tractor parts is imperative. The grain supply of Palestine is constantly on the verge of disappearance, for too much of the crops that used to be bought in Jordan, Syria, and other neighboring producers is diverted to other consumers (including smugglers and black marketeers) or hoarded for speculative or precautionary purposes. Yet several times before, the parts dealer had to be informed that "a higher instance" had disapproved the license provisionally granted by the Palestine Government; some muttering about the "Middle East Supply Centre" as the source of all trouble had accompanied the regretful communication. But the Board will try again. The local M.E.S.C. representative is consulted. He is encouraging. An import license is granted to the dealer, subject to "approval in Cairo and Washington."

Meanwhile staff members of the War Supply Board are at work compiling the total overseas import program for Palestine for the next month. A list is prepared of the various quantities and commodities which the Palestine Government deems crucial enough to justify a claim on Allied shipping and production; somewhere down the line, under "agricultural machinery," the dealer's pistons take their place. Details on the other licenses granted to him are appended to the list. A special meeting of the Board subjects the "program" to a careful review in the light of directives received from Allied authorities and information collected on the latest development in Palestine's food and industrial picture; the latest progress reports on imports ordered and authorized in previous months are also considered. Then the "program" is cabled to Cairo, in care of the Director General of the Middle East Supply Centre.

In Palestine, the licenses for pistons were conspicuous items in the list of necessary supplies serving the needs of 1.6 million. In Cairo they submerge meekly in a long line of claims summarizing the needs of 100 million. The Middle East Supply Centre will decide whether the small voice of the parts dealer in Palestine will be transmitted across the Atlantic strongly enough to move the supreme arbiters of Allied resource allocation.

Despite heavy preoccupation with the overall supply strategy for the Middle East, the Palestine program in general and the pistons orders in particular come in for elaborate scrutiny by various organs of the Centre. The representative of the British Minister of State examines the political implications of the Palestine requests. Is there rural unrest in neighboring Syria which may be alleviated by giving preference to agricultural machinery deliveries to that country although their use would be less efficient among farmers only recently converted to the use of machines; have there been ominous Arab outcries against favoring Jewish Palestine and Jewish dealers and farmers too much? The Minister also is concerned with another question: Is there any valid reason for ordering agricultural machinery parts from the United States when before the war they were as a rule obtained from Britain?

The representative of the United States Government also weighs the implication of the Palestine program in terms of American policy. Meanwhile, the Food Division checks the latest balance sheets of crop forecasts, grain reserves and food needs in order to calculate whether or not an impairment of agricultural output in Palestine can be absorbed by the region without calamity. The Materials Division consults its files and agents to see whether tractor pistons cannot be procured from surplus or salvage stocks in other parts of the Middle East. Both divisions study available records likely to show whether past shipments to Palestine and the GM parts dealer went into authorized channels or disappeared in black markets. The representative of the British Ministry of War Transport is asked for a forecast of Haifa's capacity to unload such cargoes as may arrive perhaps six weeks hence, expeditiously and without loss to pilferage and inept handling; there has been a recent report indicating some congestion for the months ahead. The Transport Division looks into the availability of land transport in case Palestine bound shipments have to be unloaded in Alexandria, Beirut, or Iskenderun and forwarded from there. The Director General weighs the significance of a cablegram just received from the British Ambassador in Iran stating that M.E.S.C. and the Allies are severely criticized for failing to send certain tractor parts promised (so it is alleged) by him when he visited Teheran last month. The representative of the Middle East Command is approached to ascertain whether the military still insist on getting the whole Middle Eastern allocation of tractor parts to carry out emergency reconstruction in occupied enemy territories of Libya and Eritrea. A cable is dispatched to Addis Ababa to check on the progress of a project to ship several reclaimed Italian tractors over a hazardous land route to Egypt.

For some days the dealer's order hangs in precarious balance; then the recommendations come in from the various posts of scrutiny. The consensus is favorable. The next meeting of the Licence

Committee is at hand. Quick eyes and hands process the form dealing with the order of pistons from America. The outcome is: Yes.

This yes does not yet mean the pistons will come to Palestine. It only means that like all other licenses whether approved or not, this one will be forwarded to Washington (with an information copy to London). The program section will draw up master lists on which all orders processed by M.E.S.C. will be recorded by commodity categories with their classification grades and preferred source of purchase stated in separate columns. This program is cabled to Washington and London. But the pistons for Palestine enjoy a great advantage as they face a new and even sharper scrutiny: they have a top priority rating from M.E.S.C. They are classified "A".

Just as the Palestine import program had to stand the test of urgency within the larger framework of Middle Eastern needs—twenty-odd territories—so the Middle East's claim to the Allied larder now has to take its modest place in the gigantic breadline of the non-Axis world—nearly one hundred lands and territories and nearly two billion people. While the cable carrying the monthly import recommendations of the Middle East Supply Centre is decoded in Washington, dozens of clerks disentangle the code of hundreds of other wires requesting tanks for the Italian front, trucks for the Russians, tools for a Bristol machine shop, syringes for a hospital in New Caledonia, leggings for Free French soldiers in Algeria, submachine guns for Chinese guerrillas, chemicals for a tannery in West Africa, Cadillacs for an important neutral chief in Latin America, tractor pistons for encircled Switzerland, canteen equipment for a battle-weary Marine division in the Pacific, a small generator for an occupied town in Italy, gasoline for the account of the Spanish government, newsprint for a propaganda sheet in Lisbon, emergency food and pharmaceuticals for a flood stricken province in India, railroad cars for the transport of South African manganese, synthetic rubber for Australian scout cars, books for Samoans, bulbs for Bolivians, and bundles for homesick Americans in every corner of the globe. After the message is decoded it is sent to the appropriate desks at the start of the long bureaucratic chain.

For the Middle East Supply Program the journey through the gamut of scrutiny at the Allied resource summit begins in the office of the Combined Agency of Middle East Supplies. The positions of various agencies of the United States Government and the British Government interested in the recommendations of the Supply Centre are known. The Middle East Division of the Foreign Economic Administration had studied its fact sheets to establish the food and employment situation in the Middle East and Palestine's role in it. The present status of "reimbursable lend-lease" accounts under which some of the commodity trade with the civilian sector of the Middle East is settled had been reviewed,[7] in order to determine the continued eligibility of items on M.E.S.C. lists. The U.S. Treasury had given a report on the strong dollar position of Palestine (due to the permission received from the sterling area pool to dispose freely of Zionist contributions collected in America). The U.S. Department of Agriculture and the U.S. War Food Administration had sent a reminder of the always insatiable equipment needs of the American farmer, supreme provider of the Allied world and its armed forces. The man from the War Production Board had related to his CAMES colleagues the production outlook for agricultural machinery parts in the United States and correlative information on stocks. The agent of the British Colonial Supply Mission, as spokesmen of Palestine's import needs, had parried searching questions that tended to minimize the importance of certain items requested, among them tractor pistons. The British Supply Mission representative had stated Britain's present inability to meet the Palestine requests. The U.S. War Shipping Administration had expressed concern over the strain that the new demands from Palestine could place on an overtaxed pool of Atlantic shipping. Several pronouncements of the Anglo-American Combined Boards for Raw Materials, Shipping Adjustment, Food, and Production and Resources had been cited. Out of all this a half-year supply allowance for Palestine had been formulated for CAMES to deal out.

The small executive committee of CAMES reviews the Palestine licenses sent this month by M.E.S.C. in the light of the half-year projections for the Middle East and the previously stated position of the Policy Committee. The political, economic and strategic needs of the world which might dispute or support the appeal of the Middle East, of Palestine and of the GM parts dealer to the much tested munificence of America's production and her merchant marine have been re-examined. A number of export releases is finally granted. One of them covers the dealer's license. The biggest hurdle is mastered. Once more the appraisal of the Middle East Supply Centre of the legitimate need of its region and Allied capacity to meet it has found vindication. The dealer will have his pistons.

But when? CAMES approval bespeaks a consensus among interested Allied agencies and departments that the delivery of pistons to Palestine is in the interest of the war effort and therefore represents a legitimate claim on American resources. They have received a certain priority label. But this by itself does not generate the raw materials and manpower and vessels needed to make and ship them. These resources remain as scarce as ever and now the piston priority must battle against similarly recognized priorities held on behalf of other civilian interests (including the American consumer) as well as the military for a War Production Board priority; once this is obtained another battle ensues in the office of the supplier of raw materials against holders of similar priorities and the process repeats itself at the plant of the manufacturer. And, while machines turn out the valuable tractor parts, pleas must be entered with the War Shipping Administration for early shipping space across the Atlantic, the Office of Defense Transportation must issue an inland priority, and the Office of Cargo Clearance in New York must be induced to translate the shipping priority into an early sailing date.

It is a long and hazard-ridden route that leads from CAMES to the loading of cargo. At any point along this route danger looms from new superseding priorities and directives arising out from military and political developments on land and sea throughout the world. CAMES, as U.S. representative of M.E.S.C., renders invaluable service as an expediter, escorting the various parts of the M.E.S.C. program including the pistons for Palestine through the various waystations by correspondence and personal representations. One signal advantage which the Middle East enjoys in this procurement battle is the special arrangement concerning the grant of export licenses, made possible by M.E.S.C.'s half-year forecasts. If standard procedure prevailed, each item on the M.E.S.C. list would have to become the subject of an individual license application, examination and issuance, by officials of a harrassed, overtaxed Foreign Economic Administration. In the case of the Middle East, largely because of the confidence reposed in the forecasts of the Middle East Supply Centre, F.E.A. grants every six months a general "program license" to CAMES. This lets CAMES issue individual licenses against the overall allowance.

Before the pistons finally come to rest in the hull of the S.S. *Davenport* awaiting the next convoy departure, the interested parties also have reason to thank the most active New York office of CAMES. In the early days of the war this had been the New York Office of the United Kingdom Commercial Corporation through which

American exporters dealing with the Middle East had received space on British ships, if M.E.S.C. approved their shipment; the U.K.C.C. office also had been active as an expediter in Washington for orders approved by M.E.S.C. but delayed there in their processing on the Potomac's shores. In 1943 this office was integrated into CAMES.

Now the ship carrying the pistons is at last at sea. The last hazardous phase begins. The ship may be sunk by submarine. It may be delayed by engine trouble, congestion at intermediate ports, or sudden changes in warship disposition which may cancel a convoy two days out of New York. It may suffer the fate of the S.S. *Princess Margaretha* which owing to a combination of mishaps took more than a year to journey from New York to Alexandria around the Cape of Good Hope.

But at least one thing is certain. If the S.S. *Davenport* does come through to Haifa the goods will be speedily unloaded and forwarded inland under the watchful eye of local M.E.S.C. representatives. There will no longer be the horrendous port congestion and delays of earlier days. The rationing and management of overseas imports by M.E.S.C. has had its effect in keeping the ports uncongested most of the time. The pistons will have arrived. If the parts dealer does not succumb to the lure of the black market and if government supervision is effective, the pistons will be delivered to the *kibbutz* and to other farms. And there will be a little more food for Palestine and a little less tension in the Middle East.

Seen only from the molehill view of the dealer and his small package of pistons, this long exercise appears like the roaring labors of a mountain stung by the nibbling of a mouse. Would a simple rule-of-thumb applied in Washington and London after a cursory study not have been adequate to extract a few pistons from the mighty Himalayas of Allied war production without impairing their majesty? Yet, the trouble is that there are many such dealers, and their joint demand totals thousands of pistons, hundreds of thousands of bushels of grain, millions of tons of shipping. Be lax with the demands of one and a deafening cacophony of outraged protest will arise in various lands, and amid the multiplicity of racial and political pressure groups, sown so uniquely across the Middle East. Besides, to spread the habit of economic discipline throughout the region, the rod must find every corner of wastefulness, every leakage of war potential. There must be daily awareness that each pound of supplies from across the seas is paid with the life risk of a seaman, the privation of others in need, and the neglect of a soldier of nations waging a war to the finish. Otherwise, a huge subcontinent waiting out the war in monumental indifference and personal detachment, asking a high price merely for not being a nuisance, can become a bottomless sink for the central provisioner.

Thus, the delivery of a few American-made pistons to a farm in Palestine is not a commercial transaction needlessly cluttered with bureaucratic detail. It is a small but meaningful victory in a sector of the front.

In Palestine many people will rejoice. But in Cairo, the men who made the decisive sally in the battle of procurement take only perfunctory notice of this minor victory. More than 80,000 import licenses pass through their hands annually, many of them vastly more important than that covering the pistons; hundreds of import emergencies arise every day in various corners of M.E.S.C.'s vast domain, and no sooner are they met when new ones arise. Hundreds of recommendations pass safely through the cordons of control in Washington and London; but M.E.S.C. must worry about dozens of others that appear to get caught in the web of negative decisions.

A report has come in that a promised shipment of Australian grain may face tough sledding at the next weekly meeting of the Shipping Committee for Civilian Requirements in London. The Colonial Office wants ships for two shipments of rice for Ceylon. The Ministry of Production is reportedly annoyed at the inroads which civilian shipments to the colonies and the Middle East have made on raw material shipments for United Kingdom industry. The matter is urgent. In Teheran, the wheat reserve is down to a two-week's supply and shrinking fast. There will be trouble in the streets if another shipload does not arrive soon from Australia. M.E.S.C. dispatches a man to assist its spokesman in London in the argument for special shipping priorities. He is taken along to the Ministry of Transport as soon as he gets off the plane because this is Wednesday, time for the weekly meeting of the Shipping Committee.

The meeting is called to order and the Chairman, with the current position of world shipping and the latest losses in his mind settles down to listen to the various claimants. "It is surprising," relates an eyewitness, "how quickly business goes forward. The big demands have been submitted to the Committee on paper beforehand, and each representative will give a short explanation. But now comes a tussle. There are only five ships loading in Australia.

Ceylon wants three; two must go to the Persian Gulf, and three must go to the Red Sea. How are five ships made into eight? Each representative will give a statement of stocks on hand and the harvest prospects. The Ministry of Food perhaps will throw in some information about world crops. The Committee will ask the American representative if there is any chance of an American ship to help the Red Sea program. Finally they come to a decision— perhaps there is one ship to Ceylon, two to the Persian Gulf and two to the Red Sea, with a chance that a further ship may be available later in the month from the American War Shipping Administration, or a request to India to help even more. The meeting breaks up, and the telegrams go out from different offices, and in far off Australia the Ministry of War Transport representative gives sailing orders to the merchant captains, with perhaps 9,000 tons of Australian wheat packed in each hold." [8]

Without the last-minute arguments thrown in by the M.E.S.C. representative fresh in from the scene there might have been no ship heading for the Persian Gulf. While he makes out his report on the plane that takes him back to Cairo, his colleagues there grapple with another rash of emergency appeals. Almost every import program that reaches the Center from its various territories is accompanied by spirited and sometimes desperate efforts of governments and individual beneficiaries to secure a favorable recommendation by M.E.S.C. for a specific import or for the whole list. A gigantic lobby working through telegrams, letters, telephone calls, and personal visits dogs the steps of M.E.S.C. officials down to the lowliest clerk in a division. Some of the pressure stems from shameless greed; some from unashamed panic; much from the normal repercussions of all lobbyism: the belief if no lobbying is done for a specific case then awards will go to other campaigners by default.

The Governor of Cyprus cables that for lack of machinery replacements a copper mine may have to close and render hundreds of Cypriots unemployed; he also pointedly asks M.E.S.C. not to forget the extra drain on the island's resources caused by the swelling camps for illegal Jewish immigrants to Palestine. The Political Resident in the Persian Gulf sheikhdoms telephones to warn that babies of European personnel may be dying soon for lack of milk— and how about getting some aircraft passenger priorities for soldiers and officials who have been waiting for months to spend a few days of hard-earned leave away from the maddening heat at their stations? A high official in the Egyptian government who has been

most helpful in assisting M.E.S.C. policy sends word that he is gravely ill and pleads for a small shipment of penicillin to save his life; another equally high official in Egypt complains vigorously because it seems he will not get the American refrigerator he ordered for his home. The British Ambassador in Teheran urges favorable consideration for Teheran's request for trucks to save the impending new wheat crop from rotting on the ground; another diplomatic source in the same capital drops a hint that the Cadillac requested for a certain cabinet member may be "essential" in an indirect way because the man "could cause us a great deal of damage." [9] The M.E.S.C. man in Baghdad transmits an angry inquiry of the British military commander there: When will the Iraqi railroads get some new rolling stock?

The word from Damascus is that bread riots may erupt if transport between the countryside and the cities breaks down due to lack of truck tires. A Lebanese manufacturer appears in person to ask how he is going to sell shaving sticks to N.A.A.F.I. (the British Army's service unit for off-duty soldiers) if his license from the import of stearine is not approved; in the next office the Cairo agent for a Persian company accuses M.E.S.C. of sabotage because he is not getting sodium carbonate for his window-glass factory. A long memorandum from Benghazi pointedly states that Cairo may deem frivolous a demand for shellac wax to be used for the manufacture of shoe polish, but did somebody remember that the biggest customer in Libya is the British Army, particularly before inspection day? The Middle East Anti-Locust Unit telephones to discuss a possible locust invasion; it may materialize if enough sodium arsenite does not come through in time.

From the Sudan comes a righteous officer to complain that just because the Condominium has been so efficient and successful in rationing the consumer and controlling inflation it should not constantly be neglected in favor of less provident territories in the allocation of shipping. An American oil company representative alludes to the displeasure he can arouse in Washington if some of those pipes stored up for emergencies are not allocated to his refinery; a truck fleet operator serving the Russian Corridor route to Russia storms into the office in the company of a British Army officer to threaten he would go directly to the War Office in London if his spare parts allocation is not raised. From Aden comes a splutter of telegrams supporting a demand for sailcloth for the fleet of native dhows; it is not true, proclaims one cable, that these dhows are mostly engaged in smuggling between East Africa and the Peninsula—and even if they are, aren't they helping Aden relieve its constant penury of goods? And the Secretary of the British Chamber of Commerce in Egypt makes a stiff appearance to complain that too many import licenses are assigned to the United States although British firms were the traditional suppliers before the war.

Most of the situations the Centre has to meet require grim choices of alternatives or unpleasant altercations with disappointed pleaders. On occasion, human greed or ignorance deposits a tidbit of humor that adds spice to the rich folklore of administrative adventure accumulating in the mental and metal files of M.E.S.C.'s agents. Thus, a tongue-in-cheek inquiry arrives from Washington asking serious consideration for a proposal a New York wholesaler had made to CAMES. The man has heard of the problem of overpopulation in the Middle East; he has a large supply of contraceptives in the warehouse and is ready to ship them to the Middle East at moderate cost. The merchandise is defective, he says, and could therefore not be sold in the United States, but it was certainly good enough for the Arabs.[10]

This is welcome relief to M.E.S.C. officials laboring on a new shipping program which *inter alia* would call for a reduction of Egyptian imports of newsprint in line with a decision of the Combined Raw Materials Board in Washington. The implications are not pleasant. How will Egypt distribute the remaining allotment among newspapers of varying political shades? If some publications have to close down, on which will the axe fall? How, in other words, can the Supply Centre escape the accusation that it is meddling with the freedom of the press, if the blackout falls on papers opposed not only to the government but to the British?[11]

How to compose, discourage, pacify and chastise the lobby, how to distinguish the legitimate from the ephemeral, how to investigate and recommend on the basis of charges proffered, was a task as exacting as the original screening of license programs. There were never enough experts around to whom to refer delicate technical questions. Even after the organizational build-up of M.E.S.C., a single official might find himself arguing at first about buffalo hides, then about whiskey, then about manganese, and next about quinine. Regardless, however, of how competently, or objectively, or disappointingly, the "lobbyists" were disposed of, the job of dealing with them was a very vital backstage function of M.E.S.C. because it provided the Middle East with an on-the-spot court of appeal which tended to "humanize" the formality of paper controls and thus made their total impact more tolerable to the people affected than if they had come from remote moguls across the seas.

The web of M.E.S.C. controls and intervention was constantly spreading. A regional center of trade regulation could not function effectively without collateral control on the national and territorial level. One of the great achievements of the Supply Centre was the acceleration and intensification of import regulation in practically all the territories that came under its jurisdiction in the course of the war. But this too was only an interim accomplishment. Even trimmed to the barest minimum the dependence on imports shipped across the oceans would still be disconcertingly large— large enough to be a serious drain on Allied logistic capacity— unless the Middle East was edged resolutely into a stage of economic mobilization which would eliminate waste on the one hand and produce with local resources and labor much of what so far had to be imported.

8

Economic Mobilization of a Region

Industrial Expansion

IN 1954, on the outskirts of Omdourman in the Sudan there was in operation a medium-sized tannery, the only one in the young republic. For most of the last ten years, the plant had functioned at a fraction of capacity and at an annual loss to the owners. Reluctance to dismiss a faithful staff and inability to find a buyer for the property had kept operations going. So had the dim hope for a return of the seller's market which greeted the new venture when it opened in 1945.[1]

In the Sudan, a country poor in capital and almost devoid of industry, the opening of a new industrial plant is a historic event. Agents of foreign investors invariably are the stars of whatever ceremony hails the event. But no foreign investor appeared in a proprietary capacity at the opening of the tannery. Instead there were many government officials and a representative of the Middle East Supply Centre. For the new factory had neither been financed by outside capital nor equipped with deliveries from the Sudan's traditional supplier of machinery: Britain. It was conceived, planned, and built in the middle of the war by local capital and enterprise when British equipment was virtually unavailable. Nevertheless there was an important non-Sudanese partner. "This factory," the owner has stated, "was made possible by the Middle East Supply Centre."

Behind this lies an interesting story. Late in 1943, N. Seroussi, head of an old Jewish export-import firm in Khartoum, started asking himself a few pointed questions. Why were his exports to Europe of Sudanese hides stalling? The answer was: lack of shipping. Why could he not import British and Egyptian leather as he had in peacetime? The answer was: lack of shipping, plus overtaxed tanning facilities in neighboring countries. Did it make sense that raw hides were rotting in warehouses while the military and civilians in the Sudan were short of footgear? The conclusion was obvious: There was room for a tannery in the Sudan as long as the war lasted and perhaps beyond. And it looked as if the war would last for years.

Seroussi discussed his idea with officials of the Sudan War Supply Board. They approved in principle but were skeptical as to the procurement of machinery. Nevertheless, an inquiry on this point was telegraphed to the Middle East Supply Centre in Cairo. The Centre, in reply, asked for a detailed prospectus.

Meanwhile Seroussi remembered an old friend in Cairo who at one time had been his instructor at a leather trades school. Holding a transportation priority issued by the Military Transport officer upon recommendation of the War Supply Board and M.E.S.C., Seroussi flew to Egypt where he met with his friend, Hassan Abdul Aziz. Several weeks of deliberations, blueprinting, calculations, and site-hunting followed, after which Seroussi and Abdul Aziz were ready to present a detailed proposal to the Middle East Supply Centre.

The Industrial Production Section in M.E.S.C.'s Materials Division studied the proposal and solicited the advice of other Centre officials. Leather imports of countries adjoining were surveyed to measure the full extent of the market the new tannery could serve; the needs of Allied military establishments in the area were ascertained. The absorption of overseas shipping space by leather and leather products was reviewed. The availability of manpower and building materials within easy range of the proposed site in Omdourman was investigated. The possibility of transporting conveniently part of the output to other countries—not only to the Sudan's neighbors but to the rest of the Middle East—was explored. Rough comparative studies were made to determine whether another site inside or outside the Sudan might not be more economical. And, finally the most important question, the supply of machinery, was discussed with officials and merchants in Cairo, London, and Washington.

The importation of new equipment was out of the question. This was one of the tight moments in the Allied shipping and supply situation. The Middle East had passed its moment of military crisis and had receded to secondary importance as a war front: the assault on Europe was now in the center of logistic preoccupation. Only one faint hope remained: was there perhaps some idle second-hand tanning machinery somewhere in M.E.S.C. territory? This was the subject of cable inquiries addressed to M.E.S.C. representatives in the field; calls were also made at various tanning establishments in Cairo and Alexandria.

Weeks passed in fruitless search until word came from the M.E.S.C. representative in occupied Cyrenaica that the British Military Administration there had come upon some salvageable machinery in an abandoned Benghazi tannery to which the Italians had set fire before retreating. An M.E.S.C. inspector flew to the scene to examine the equipment and found it worth rehabilitating. Permission to appropriate it and take it out of the territory was secured. The occupation authorities also agreed to send a detail of mechanics from the Royal Engineers for repair and refurbishing work; a few spare parts needed were released by the R.A.F. quartermaster. In short order a full complement of Italian-made and British-remade tanning equipment made off on a journey via Port Said and Port Sudan to the outer fringes of Omdourman.

A host of other questions arising out of the Seroussi project were now tackled by officials at M.E.S.C. headquarters. The Hides, Skins, and Leather office rendered a positive verdict on quality and long-range availability of Seroussi's hide supply—which was the final go-ahead signal. A commitment to deliver to the new venture bichromates and chromic acid was obtained from a company in Cairo which was using minerals from a new mine in Upper Egypt (opened some months before, thanks to technical and important assistance from the Centre). From the M.E.S.C. pool of "technical specialists" a man was chosen to guide the installation and activation of the equipment. The Director of the Materials Division escorted Seroussi and Abdul Aziz to the Provisions Office of the Middle East Command where papers for an Army and R.A.F. contract were signed. Finally Seroussi & Company on their part formally obligated themselves to sell their entire output to the United Kingdom Commercial Corporation which, on instructions of the Centre, would distribute the stocks to the armed forces and to civilian outlets in the principal deficit areas of the Middle East, including of course the Sudan.

The new tannery was ready for business early in 1945. As it happened, the war ended much sooner than expected. Deliveries to the armed services in the end were small. But signal service was rendered to the Sudanese population during the immediate postwar period pending the resumption of cheaper imports from Europe and overseas.

This is a typical case history from the files of the Middle East Supply Centre. Almost all the elements of a characteristic intervention are there: The close liaison with territorial authorities; the detailed spadework in support of new ventures and schemes; the sovereign mastery of the keyboard of regional resources; the stern endeavor to spare Anglo-American resources all avoidable incursions by Middle Eastern claims; and the constant pressure on all enterprises receiving help to serve the needs of the armed forces and of *all* countries and territories in the region. This pattern was consistently followed in every new sphere of economic mobilization invested by the Centre—whether it was food output and marketing, the rationalization of transport, the curbing of inflation, the promotion of public health and nutrition standards, the salvage of waste products, the containment of locusts and agricultural pests, the rechannelling of trade or, as in the case of the Omdourman tannery, the stimulation of industrial production.

Middle Eastern manufacturers, operating at a slow pace through 1940 and 1941 [2] experienced a rapid and unparalleled expansion thereafter.[3] Regional statistics on this subject are scant; but the United Nations cites the following data: [4]

The index of industrial production in Turkey for 1947 was 51 per cent above 1938; the index of man-days worked in Palestine industry rose 82 per cent from 1939 to 1949 despite a letdown after the war; a partial index of industrial production for Egypt showed a rise of 47 per cent between 1938 and 1946. Electric power output in Turkey doubled in the ten years following 1938, while coal extraction rose 60 per cent. Production of steel ingot in Turkey and Egypt increased 200 per cent during roughly the same period, output of refined sugar 20 per cent, tobacco products 60 per cent, alcoholic beverages 50 per cent, cotton yarn 70 per cent, cement (in Egypt, Turkey, and Palestine) 400 per cent, paper, in the same countries, 250 per cent. Many existing industries of the region "expanded several fold during the war years, and several new industries, such as diamond cutting and polishing, vegetable dehydrating and various chemical and mechanical industries were created." [5]

These aggregate statistics do not fully convey the physical and psychological impact of wartime industrial expansion on the Middle East; by themselves the figures easily can be deprecated by the palpable warning against percentage comparisons which start with a small base. The real story lies in national and local case histories: Palestine, for example, where a diamond cutting industry rose from insignificance to an annual gross product of over 5 million Palestine Pounds (£P), or $20 million; where the number of industrial establishments increased from 1,556 to 2,441, while industrial employment expanded from 21,964 to 48,110 (1937–1946); where cement production went from 112,000 metric tons in 1939 to 176,000 in 1943; where the export of manufactured goods (exclusive of oil products), after dipping to £P470,000 in 1940, recorded an all-time peak of £P11,075,000 in 1945 (much of it going to regional destinations); where manufacturing itself, after accounting for only 18.7 per cent of the Jewish labor force between 1931 and 1939, comprised 28.8 per cent in 1945, displacing agriculture as the leading source of Jewish working places; where the share of manufacturing in the national income quadrupled as against a three-fold increase in total national income; where the number of Arab and other non-Jewish industrial enterprises employing three persons or more, rose between 1939 and the end of 1942 alone from 339 to 1,508, their gross output from £P1.5 million to £P5.6 million, their working force from 4,117 to 8,804; where total capital investment in industry in 1946 stood at £P43 million, as compared with £P11 million in 1937, and where during the same interval new capital placements advanced from £P2.5 million to £P13.5 million, yet where the import of industrial equipment fell from a 1933–1939 total of £P4,905,000 to only £P1,101,000 during 1940–1944.[6]

A rise in industrial production of this amplitude was of course not seen in all parts of the Middle East; expansion tended to concentrate in the countries most advanced industrially, like Palestine, Egypt, Syria, Lebanon, Turkey, Iran, and Iraq.[7] But where it did happen the mere visual effect was striking. A Zionist leader visiting Palestine and the Middle East in 1944 after an absence of five years was astounded by the "expansion of industry both in variety and volume" before his eyes.[8] For years afterwards the business community of the region mused about the war years as something akin to a golden age of bustle and confidence.[9]

The new manufactured goods were a blessing not only to the civilian populations but to the Allied forces. Two minesweepers were built and many other warships repaired in Palestine shipyards. The Vulcan Foundries in Haifa delivered considerable quantities of heavy armament. From factories and workshops throughout the region spewed forth a stream of goods for consumers and commissaries, including cast iron pipes, cisterns, fire extinguishers, shipbuilding tools, cranes, air compressors, transformers, pipes, flit guns, hydraulic jacks, steel castings, oil stoves and burners, wire strainers, lead tubes, barbed wire, uniforms, tents, tarpaulins, batteries, camouflage netting, knitted goods, hand tools, precision instruments, automobile parts, brass castings, accumulators, aircraft heaters, antitank mines, shrapnel balls, signal gear, window glass, electric bulbs, nuts and bolts, processed jute, tungsten, tin, chromium, refined lead, drugs, carbonic acid, sulphuric acid, sodium silicates, sodium sulphates, superphosphates, potassium chlorate, borax, lactic acids, refractory bricks, industrial diamonds, saddle soap, canteen equipment, army boots and clothing, cardboard containers, canned foods, jams, toothbrushes, drugs and medicines, shoe polish, retreaded tires, and, to the special delight of His Majesty's thirsty forces, millions of bottles of beer brewed in hastily improvised breweries in Cairo and points East.[10]

In more than one emergency at and behind the front the readiness and adaptability of industry and labor in the Middle East came to the aid of hard-pressed commanders. Thus, an Egyptian factory helped obviate the imminent grounding of R.A.F. planes during highly critical weeks in 1941, when it undertook on short notice to manufacture spare parts as R.A.F. reserve stocks reached the exhaustion point. A Tel Aviv workshop switched overnight to the output of bolts, the lack of which had stalled numerous tanks in the Libyan desert; another succeeded in developing a compass that could be used by tank crews during severe desert storms—and manufactured it from shells found in the Dead Sea. Scientific research at universities in Jerusalem, Cairo, and Beirut sparked the output of drugs that averted outbreaks of epidemics; it also made possible the operation of maintenance depots which could carry out repairs on complex electronic equipment. Poor and emaciated *fellahin* were converted after a few weeks of on-the-job training into remarkably efficient workers just when they were needed to get trucks and transport planes assembled in Iran and Iraq for delivery to the defenders of Stalingrad. "The two [assembly] plants employed over five thousand of the poor hopeless citizens of the Backward Races," remarked an admiring American observer in Basra, "and they were so shiftless and unteachable that they could do no better than learn how to turn out trucks at the rate of one every five minutes." [11]

Several forces were at work to fan industrial development. The

shipping stringency had the effect of a protectionist wall, bound to
lure some enterprising men, even in critical days, into skimming the
cream of a market so hungry for consumer and military goods. On
the other hand, the Middle East Command had started very early
with offshore procurement and thus had gradually opened up a relatively safe and (in view of the contract liberality practiced) fairly
generous source of purchases; British and American assembly camps
for tanks, trucks and aircraft and the massive Persian Corridor operation had not only been a profitable source of subcontracts for thousands of workshops and factories nearby, but a superb training
school for transplanted farmhands and handymen, which alleviated
the problem of skilled labor shortages for private industry as well.[12]

The purchasing power of the "new" laborers and the profligate
on-leave expeditures of Allied personnel stimulated the sale and
production of many consumer products and services for which demand had been discouragingly low in prewar days.[13] Once Rommel
had been defeated, and with him the paralysis of uncertainty, it
was indeed a good time for men motivated by aspirations for prestige and profits to go into industry. Never had the social standing of
the manufacturer, his opportunity to throw his weight around in
business and society been greater. In peacetime his products were
spurned by consumers who for generations had learned to pay tribute and respect to European and American labels.[14] He had been
treated with condescension if not contempt by wholesalers and retail merchants who preferred the prestige and profit potential of imported merchandise. But now consumers and traders were beating a
path to his doorstep, and generals, politicians, and public opinion
sang his praise.[15]

In the background was the music of inflation, shrill to the ears
of those who had to buy their daily provisions, but sweet and ex-
hilarating to those who had or made something to sell. Since time
immemorial, runaway prices have been a mighty ferment of production—as long as they do not gallop out of sight. Inflation was
rampant in the Middle East during the war, but under the pressure
of Allied authorities it was reined sufficiently to stop short of disaster.[16] The banks were bulging with loanable funds idled by the ces-
sation of their traditional lending preserve, the export of cotton
and citrus and the import from overseas of manifold manufactured
goods; usually reluctant to finance local industry, they now had a
change of mind.[17]

It was a good time indeed to go into industry—if one could lay one's hands on machinery and raw materials. Sometimes the Middle East Provisions office of the British forces released quartermaster supplies to its contractors or used its entitlement priorities to purchase stores on its own account from private sources in Britain, India, and other parts of the Commonwealth.[18] But in a large number of cases the only road to manufacturing capacity led through the precincts of the Materials Division of the Middle East Supply Centre.

The principal assignment of this Division originally had been the determination of overseas import needs for items other than food.[19] Because of the enormous scarcity value of all foreign manufactures, the scope had been expanded to include the strictest regulation of their distribution, lest they disappear in the black markets; for items like paper, textiles, coal, and leather, the distribution was taken out of commercial channels altogether and entrusted to the U.K.C.C. This logically led to their centralized purchasing in Britain and the United States. When shortages came to their highest pitch in these two "loading areas" centralized purchasing became a double blessing. For it soon developed that American and British manufacturers overloaded with massive war contracts paid little attention to small isolated orders such as private traders in the Middle East acting separately were likely to place with them. By "bulking" the requirements of the whole region and blessing them with a high priority secured through the proper channels in London and Washington the Centre was able to break through this supplier indifference.

For bulk materials as well as the thousands of items still obtained through commercial channels, a system of regular "inventory keeping" was gradually developed. It was a gigantic job. Throughout the vast domain of the Middle East a constant check was maintained on the rate of utilization of stocks—and the legitimacy of the end-use—of caustic soda, marine engines, coal, tobacco, insecticides, baby foods, cigarettes, hides, newsprint, oils, industrial diamonds, pyrethium, sisal, steel, sulphates, photographic materials, and many other scarce materials which had been wrenched with such exertion from the jealously guarded *Nibelungen* hoard overseas and carried across the seas at such risk of Allied lives. In due course a large variety of locally produced materials useful to industry—and scarce— was added to the purview of regular stockkeeping. Then surveys were made of industrial plant capacity and mines, as well as of surplus stocks held by the armed forces. In the end, the files of the Materials Division were a gigantic, stationary mail order catalog from which procurement information could be ladled out to distributors, producers, the armed services; one frequent "customer" was the United States Commercial Company (u.s.c.c.),[20] scouring the world on behalf of U.S. war industries.

Under the prevailing circumstances no more than rough approximations or estimates of stocks could be hoped for in the case of many materials. Yet, Marshall Macduffie, the Director of the Division, and his staff took special pride in the promptness and relative reliability with which they could service inquiries from the trade, from the Middle East War Council, or supply authorities overseas. Such became the reputation of "Macduffie's Department Store" that protests had to be lodged on occasion against excessive demands for minute detail coming from Allied agencies in Cairo or Washington; some officials, it seemed, expected m.e.s.c. to be on the track of every pound of chemicals or every handful of nuts and bolts in the twenty-seven territories under its jurisdiction.[21]

The Materials Division was not content to be a mere store and score keeper. During 1942 and 1943, two new sections were set up and quickly evolved into major operations. The first, a sub-section for salvage, sparked the organization throughout the region of drives aimed at salvaging every usable piece of scrap and slag that could be made to replace an import.

Salvage in the Middle East did not mean sending teams of volunteers to kitchen doors and vacant lots in search of paper, tin cans, and other household discards. A population whose national income per capita is in the lower teens (stated in dollars) is not in the habit of throwing things away and needs no encouragement, in war or peace, to go out and collect the leftovers from the few rich or from industry. What was needed were new methods—and priorities—for the leftovers of industry and the armed services, besting the endless hordes of amateur scroungers who could strip a stranded or parked vehicle in minutes and could build whole villages from petrol and water *bidons*.

In due course, the practice developed of requiring, wherever possible, the surrender of old equipment and parts before approving an import license for tools or raw materials. New ways of using and recycling industrial refuse were developed in m.e.s.c.'s own Cairo laboratories or in research institutions under contract to the Centre. As soon as they were tested successfully, the new processes were broadcast to each territory and import quotas adjusted accordingly.

Before the war, for example, considerable quantities of sulphuric acid resulting from the refining of kerosene were thrown into the sea. Now the acid was collected, purified and turned into superphosphate fertilizers. An ingenious process was developed to recover from petroleum refineries large quantities of sodium sulphide—an important material for leather processing. Tin was newly recovered by a special electric process which succeeded in separating the pure metal from all types of scrap. An immensely useful method was discovered for the purification of lubricating oil after it had been used for some time; the oil became as good as new after the cleansing. M.E.S.C. initiated the opening of an electric furnace where scrap steel was transformed into castings. And so it went.

As with all other services and commodities subject to M.E.S.C. action, the salvage of material was put to regional rather than localized use. Thus transfers of large quantities of scrap and refinery waste across the region to points of acute need took place under the aegis of the Centre.

Much of what the salvage subsection accomplished served to bolster the effectiveness of the Centre's industrial development program administered by the Assistant Director of Industrial Production and a "pool" of industrial engineering experts. In a larger sense, this too was a salvage operation: Mobilizing talents and enterprise that had been incarcerated by submissive poverty, government ineptitude, social ballast, and vassalization. The record of M.E.S.C. reveals no grandiose schemes; for that the tenure was too short, the requirements too immediate. Nor is there an impressive tally of gleaming new factories; they could not have been started without massive machinery imports outside the region. The bulk of the work of the industrial production section was done under the prosaic heading of "Technical Field Work."

> Industrial experts are continually visiting plants, and whenever required giving necessary advice as to process [sic] and specific consumption of raw materials. Extension of production facilities, use of local raw materials, application of improved methods, and the manufacture of new products are among the subjects generally treated. Wherever assistance in the form of urgently required materials, equipment, allocation of transport facilities etc. is required, the visiting officer attends to the necessary action.[22]

Prosaic and unspectacular, perhaps; but it was the kind of service for the lack of which many fledgling industries had fatally stumbled in peacetime years, unable to meet overseas competition or standards; often the reason for foregoing it had been the expense. What the organization chart of M.E.S.C. called the "pool of technical specialists, varying grades employed as available" proved to be in effect a "skill bank" of extraordinary scope to which the smallest and poorest entrepreneur anywhere in the region had ready access if his line of endeavor were deemed essential to civilian welfare and a relief to the region's shipping quota. On call through the "bank" were ranking specialists of the United States, Britain, or the Middle East. If need be they were drafted from other pursuits, including the ranks of the armed services on temporary duty. Sometimes they were flown in posthaste from Britain, India, and other parts of the Commonwealth, and even from the United States. Here was a glittering roster of first-rate talent such as never before had bent their heads in unison over the mountainous problems of industry in an underdeveloped area. For years afterwards, their praises were still sung in industrial plants all over the Middle East.[23]

There were other functions and accomplishments. The Industrial Production Section of M.E.S.C. was constantly consulted by supply officers of the armed services who were in search of production facilities to do repair work or replenish dwindling stockpiles of war materiel. A census-in-depth of all industrial establishments in the region was started. Soon the services and the trades could locate, in the time it takes to exchange telegrams, the only plant in the East making surgical instruments, for instance. Through the intermediary of M.E.S.C. small businessmen were able to pool their orders with one particular plant and thus save money and time. The expansion of plants was often encouraged by inducing customers, including the armed services, to place orders on a long-term basis so that the addition of facilities could be programmed with confidence. Buyers —and consumers—were protected by making M.E.S.C. assistance to industrial enterprises subject to an undertaking to restrain profit margins. On occasion, the Industrial Production section was able to persuade the armed services to loan raw materials or machinery to an enterprise stymied by a temporary shortage or delivery delay.

Typical of the restless quest for means to encourage production and productivity was the scheme to sanction the importation of a small quantity of semi-luxury consumer goods from overseas normally vetoed by the Centre. They were put on sale in industrial plants as means to give greater value to wage earnings and, therefore, an encouragement to sustained or increased work schedules. A new phrase appeared in the administrative vocabulary of the

Centre, the "extraction rate." This described various degrees of productive reaction in factories to the exclusive appearance of a specific
type of consumer goods.

In general, what happened at "Materials" in M.E.S.C. was a long
list of small doings. But these were the doings that were largely responsible for the "mushrooming" of industry in the Middle East
which struck so many observers, including the spies of the enemy.
Nevertheless, the Materials Division participated in one large effort
that by itself freed many thousands of tons of shipping capacity for
military use. Late in 1940 the British Embassy and General Wavell
began to press the Government of Egypt for action that would gradually convert the Egyptian state railroads to the use of local oil instead of coal imported from Great Britain. In 1941, a Joint Anglo-
Egyptian Committee was appointed which initiated and brought to
conclusion the desired conversion. The British side on this Committee was represented by the Middle East Command and the Middle
East Supply Centre with the latter playing a leading role in the difficult engineering adjustments to be made. This was part of a general program of coal-to-oil conversion which also involved such
coal-burning facilities as irrigation machinery and water condensers.
Along with the conversion of cotton acreage to cereal cultivation
(see below), this was probably the most notable feat of logistic assistance accomplished by civilians in the Middle East during World
War II.[24]

While the impact of M.E.S.C. on industrial production in the Middle East cannot be measured statistically, because of the undistin-
guishable presence of other stimuli, the following statement of the
Palestine War Supply Board on "local manufacture" in 1942 should
be noted: "The industries showing the greatest increases are those
whose development locally affords most direct assistance in the saving of shipping space." [25] Earlier, on the same subject, the Board
said that "the first year of the war was one of industrial depression
in Palestine." [26]

Feeding the Middle East

The first and foremost concern of public authority in a beleaguered
fortress, after organizing the defense and providing for the defenders, is food for the people. On the shipping lanes leading to the

Middle East, grains, aids to grain output (fertilizers), and sugar had been the heavy users of cargo capacity before the war.[27] In 1941 the food deficit was accentuated by a disastrous crop failure.[28] Food and agriculture therefore held high priority in m.e.s.c. activities from the very beginning.[29] Under the direction of Dr. Keith A. H. Murray, a leading British agronomist, the Food and Agriculture Division spearheaded the Centre's most notable victories in the battle for stability in the Middle East and for shipping economy on the high seas. Its principal allies were the British Ministry of Food, the U.S. War Food Administration, the ministries and departments of agriculture of the Middle East, the United Kingdom Commercial Corporation, the British Army, the Office of the Minister of State, and a "floating" pool of British and American experts on call for whatever surveys, planning and emergency duty the growing, sheltering, and distribution of food in the region required. Their combined labors steered the region past the threat of famine and bread riots, past the leech colonies of hoarders, profiteers, and speculators, and past a serious aggravation of social conflict. Standing firm on the shored-up foundation of a secure food supply, the region could more calmly attack other wartime problems, and showed greater willingness to cooperate with the foreign host in its midst.

Dr. Murray and one of his principal collaborators and counsellors, E. M. H. Lloyd, economic adviser to the Minister of State, have published detailed accounts of this great Allied undertaking.[30] The story is dramatic even in the most sober and technical account. There are desperate races between grain ships from Liverpool and Sydney on one side and dwindling flour reserves in Teheran and Damascus, on the other side. There are improbable scenes showing British envoys in the Middle East pleading, arguing and even quarreling with Ministers of the Crown about a few tons of wheat and fertilizers for Iran or Egypt. There is the Egyptian cereal crisis of Spring 1942.

The Joint Anglo-Egyptian Supplies Committee early in 1942 listens amid gathering gloom to tidings of ill import: grain stocks in private and government hands are not expected to last until the end of March; the next crop will not start coming in until 10 June; no shipment from overseas can be expected for the time being, and no help from neighboring countries; the only available reserve in the Middle East,—the emergency stocks held by the armed services —even if *all* could be released to Egypt, would only last until the end of May, and this only if there are further admixtures of coarse grains to the constantly graying bread and if rations are cut to the very bone; unrest is spreading among the populations of Cairo, Alexandria, Port Said, Suez, and Ismailia and ready to spill over any minute; and General Rommel is reported poised for a new offensive west of Tobruk around the beginning of June. At the very best, the cities should be without bread around 27 May, and security officials can almost predict to the hour when riots and wildfires of civil disturbance will begin to sweep the streets. Meetings of the Committee multiply as the day of reckoning approaches. The Army, on appeal from M.E.S.C. and the British Embassy, releases driblets of grain every day while cutting the bread ration of its own soldiers up front. Its stocks are down to 8,000 tons, and now urgent appeals pour in from Turkey, Iran, and Cyprus. Then, mere hours before the dreaded deadline, good news is telephoned from the Egyptian Ministry of Finance: The new compulsory grain collection scheme has surpassed all expectations. The crop is coming in almost three weeks earlier than expected. The first grain trucks roll into Cairo and new flour is delivered to the bakers' shops, just as further west a new German offensive gets under way that will capture Tobruk and carry the Afrika Korps to the threshold of the Nile Delta.[31]

Never again during the war must matters reach such extremity. This was the mandate of M.E.S.C.'s Food and Agriculture Division.[32]

Two subdivisions or sections were created: Food Supplies and Agricultural Production. One dealt with the programming of imports and food supplies imported or home-grown; the other with the technical needs of local production. As in the case of the Materials Division, measures to rationalize available supplies dominated the early phase.

The first responsibility of the Middle East Supply Centre was to bring order into a chaos of grain procurement, a free-for-all where individual countries and the Army authorities were bidding against each other and against the U.K.C.C. which had begun to assemble central reserve stocks on a modest scale in the spring of 1941 for distribution in trouble spots. The confusion reigning then and the gradual emergence of rational management is related by Lloyd:

> The first detailed proposals for centralized supply of cereals came from London in August 1941 following representations from the Minister of State. For some months, however, the situation continued to be confused and unsatisfactory. Such imports as were being obtained by private trade were irregular

and insufficient, and the prices at which they were being sold were exorbitant and constantly rising. Government action in Egypt, Palestine, Syria, Lebanon, Cyprus, and Turkey became necessary to assure supplies and ward off famine. Palestine and Cyprus were appealing to the Colonial Office for help; Egypt's and Turkey's requirements were being pressed by the British ambassadors in Cairo and Ankara and sponsored by the Foreign Office in London. Uncoordinated attempts to buy by private traders and Middle East governments upset the markets and cut across the bulk purchase and loading arrangements of the British Ministry of Food, which complained of Palestine enquiries for wheat in Australia, Egyptian bids for maize in South Africa and for wheat in Canada, and Syrian attempts to buy wheat in India.

Meanwhile, such cargoes as were arriving in the Middle East were consigned to particular territories and therefore could not be allocated to meet the most urgent needs. At first the only wheat for emergencies at the disposal of M.E.S.C. was a few cargoes that had been diverted from Greece and Yugoslavia after the German invasion of those countries. Small quantities of lend-lease flour were also beginning to arrive for the U.K.C.C. stockpile. M.E.S.C. had as yet no precise knowledge of the level of stocks in each country, though a request had been made for monthly stock returns. The British forces were still buying cereals and flour locally, and some months elapsed before the War Office in London and General Headquarters in the Middle East agreed to obtain imported cereals and sugar through U.K.C.C.

In August 1941 it had been agreed in principle that all cereal imports required for the services and for civilian consumption should be co-ordinated in a single program to be submitted by M.E.S.C. to London and that the entire quantity required from outside the area should be purchased by the Ministry of Food. On arrival, cereals would be allocated by M.E.S.C. in the light of its estimation of needs. To enable the system to work smoothly, it was agreed that a central reserve stockpile would be essential. But owing to the stringency of shipping at the time, the best that London could offer at the outset was to ensure that there would always be 50,000 tons of wheat or flour and 20,000 tons of barley or maize afloat in the form of cargoes already bought and consigned to the Middle East. This gave no insurance against delays or losses at sea nor against last-minute diversion of ships to other destinations, and thus was far from satisfying the need for an assured stockpile to be drawn upon as required. Indeed, throughout the winter of 1941 and the first six months of 1942 the flow of cereals to the Middle East was on a hand-to-mouth basis, and the greatest difficulty was experienced in allocating irregular and insufficient arrivals between the competing claims of Syria, Turkey, Palestine, and Egypt. . . . The final result was that between October 1941, when centralized buying first became fully effective, and June 1942, when the harvests began to come in, only 480,000 tons of wheat and flour had been delivered to governments and the armed forces, compared with an agreed program of 550,000 tons.

By the middle of 1942 the system was working satisfactorily and it was clear that the cereal crisis of the previous year could only have been dealt with by pooling imports. To avoid breakdown in the future it was essential to have adequate stocks; but the maintenance of a three-month strategic reserve in each Middle East country would have been wasteful and uneconomic. So long as each was able to share in a common pool, to meet both current needs and unforeseen emergencies, they were in effect enjoying a system of mutual insurance.

Centralized buying was gradually extended to sugar, fats, oils and oilseeds, tea and coffee, canned milk, meat, and fish as well as to rubber, tin, medical supplies, jute sacks, and some other items. As u.k.c.c. took over, private import came to an end or was prohibited. Monthly allocations were determined by m.e.s.c. and deliveries were made by u.k.c.c., sometimes from pool stocks and sometimes from cargoes as they arrived. An essential feature of the pooling system, which was only gradually accepted by governments, was that stocks held in any country were not earmarked for the use of that country but could be allocated by m.e.s.c. to any territory that most needed them. Special agreement had to be reached whereby u.k.c.c. stocks were not liable to requisitioning by the governments of the countries where they were situated. Another important corollary of pooling was that the armed forces ceased placing orders independently for wheat and flour, sugar, rice, and other staple foods, and agreed to submit their requirements to m.e.s.c. and buy from u.k.c.c. Army supplies were programmed along with civilian requirements and allocations were made by M.E.S.C.; but demands from the armed forces were entitled to priority over civilian needs.[33]

This was the beginning. Supplementary measures came with the virtual elimination of processed food imports (except for small essential requirements such as baby foods), firm controls over fertilizers (which included unceasing efforts to secure as large allotments as possible from the shrinking world supply) and the enforcement of high priorities for food shipments on inland transport facilities. A great deal of housecleaning remained to be done by local governments as well. They had to be aided, advised, admonished and at times compelled to do what was unpopular, unaccustomed and often beyond their administrative talents.

Take any of the numerous postwar studies on agricultural deficiencies in underdeveloped countries and multiply the variety and depth of the problems by the factor of war; consider further the time factor—the emphasis on quick results, the impatient demands of epochal events telescoped into a few weeks or months—and the scope of the task to mobilize Middle East agriculture becomes vaguely comprehensible. Probing for weak spots on their own initiative and meeting requests as they arrived, in growing numbers, from local governments and producers, the Food and Agriculture Division of M.E.S.C. found itself facing such questions as how to institute and administer food rationing; how to improve forestry and animal husbandry and expand fisheries; how to combat plant pests and diseases, such as the senn pest and rust; how to use locally available components as a substitute for unavailable overseas fertilizers; how to initiate soil conservation programs; how to expand experimental rubber plantings; how to organize cereal collection schemes; how to improve grain storage methods; how to make better use of irrigation facilities and to extend their area; how to operate, service and repair new tractors and other agricultural implements on farms unaccustomed to mechanization; how to reduce fallowing periods on farm land, alter the crop rotation and switch from unmarketable cash crops (such as cotton and citrus) to urgently needed food crops (wheat, corn, rice, barley, and potatoes); how to promote and expand truck farming and "victory" gardening; how to provide more effective "extension" service to farming, along American lines; how to reduce the incidence of foreign matter in shipments of cereals, fruit and other food crops; how to organize and schedule the transport of crops from outlying areas; how to stretch the supply of wheat by higher flour extraction rates and admixtures of coarser grains; how and where to obtain extra labor during peak activity periods and how to pool it where unavoidably scarce; and how to assemble and present agricultural statistics and reports for local and regional assessments of production, and forecasts of future crops.

Not that this knowledge was completely unavailable in the Middle East; to assume this would grievously insult the useful and dedicated work long carried out in many parts by government departments and research stations; universities; projects like the Gezira Scheme in the Sudan; centers like the Chaim Weizmann Institute in Palestine; and the great localized wealth of traditional skills and ingenuity found on even the smallest farm tilled during the millenia of unbroken cultivation in the Middle East. Nor had access to Western skills and science been new to the region. Colonial governments, missionaries, and Middle Eastern students at Western universities and schools such as the American University of Beirut, had brought with them the seeds of British, French, German, Italian, and American technology and agronomy. What the Middle East Supply Centre could and did do was first of all to produce a powerful burst of new interest in the application of new methods; to furnish a clearing house through which localized experiments and experience could be shared by the whole region; and to set up a large pool of Western specialists ready to rush in from Cairo on short notice, among them many whom normally all the treasures of Harun al-Rashid could not have lured to the heat and flies and primitive plumbing of Araby.

The ways in which M.E.S.C. rendered these services to the development of food management and agricultural production were innumerable. They occurred on the governmental level, in contacts with scientific institutions, in communications with business firms supplying and servicing agricultural equipment, and in face-to-face meetings with the cultivator on tours of many prime agricultural regions.[34] Besides the exchange of personal visits there were consultations by correspondence, telegraph, and telephone. There were numerous surveys and special studies on everything from crop rotation to land tenure.[35] And there were several regional conferences dealing with such matters as cereal collection, food distribution, rationing and agricultural development to which local experts from all corners of the Middle East as well as specialists from Western countries came in droves to participate in a generous exchange of knowledge and techniques.

A number of major projects bore the special brand of M.E.S.C. initiative and intervention. They included new irrigation schemes in Syria, Lebanon, and Iran; the opening to cultivation of thousands of acres in Syria and Cyrenaica; cereal collection systems in the Levant, Egypt, Iran, and the Sudan; cultivation shift from export to food crops in Egypt, the Levant, Iraq, Iran, and the Sudan; the introduction of potato growing in Palestine and the soya bean in the Sudan; and the great anti-locust campaigns of 1943 and 1944. A detailed account of the cereal collection scheme for Syria and Lebanon and the anti-locust drive will exemplify this work.[36]

In normal years the two French mandates in the Levant had been a net exporter of cereals and livestock products; a leading customer had been Palestine. But poor harvests in 1939, 1941, and 1942 plus speculative and fright hoarding had transformed Syria and Lebanon into deficit countries. In order to prevent a recurrence of the World War I famine, as well as to counteract Axis and Vichy influence and "break" the speculators, M.E.S.C. joined hands with the British Military Mission in the Levant (the Spears Mission) in securing from overseas more than 100,000 tons of wheat for distribution in the two newly liberated states. The hope that the sale of these cereals at controlled low prices might force the hoarders in the cities and rural areas to disgorge their holdings failed to materialize. New measures were debated. A Free French proposal to confiscate the hoards with the assistance of troops was discarded as politically unwise. Instead M.E.S.C. and the Spears Mission obtained from the new governments of Syria and Lebanon approval for the formation of a Wheat Commission, known locally as Office des Céréales Panifiables (O.C.P.), in whose hands was placed a total state monopoly for the purchase, transport and distribution of bread crops in the country. Represented on O.C.P. were the new independent governments of Lebanon and Syria, the Free French Delegation, and the Spears Mission. Technical advice and key personnel were provided by the Middle East Supply Centre which also agreed to make recommendations to London and Washington for the allocation of agricultural implements and fertilizers for the two countries as well as special allocations of consumer goods that could be offered to farmers at controlled prices so as to make price ceilings for their compulsorily collected produce more acceptable.

O.C.P., also known as M.I.R.A. (Mouvement interne du Ravitaillement), in due course became a household word in the Levant, a thing cursed by some, blessed by others but known to all. Without a permit issued by o.c.p. not a single bushel of grain could be sold or transported legally anywhere in the Levant; if anyone was caught by gendarmes or the o.c.p. trying to move grain, be it by truck, rail, cart or camel, without a license, the man, the camel, and the grain were confiscated—the man to go to jail, the camel to be sold and the grain to be transferred into the government pool. Under the aegis of o.c.p. dozens of details of Frenchmen and Britishers who in peacetime might have been bank clerks, teachers, export managers, or tavern owners and who more recently might have marched with General Wavell or Leclerc became as familiar to the Syrian country-side as the proverbial tax collector. Visiting each farm up to the re-motest mountain hamlets, they succeeded where mightier men had failed time and time again: the collection at *controlled prices* of most of the cereal crop above the portion needed for home con-sumption and next year's seeding. Other agents of o.c.p. sat in the cities and carefully doled out flour grain to strictly controlled mills and bakers' shops where bread was sold at fixed prices against ration cards. In Beirut the executive committee of o.c.p. determined the size of reserve stocks to be laid up and the transfers to be made to the regional reserve stocks administered by m.e.s.c. On 25 September 1942, one month before the battle of El Alamein and one month after the start of o.c.p.'s first full-scale collection drive, Beirut could report to the Middle East Supply Centre that it had in store 55,675 tons of cereals, equivalent to a three-month reserve, and that no call would be made on Allied shipping for imported wheat and flour during the first six months of 1943, by the two countries which in 1941, on the brink of famine in the cities, had absorbed more than a hundred thousand tons of Allied grain and shipping space within a few months. In 1944 Syria and Lebanon furnished a large contri-bution to the Middle East Reserve Pool.

Meanwhile in Cairo, while celebrations of the victory of the Eighth Army filled the air, quiet consultations were going on in the offices of m.e.s.c.'s Food Division in preparation for another spectac-ular battle, one which was to make no headlines and earn no med-als or citations for anybody. The battle was fought and won against an enemy which had waged war against man in the Middle East since biblical times and had never been defeated. Were it not for the short lives of his soldiers, their propensity to return to their homes after devastating the lands of their invasion, and their habit of attacking only in cyclical thrusts after long intervals, this enemy might have ruled the Middle East in all the centuries that separate the earliest pharaoh from Faruq, Abd al-Nasir, and Ben-Gurion. The commander of the first army to repeal this enemy before he could invade was not a five-star general but a scholarly agronomist heading the Food Division of the Middle East Supply Centre. His chief of staff was the anti-locust officer of the Division, his retinue the Middle East Anti-Locust Unit and his chief campaign adviser Dr. B. P. Uvarov, founder and director of the world famous Anti-Locust Research Centre in London.

The main breeding grounds of the Middle Eastern or "desert" locust are in the Rajputana Desert in India, the coasts of the Persian Gulf, and many parts of the Arabian Peninsula and the swamplands of East Africa. For six weeks after birth the insect is earthbound. To feed itself it marches with millions of its brothers and sisters in an almost straight continuous line, miles in breadth, across the land devouring every plant growth in its path. Then it becomes airborne. Swarms large enough to darken the skies of a large metropolis billow across the chosen lands. They settle down during brief "fueling stops" in places where the corn and grass is succulent, and leave vast areas of wasteland behind them. They are strictly cosmopolitan and have nothing but contempt for man's eternal ambition to build little fences with flags on top. They may breed in one country and attack in another; sometimes, as if heeding a regional commander, they join from separate roosts to attack together; if campaigning separately one swarm is certain to invest places bypassed by others.

There is only one place at which to meet the armies of the locust on even terms—at or near the breeding grounds. There is only one time to battle them to destruction—before they take wing. There is but one way for the nations of a region to avert a locust invasion— to form an alliance and counter-attack everywhere at once, regardless of border markers. To attack one breeding sector alone is useless. When the attack phase comes in the locust cycle they all attack from everywhere. The destruction of one swarm alone merely gives more pasture to the others.

Not until World War II did cooperation and technology in the Middle East region reach a stage where a frontal attack could be planned, organized, and pressed to conclusion.

The locust breeds and migrates in long cycles. Years of research on its habits have established something akin to a twelve-year rotation in its visitation upon the Middle East. All signs pointed to an invasion during 1943 and 1944.

The first warning was sounded by Dr. Uvarov whose center had been a focal point of reports on locust breeding and movements from all over the world since 1926. Action followed almost immediately; there were enough old hands around in Cairo who remembered how much the Allies had been helped during the First World War by the locust destruction of crops in Syria and other enemy-held areas of the Middle East. In May 1942 the Middle East Anti-Locust Unit was formed as part of the Food Division of M.E.S.C., with O. B. Lean as chief anti-locust officer. Through this office field investigations were initiated in potential breeding areas. Their reports were correlated at the Middle East Anti-Locust Conference called by M.E.S.C. in Cairo in July 1943 under the presidency of the Deputy Minister of State, Lord Moyne. Delegates from India, Egypt, the Sudan, Syria, Lebanon, Palestine, Eritrea, Cyrenaica, and Tripolitania, met with M.E.S.C. officials and Dr. Uvarov to lay out the campaign against the locust whose imminent appearance had been confirmed by the field investigators.

With M.E.S.C.'s Anti-Locust Unit acting as coordinator, equipped with materials and equipment secured by the Centre, "combat missions" went out to reported breeding areas in the Sudan, in Southern Arabia, the Persian Gulf, Upper Egypt, Ethiopia, Eritrea, Tripolitania, as far as Kenya. Poisoned bait was disseminated by trucks and planes. Most advancing swarms were caught on the ground and destroyed. Some could not be prevented from reaching the flying state but were substantially checked by poison spray from planes of the R.A.F. and Soviet air forces.

The magnitude of the operation and the unprecedented scope of international cooperation attained in this historic undertaking stand out as probably the most important single achievement of the Middle East Supply Centre.

The successful outcome of the campaign, which in size, scope, and extent of international co-operation was unparalleled before or since, was mainly due to a combination of three factors: first, a team of British and American technical experts and M.E.S.C. administrators, who entered upon this novel and arduous work with something like missionary zeal; second, wholehearted cooperation from the military and air authorities in providing personnel, transport, and wireless facilities; and third, financial assistance provided by the British Treasury at the instance of the Inter-Departmental Committee on Locust Control in London. None of these would have been forthcoming in such full measure if the fight against locusts had not been recognized, thanks to Uvarov's pioneering research, as an urgently needed and practicable method of saving shipping and safeguarding the food supply of the Middle East. In Sudan, Egypt, Ethiopia, Eritrea, and Libya, as well as farther afield in India, East Africa, Turkey, and the U.S.S.R., governments and local administrations intensified their normal control measures and contributed and received technical information of the greatest value. Fortnightly reports about the appearance of swarms and the discovery of breeding areas were centralized in Uvarov's Anti-Locust Research Centre in London. M.E.S.C.'s main contribution lay in the work carried out, with the aid of the army and the Royal Air Force, by technical missions sent to Saudi Arabia and to Persia. The Arabian peninsula had long been regarded as the stronghold, hitherto undisturbed, of the desert locust and the strategic center for a coordinated campaign. Swarms arrive there from both India and Africa and multiply during the winter months. To meet the threat of infestation spreading to neighboring countries, the plan was to seek out and exterminate the locusts in their breeding grounds in Arabia. . . .

King Ibn Saud took a personal interest in the work of the missions and overrode the scruples of some of his advisers who were lukewarm if not opposed to the extermination of locusts. It must be remembered that locusts are a prized article of diet among the nomad tribes, and the government was rightly concerned about the risk of human beings and animals being poisoned. There were also some difficulties at first in obtaining permission for almost a thousand uniformed British troops to enter Saudi Arabia. But with good will on both sides most of these were solved. In particular the wearing of an Arab headdress—a *kefia* and an *algal*—as part of the uniform added a touch of glamour to the expedition and (at the same time) allayed the misgivings of the Saudi Arabian authorities.

General Headquarters was prevailed upon to provide two Palestinian transport companies and two platoons of a tank-transport company equipped with ten-ton trucks, with a total strength of 24 officers, 800 other ranks, and 329 vehicles. M.E.S.C. was responsible for providing the civilian specialists as well as bait and other technical equipment. For the actual killing of locusts, Saudi Arabian labor was recruited to work under the supervision of Sudanese foremen. . . .

Periodical plagues of locusts still constitute a threat to the food supplies of the Middle East. What was done during the war, particularly in Saudi Arabia, has set an example for later campaigns conducted by entomologists working together in the Middle East. But the resources mobilized during the war exceeded anything attempted before or since, with the result that no severe outbreak occurred involving serious loss of food during what were expected to be the peak years of the locust cycle. Prevention of crop failure, famine, and famine prices by fighting the locusts in their breeding grounds may have saved the diversion of hundreds of thousand tons of Allied shipping which would have been needed to bring relief.[37]

This incidentally was the only instance in which the Soviet Union responded to overtures of the Supply Centre. An invitation to the Russians to join the Anglo-American-Iranian committee supervising the Teheran office of M.E.S.C. was ignored.

What were the results of M.E.S.C.'s food program? Between 1939 and 1943, the tonnage of merchant ships entering the ports of Egypt, Iraq, Lebanon, Palestine, and Iran from foreign points of origin (including some intercoastal shipping) declined from 50.8 million to 19.4 million net registered tons.[38] During the same period, the sea-borne civilian imports of the same countries declined from a prewar average of approximately 5 million tons to an estimated 1.5 million tons.[39] Under these conditions, how was the Middle East fed? How was agricultural production maintained in the face of the multitude of disturbances, including a disastrous crop failure in 1941 and the lack of fertilizers?

On the latter point Lloyd has compiled cereal production data for Egypt, Sudan, Palestine, Syria, Lebanon, Cyprus, Iran, and Iraq from official sources and shows that average output during the 1940–1945 period was slightly higher than during the 1934–1938 span: 10,600,000 tons as compared with 10,362,000.[40]

As for the level of food consumption no direct statistical measurement is available, or possible, considering the low state of statistics in the Middle East during this period. Lloyd suggests however the use of infant mortality statistics as an indication of what happened. Such data were recorded during the war for Egypt, Palestine, and Cyprus. They show that in all three countries the 1940–1945 average was below the average for 1934–1938, in Palestine substantially so both for the Jewish and Arab population. The correlation between food and infant mortality is clearly revealed by the fact that infant mortality rose sharply in the three countries during 1942 following the 1941 crop failure. Lloyd also cites, by way of comparison with the Axis area, a definite contra-secular rise in Italy and the Netherlands.

Beyond the raw statistics, there is the indisputable fact that all accounts of the wartime years whether from Western, Arab, or Israeli sources, agree that no serious food shortages developed for any length of time. Certain foods were short of course, and brief bread riots occurred in Teheran, Ahwaz, and Damascus. Famine conditions, resulting from crop failures and bad communications were experienced in Hadhramaut and in parts of British Somaliland.[41] These were exceptions to an overwhelmingly different trend.

Far from being a province of famine the Middle East proved capable of adding to the provisioning of other regions and, of course, the Allied forces. Egyptian rice stemmed a critical shortage in Ceylon and sustained the diet of Indian troops in the North African and Mediterranean Theaters of Operations. Barley, onions, potatoes, jams, citrus, poultry products from Egypt, Iraq, Palestine, and Lebanon supplemented the food rations of the Middle East Command. In 1944, the Middle East Supply Centre began to assemble food stocks for Greece and other Balkan countries to be distributed upon liberation. They were placed under the wings of a new Middle East Relief and Rehabilitation Administration and formed the first harbinger of better fortune that followed the liberation of Greece. They also were a source of contribution to the stocks of UNRRA.[42]

Regulation of Inland Transport [43]

In Iran there was a black market for standing room on railway trains going cross-country ($500 per person); in Kuwait, British personnel had to postpone their leaves for as much as a year for want of passenger flight space; in Cairo, a set of retreaded tires sold under the counter for $2,000 to $3,000 and in Aleppo truck tires were retreaded under contract for the French and British armies for $400 per tire; in Khartoum "Jolting Mathilda" taxis and in Aleppo trucks rolled on tires patched with scraps of rubber held in place by nuts and bolts. The absence of modern equipment made the manufacture of new tires difficult and impractical. In Aleppo, the owner of a retreading business manufactured six new tires in 1943— perhaps the first ever made in the Middle East and the only ones to be made in the area during all of World War II—and sold them for $2,500 each. Such was the situation of civilian transport in the Middle East during World War II.

It was part of a paradox. Never had there been more trucks and utility vehicles on the roads. Never had there been more railroad and highway construction. Never had there been larger stockpiles of tires and spare parts, nor more expert mechanics on duty, nor more well-equipped service stations. There were more new airfields than decent soccer fields. In Khartoum, Cairo, Beirut, Basra, and Teheran transport planes shuttled in and out with the frequency of bus schedules. And the easiest thing to get was petrol. But all this accumulation and activity was part of an enclave, vast, mobile and largely foreign, to which the average dweller of the region could get access only by special sufferance, through occasional charity, or by theft. Contrasts such as these could be found all over the world in those years. They set dweller apart from defender or occupier, in matters of food, clothing, comfort, recreation, tools and waiting lines. Usually it was in transport that contrasts were most visible.

The abundance of trucks and trailers churning up the roads of the Middle East under military auspices was of course not extravagance. Every vehicle had been wrenched from tight quotas in the places of origin. They had come from countries that themselves lived under severe restrictions. And they had been carried overseas at the risk and the actual cost of many lives. They had been sent to make war on the Axis. The sacrifice these vehicles represented was not made, and would not be made in the future, in order to provide joyrides to noncombatants.

The demand for nonmilitary travel by motor was great in the Middle East precisely at this time. Vacation travel to Europe was suspended; instead of boarding ships or an intercontinental *wagon-lits,* holiday travelers had to seek out busses or taxis, or hitch-hike on trucks to nearby beaches and mountain resorts. Villagers able to sell their crops at wartime prices had plenty of money in their pockets and were anxious to reach the cities to spend it. Many persons had followed the lure of new jobs in places away from home, particularly in army camps and assembly depots; they wanted to visit their families or just return home. Students once bound for European universities now flocked to institutions in Cairo, Beirut, Jerusalem, Baghdad, and Teheran—and back home during the vacation. Pilgrims, though not as many as in peacetime, were straining for Mecca. At the same time, civilian travel on the region's sparse railroads was restricted. The British military were controlling most of them and gave special priorities to soldiers and other Allied personnel. Moreover, they had under contract large fleets of privately owned motor vehicles, for service in Iran and elsewhere. Quite literally, civilian travellers were pushed off the road and squeezed out of railroad compartments.

But joyrides—and more urgent travel—were not the only non-military calls on railroad and motor facilities. Goods had to be moved—food, chemicals, clothing, toothbrushes, boots, drugs, paper, leather, machinery. New patterns of trade directed many shipments to routes other than traditional thoroughfares that connected ports with inland centers of distribution; cross-country traffic was on the increase; the very scheme of regional self-sufficiency which the British Minister of State, the British Middle East Command, and the Supply Centre had foisted upon the economy demanded efficient and readily available inland transport. Egypt and Iraq were asked to deplete their individual cereal reserves and place trust in a central emergency reserve in Beirut, Damascus, or Haifa. What if the emergency came and there were no trucks or freight cars to carry the grain? Industrial expansion was encouraged and aided by M.E.S.C. on the prospect of markets all over the region. Who was going to make the actual deliveries? A highly critical point were the compulsory grain collection schemes promoted by the Centre; cereals instead of being transported in outlying villages by camel, donkey or cart were now to be collected by truck and ferried to the nearest railhead or directly in the city. At harvest time therefore, motor transport must be available in greater numbers than ever before.

To provide a positive answer to these questions the Middle East Supply Centre established a Transport Division under the direction of Harold Elliott, a British transport specialist. More than any other division, Transport had to turn deaf ears to civilian demands for imports of transport equipment from overseas. With the British and American forces in the Middle East receiving large consignments of material to expand the Trans-Iranian Railway, to build a new rail connection between Haifa and Tripoli (Lebanon), to construct a transdesert highway from Damascus to Baghdad, a new port in Khorramshahr, a new airfield near Cairo, and with thousands of lendlease trucks assembled each month in local military depots, it was futile to implore the governments of the United States and Britain to approve shipments of similar items for civilian use. Although this might not have been officially stated, in transport matters the civilian in the Middle East usually was expected to get by as a scavenger.

It was necessary therefore for the Transport Division to seek concessions from their colleagues in the Middle East Command. It was suggested that vehicles, tires, and spare parts which had become surplus, or at least not urgently required, be transferred through M.E.S.C. to essential civilian transport operations. An agreement was sought under which it would obtain the temporary assignment of Army equipment and personnel to such transport emergency tasks as would arise during harvests, anti-locust drives, and the shipment of M.E.S.C. reserve stocks to cities exhausting their flour stocks.

It was fortunate that the Director General and the field agents of M.E.S.C. had from the start worked in exemplary harmony with the military.[44] It was equally fortunate that the British commanders were alive to their political and psychological responsibilities.[45] The result was an exceptionally well-integrated military-civilian transport policy.

As long as the services controlled the railroads and air traffic (and, by the way, river transport) facilities and priorities were granted to the movement of essential civilian cargo and passengers as recommended by M.E.S.C. As the services loosened or relinquished their hold, certain controls were, *pari passu*, taken over by the Centre. The most sweeping transfer occurred in 1944 when maintenance for all the civilian motor transport hired by the British and American military establishments to help carry supplies through the Persian Corridor to the Russians was entrusted to the Supply Centre and U.K.C.C. Some 2,000 privately owned vehicles were running this 700-mile route, from Basra to Tabriz, under road and weather conditions as bad as could be found in any part of the world. To be given this job was one of the great challenges of M.E.S.C.'s career and demonstrated its high standing with the military.

In 1944, M.E.S.C. also assumed the task of presenting to the Allied governments the carefully screened requests of the region's railroads for new rolling stock and replacement parts—something done heretofore by the military. A report by a team of M.E.S.C. experts on the Iraqi State Railroads, for example, served as basis for the allocation of rolling stock to Iraq through lend-lease channels.

On numerous occasions, the army answered promptly the appeals of M.E.S.C. (and other civil authorities) for emergency assignment of transport and personnel. Certain phases of the cereal collection schemes in Egypt, Syria, and Iran were rescued from fatal delay by such timely intervention. In the process the British exposed themselves to charges by ever-suspicious local populations that they were confiscating the crops they were trying to rescue; on one occasion furious demonstrations almost blocked their progress.

The military quartermaster also came to the rescue on occasion with quick releases of tires and spare parts and the opening of its servicing facilities to stalled civilian vehicles.[46] Here however, its capabilities were limited in face of the mountainous demand. In contrast to the procurement of entire vehicles, there was a relatively large irreducible minimum of tires and spare parts and servicing equipment that had to be brought in from overseas if civilian transport was not to collapse, and here, M.E.S.C. took on its familiar function of screening, recommending, and controlling end-use.

Tires, the worst bottlenecks, were imported in bulk by the Supply Centre through the U.K.C.C. which doled them out through established commercial dealers. Bulk orders were placed overseas only after combing all reported requirements in the territories down to the minimum and after full use had been made of retreading and repair facilities sponsored by the Centre and supervised by its technical experts. Claims on overseas resources and shipping were reduced by inducing all governments to organize the collection of worn-out tires; the latter were shipped to rubber reclaiming plants in the Middle East, Africa, and India. M.E.S.C. also initiated a system of regular inspection so that tires could be salvaged before they were past the retreading stage.

Both the distribution and procurement of spare parts was left in private hands, but each local import license and corresponding order was checked for justification. A census of essential vehicles, their number as well as their state of repair, was organized in several countries, and constant check-ups on stock of spare parts were made, to render possible the formulation of half-year M.E.S.C. forecasts of needs for U.S. and U.K. consideration. Technical assistance and special import concessions enabled local governments and firms to expand facilities for the reconditioning of worn-out parts. In co-operation with the Materials Division, the opening of a few plants capable of manufacturing new spare parts was facilitated. In cooper-ation with the Agricultural Production Section rubber planting was encouraged.

Transport scarcity provided a highly combustible fuel for the fires of inflation. A thriving black market in tires and parts had to be checked. The Transport Division attempted this by holding each government and major distributor responsible for the proper assign-ment of each piston or tube. Neither could hope for approval of an import license if an allotment went astray into unauthorized chan-nels. No request for new parts was considered, even from authorized vehicle operators, unless the old, worn-out part was surrendered at the same time. To keep markups of dealers down (and block vehi-cle operators from blaming higher carrying charges on supply cost) no import licence was approved by M.E.S.C. lest it carried a commit-ment to limit middlemen's profits. Finally, the operators of trans-port facilities themselves were watched as far as possible so that only essential cargo and travel was accepted and that only prescribed rates were charged. In this manner a black market in freight and passenger travel which threatened to cripple transport planning in Iran and Iraq was ultimately brought under control.

The Organization Manual of M.E.S.C. identified four basic prob-lems confronting the Transport Division as it pursued its assign-ment with the help of outstanding transport specialists from Brit-ain, the United States, and the Middle East. Three of them were structural deficiencies that had long retarded the development of ef-ficient communications in most parts of the region and, in conse-quence, retarded economic development.

One was the lack of an adequately developed motor vehicle ad-ministration, if not its total absence, in various territories. This was but one aspect of a major difficulty: Governmental indifference if not hostility in regard to motor transport in general. At the root of this lay in part the low standard of living which permitted rela-tively few people to own cars—most of them foreigners; the expen-diture for an elaborate administration appeared extravagant, while spending on highways might have been resented by the masses as subservience to the rich. Another basic element was the state owner-ship of railroads; governments were naturally reluctant to incur def-icits or reductions in income on their facilities by assisting competing motor conveyances. One of the lasting bequests of the wartime control and regulation of motor transport in the Middle East was public recognition of motor transport needs and a framework of administrative procedures (e.g., registration) transplanted by M.E.S.C. experts from the motorized West.

The second structural obstacle was the fragmentized ownership of commercial vehicles. While not objectionable per se, even on grounds of efficiency, it was a nuisance to transport regulation and economy because of the illiteracy and spirit of technical nonconformism of most of the individual owners. The controls and projects sponsored by the Transport Division of M.E.S.C. favored the operators of large fleets or the formation of cooperative groups among individual operators, both more competent in the execution of a national transport policy and more efficient in the propagation of better techniques.

As the third obstacle the M.E.S.C. statement listed the dearth of service and repair stations particularly outside the larger towns coupled with what it called in the quaint language of prewar days the "oriental attitude of mind." The latter refers to a propensity to allow equipment to wear out to the point of in-service collapse instead of practicing life-prolonging maintenance. This was the special responsibility of the "vehicle supplies and transport rationalization officer" in the Transport Division. Technical advisers were dispatched to most of the territories to bring about government pressure for an improvement of service station procedures and equipment, better utilization of available mechanical skills, and indoctrination of all truck drivers in the fundamentals of servicing and maintaining their vehicles. Steps were also taken to persuade local authorities or established automobile dealers to enlarge existing servicing facilities and to set up new workshops in outlying areas.

The fourth problem was also structural but it was not one of scarcity. More than once, officials of the Transport Division must have expressed the fervent wish that the folks back home had such a "problem." There was an abundance of gasoline as the wells and refineries of Iran, Iraq, Bahrein, and Saudi Arabia were unable to ship a large part of their output overseas, even after operations had been curtailed. One of the most convenient "natural" tourniquets for the excessive flow of motor traffic in the Western world—the shortage of fuel—was not present and had to be created artificially. Gradually almost all countries of the region introduced, under

M.E.S.C. pressure, gasoline rationing—not to save fuel but to save vehicles.[47]

The effort to provide a focus for a civil transport policy in the Middle East under wartime conditions had its quick moments of high drama along with weeks and months of tedious routine collecting statistics, checking stock rooms, explaining patiently through interpreters the rudiments of engine maintenance, or arguing meticulously over the whereabouts of a few tires, a dozen water pumps, a set of retreads. The dramatic rescue dash of army convoys rolling into remote villages to save a crop after a brief telephone call from a cluttered desk at headquarters of M.E.S.C. were badly needed morale-building reminders for the men of the Transport Division that they were indeed a factor in winning the war. On the other hand, the endless "insubstantial pageant" of petty interventions in the affairs of a fragmentized and ferociously individualistic industry, and the constant stream of little calamities occasioned by washouts, storms and, above all, a truly dismal system of roads, could not help but drain the enthusiasm of administrators who generally came from an environment that detested the flour sifting of an officious bureaucracy. But the months of minute detail were no less important to the success of the enterprise than the hours of dramatic elation. On the sparse and cramped mountain roads of Iran or Syria a broken axle or leaking radiator could impose fateful delays on long convoys headed for supply points near battle stations or carrying grain to cities on the verge of bread riots. Not only must there be constant watch over the state of repair of practically every vehicle; many small men used to a life of insignificance and then suddenly catapulted into great importance by virtue of sitting behind the steering wheel of a truck somewhere in a long *cortège* of vehicles had to be taught by daily example the worth of equipment and the values of self-imposed discipline in the motor age. And their governments had to be awakened to the responsibility they shared with them.

To effect this latter task—to bring to the roads and garages of Middle Eastern countries the constructive acceptance of transport rationing amid an abundance of military transport and flowing petrol—was a task that would have been quite beyond the capacity of the small M.E.S.C. corps had it not been for the work of national transport advisory committees set up in thirteen countries at the suggestion of M.E.S.C.. In Palestine, for example, such a committee comprised representatives of M.E.S.C., the War Supply Board, interested government departments, the Army, and the transport industry. These committees not only speeded up the adoption of such measures as the revocation of permits of non-essential operators, the strict licensing of motor car and tire sales, the rationing of gasoline, the institution of vehicle registration (where not yet extant), and the creation of statistical services, but they were also instrumental in launching public information and educational campaigns through which both the need for, and the ways of, transport regulation were explained to the masses.

The record speaks clearly in praise of the job done by the Transport Division of M.E.S.C. At no time did a serious transport emergency of any length arise.[48] Few local food calamities developed because of a lack or breakdown of transport. Beyond that, the civilian transport system of the Middle East was in a position to support without collapsing the additional weight placed on it by the intensified economic traffic between the countries of the Middle East. Here was one of the keys to the success of the regional policy pursued by the Centre. For the basic problem of intraregional exchange in the Middle East had long been symbolized by the following classic story: The Maronite Patriarch of Lebanon was once offered a gift of Syrian wheat for one of his relief projects. He regretfully declined: It was cheaper to *buy* grain f.o.b. Marseilles and bring it in by ship than to pay the transport cost from the mountain village.

Battle Against Disease

The yearly imports of medicines into the M.E.S.C. area in times of peace could most probably be accommodated in one medium-sized cargo ship. In creating a special full-status Division of Medical Requirements under one of America's outstanding public health specialists, Dr. Henry Van Zile Hyde, the Middle East Supply Centre manifestly was not motivated by apprehensions over shipping space. In this rubric of activity, measures and policies were governed primarily by pharmaceutical shortages in Britain and the United States, on the one hand, and keenness to maintain an adequate public health situation in the Middle East despite import cuts.

The existence of this Division [49] and its full participation in the processing of import licences also showed clearly a general shift of emphasis in the objectives of M.E.S.C.. Planning was clearly shifting from shipping economy to insuring adequate supplies to the Middle East from a heavily strained source.[50]

New, powerful antibiotics had begun to be produced in quantity in the United States, among them a new highly effective anti-typhoid drug. But the armed forces of the United States and her allies were absorbing almost all of it. It was the hope that through an Allied agency like M.E.S.C. at least a small share could be squeezed out for the Middle East's most pressing civilian needs.

Caring for public health in the Middle East on short notice and term was like setting up a small sick bay on a huge trireme that should have been in permanent quarantine instead of floating on the high seas. From the bottom tier the doctor had best keep away, except in mass emergencies. There among the teeming masses was the empire of creeping, entrenched diseases, where flies and bacteria had generous and permanent squatting rights, where a large percentage of dwellers had one or two debilitating diseases; where malnutrition, festering skins, and wasting bodies were a birthmark, and where dirt and the disdain of hygienic practices were almost a badge of community conformance.[51] Only the work of a generation could bring the cleansing waters of a massive cure.

Further up was the tier of the galloping diseases—explosive epidemics which must be kept under lock and key, or quickly manacled in case of escape lest they decimate the crew. Finally there were the compounds of health, foremost among them the conglomerations of Allied military and civilian personnel or longtime foreign residents whose bodies were sound and could be kept in good repair by precautions, inoculations, incisive instructions, a relatively small supply of drugs and ministrations to temporary sickness.

In order to bring to bear upon problems of public health and of medical supply the best informed judgment available, the Medical Requirements Division of M.E.S.C. and the Minister of State called into being the Middle East Medical Advisory Committee (M.E.M.A.C.) —one of many consultative and advisory bodies that complemented, indeed upheld, the work of the Supply Centre on the regional and local level in such matters as local import controls, grain collections, transport regulation, supply planning, waste recovery, scientific research, tractor operation, refugee relief, locust control, and others. The Surgeon General of the British forces in the Middle East ("Director of Medical Services, M.E.F.") was chairman of M.E.M.A.C. Along with representatives of the Minister of State, M.E.S.C., and the U.K.C.C. sat eminent medical and public health specialists from the British and American forces as well as the medical profession in Middle Eastern countries. Serviced by the facilities of the Medical Requirements Division of M.E.S.C. this committee was a focus of technical assistance to local health authorities and a general staff for anti-epidemic campaigns. Their job was humanitarian as well as utilitarian: Saving human lives, protecting Allied soldiers and averting political embarrassment where ignorance and superstition could easily be played upon by enemies within and without in case of epidemics.

As an instance of the type of help rendered by M.E.M.A.C. might be cited the case of Iran in which the port of Khorramshahr, highly important to the war effort, was threatened by the advance of typhus from the inland area. The Government called for help in fending off the danger. A special meeting of M.E.M.A.C. was called to consider the problem. Immediately after the meeting the Quartermaster Department of the British Army started work adapting flit guns for anti-louse work; the British Directorate of Medical Services released six tons of anti-louse powder, the Ministry of War Transport made shipping space available to the threatened port, the U.S. Typhus Commission dispatched two officers and the R.A.F. one noncom specialist to survey the situation and to instruct and train local personnel; the Typhus Commission also released thousands of doses of vaccine and M.E.S.C. the required numbers of Lend-lease syringes; the R.A.F. provided air transportation for men and supplies. Within two weeks the full force of all British and American agencies that had any material, facilities or personnel needed in the protection of the threatened port had been brought fully to bear upon the typhus problem. As a result, no typhus reached the port and trained native groups continued carrying out effective anti-typhus control measures at stations in all the interior in an orderly attempt to stamp out the disease.

In between dramatic incidents like this there was the long, patient work of advising governments how to preserve their stock of pharmaceuticals, how to get after hoarders and unscrupulous profiteers trying to extort fortunes for a scarce medication, how to modernize hospital procedures, how to organize mass inoculations. In some places new facilities had to be nursed from scratch; in other cases one could build on solid achievements of the past.

A very useful initiative of the Division was the distribution of a "Middle East Formulary," a guidebook for doctors and pharmacists modelled after the United Kingdom War Formulary. It contained prescriptions for a long list of common Middle Eastern diseases based as far as possible on regionally available drugs, herbs, and ingredients, or on pharmaceuticals not in short world supply. This was a corollary to the Division's encouragement of local pharmaceutical industries and a campaign to inspire confidence in local drugs among patients brought up on foreign drugs and long indoctrinated with distrust of native doctors, hospitals, and medicines.

Control over the import of drugs and related products was one of the strictest practiced in the M.E.S.C. organization. Cosmetics and items such as toothbrushes, toothpaste, and soaps were completely excluded. Private importation of all essential medical supplies was suspended and replaced by the "bulk indent" system. Governments or specially constituted and representative national committees had to present the periodical requirements of their countries to the Middle East Supply Centre which submitted them to the Advisory Committee. A bulk indent was then forwarded overseas for the usual processing. Once approved there, the various items were procured through the Ministry of Supply in England and CAMES in the United States, in the latter predominantly on a lendlease basis. Distribution through private trade channels was authorized in several countries but under the step-by-step supervision of a public agency or committee, to insure efficient use and to curb black markets and profiteering. Generally, the cooperation of the suppliers in the United States and Britain was prompt. In view of the inexperience of governmental agencies in the Middle East in estimating requirements, and to cope with emergencies that might arise from epidemics and submarine sinkings of supply ships, a central reserve for the whole region was placed into the hands of U.K.C.C. to be administered under the direction of the Centre and the Advisory Committee.

In the later phases of the war some consultations were held and studies made with a view to assisting local governments in the propagation of better nutritional habits and standards in their lands. The Division also had a voice in the shaping of such M.E.S.C. measures as grain extraction rates, bread mixtures, and selecting "incentive" foods for agricultural and industrial workers; it advised the U.K.C.C. on safe storage methods for central grain and pharmaceutical reserves; and provided sanitary guidance for food processing plants established in the Middle East with M.E.S.C. help. In addition, the interest of local physicians and medical associations was stimulated in a continuation and expansion of cooperation and consultation with their opposite numbers in other countries of the region.

There were no large uncontrolled epidemics in the Middle East; there was no decline in general health and nutritional standards; locally produced pharmaceutical products were widely prescribed and accepted, even purchased in certain quantities by the armed services. Scarce and valuable antibiotics were made available in cases of extreme urgency. For all this, the Medical Requirements of M.E.S.C. and the Medical Advisory Committee has received recognition, if not in the wider public, at least among government officials and the medical profession.

There were several legacies. Whereas in World War I huge numbers of men, women, and children had been felled by disease in the Levant and Persia, general health conditions were probably better in these and neighboring areas during World War II than in the peacetime years before—if the statistics on infant mortality, for example, are any indication.[52] Furthermore, there was significant progress in the production and public acceptance of locally produced medications; more of this would be visible today if Israel, on whose territory most of the new pharmaceutical manufactures came to life, had not been quickly isolated from its regional market, first by private boycott and then by the concert of Arab League governments. A more subtle yet highly significant bequest was the great stress laid in the wartime years on preventive medicine. As Worthington has stated, medical services in the region, often following the bent of French medicine, had been oriented primarily toward healing the diseased while not stressing sufficiently the prevention of diseases; moreover the training and employment of physicians tended to stress the practice of specialized medicine rather than the goal of providing a foundation of general practitioners.[53]

9

From Regional Coordination
to Postwar Planning

Coping with Inflation

IN the course of World War II, Cairo was the scene of many international conferences. Roosevelt, Churchill, and Chiang Kai-shek gathered there in one of the great summit councils of the Allied world. As the seat of several governments-in-exile, the city was the feverish meeting ground of many European leaders plotting the downfall of the present occupants of their countries and preparing for their own homeward return. As the residence of the British Minister of State and the American Economic Mission, the Egyptian capital was host to many briefing sessions for groups of British and American envoys in the Middle East, often in connection with high state visits as that of the Eden-Dill mission of February 1941. As site of the huge headquarters of the British Forces in the Middle East and the smaller offices of the U.S. Forces, the palaces and hotels beneath the Pyramids provided the background for innumerable convocations of military commanders, occupation chiefs, and civilian proconsuls on duty throughout the theater of the Middle East Command, including the Middle East War Council, the Middle East Supply Council, and their committees. As head city of what was gradually becoming the pilot nation of the Arab world, Cairo also received a swelling stream of emissaries from sister nations coming on political, economic, and cultural errands related to the slow germination of Arab unity schemes.

There was therefore hardly more than a ripple of comment in local newspapers about a brief announcement in April 1944 that a Middle East Financial Conference had met in the Nile metropolis, attended by five ministers of finance and about seventy senior officials from fifteen countries, including representatives of the United States and British treasuries.[1]

Although the intrusion of greater events combined with censorship and the dearth of newsprint to deprive it of front page treatment, this conference had high symbolic and administrative significance. Of its symbolism more will be said later. Administratively, the deliberations touched on some of the thorniest economic problems inflicted on the people of the region in the later phases of the war. The delegates talked of many familiar grievances: Taxes, the public debt, the need for thrift, rationing, the follies of bankers and the pestilence of black markets. But the central topic was inflation.[2]

The Middle East Supply Centre was prominently represented at the Conference. It also was the subject of many pointed statements, some made in praise and some meant to criticize.[3] Together, these words gave testimony, negative and positive, to the commanding position which the Centre had attained in the affairs of the Middle East. They also shed light on a dilemma which had dogged many decisions of the Centre and had entangled its members in some complex theorizing.

The daily pressures of improvisation and organization, of protests and petitions, left little time for theorizing. But certain policy implications had to be weighed from time to time. One subject that gave rise to much speculation among M.E.S.C. officials was the "point of no return" of shipping economy, or, as Macduffie called it, the "price tag on a ton of shipping saved." [4]

This was the problem: Middle Eastern industrial and agricultural production stood ready to offer substitutes for many goods normally imported over the seas, from fertilizer to razor blades—but at a price. Sometimes the local product was both good and cheap but more often the stand-in could only be produced and sold at prices several times the landed cost of the import model.[5] At the height of the shipping crisis it seemed preferable to make the local consumer pay this price so that an extra ton of shipping could be spared for more urgent claims of the war. But how far could this substitution be pushed? Beyond which point would the rise of living costs do greater harm to the Allied cause than diversion from battle of a ton of shipping? By what equation could one determine whether it was more helpful to that cause to allocate more tonnage to civilians than to fan inflation?

No convenient calculus was available to measure the "relative disutilities of shipping and pricing," a term attributed to Landis.[6] There were too many variables in the formula, too many aspects on the prismatic face of inflation.

The dangerous implications were all too clear. When the Allied cause was weak and Middle Eastern opportunism strong, galloping prices, particularly on bread and sugar, were like so many torches thrown into a tinderbox of restless, hungry, xenophobe masses. Inflation was a boon to the hoarder and profiteer whether he be a merchant or a government. Governments that honestly sought to maintain equitable distribution of essentials in their countries—by rationing, price ceilings, and allocation—were the easy prey of smugglers who would carry goods across badly guarded borders from the Stygian regions of low prices to the Eldorados of inflation; and some governments in the Middle East were always ready to exact a high price for disgorging their surpluses to hungry neighbors.[7]

High mercantile profits, the offspring of inflation, seriously strained the impulse of the generosity of parliament and people in the United States and Britain called upon to share supplies and shipping with nonbelligerent foreigners far away; the consideration of Middle Eastern needs in the lend-lease program, for example, could be gravely compromised, particularly if the blame and the profits could be traced to British officials or concerns.[8]

Many an Allied representative indeed asked indignant questions during the war when he saw British or American goods, produced under stringent controls of wages, profits and prices, and carried across the seas by seamen risking their lives, help line the pockets of traders who enriched themselves with the spread between the Anglo-American and the Middle Eastern price level.[9]

Inflation was particularly unwelcome where it agitated local demands for more shipping and supplies from overseas. Not only did the reapers of windfall profits seek goods on which to spend the money, but governments used the price index to justify pressure on agencies like the Supply Centre. A strange *Methodenstreit* arose in this connection and animated many debates among economic and financial experts in the region; it also was prominent at the Financial Conference. According to some government spokesmen—those from Iran and Lebanon, for example—there was no inflation in the Middle East even where prices had risen sixfold in a few years, as was the case in Iran. With "tongue-in-cheek" recourse to the French meaning of the term, inflation was defined exclusively as a price rise resulting from large budget deficits financed by even larger fiduciary issues of money.[10] As the spokesmen told the Financial Conference, correctly, most countries in the Middle East had budget surpluses—largely because of the orthodoxy of prewar colonial administrators and advisers as well as the wartime slowdown in public improvements—and money in circulation, much as it had increased, was amply backed by gold, sterling, and dollars freshly earned from Allied expenditures in the region; high prices were basically the result of Allied supply restrictions compounded by large offshore purchases, not of "inflation." [11] From this correct analysis, the discussants drew the questionable conclusion that high prices were a matter not of local restrictions but one of more supplies from England and America. This semantic vagrancy was continually used by certain governments to resist pressures for the adoption of unpopular tax, rationing, and price control measures. The Allies had caused the inflation, was the rejoinder; it was for them to undo their work by restraining their local expenditures and by allowing more goods to come in from overseas.[12] The latter was bad medicine for the Middle East Supply Centre to which the finger was thus accusingly pointed.

But there was another side to inflation. To reduce the burden on the Allied supply line, the Middle East had to become self-sufficient to the largest possible degree. Belt tightening alone, as everyone knew, was not enough unless one meant to starve millions to death or horrible debility. There must be a surge of local production. A policy of deflation is seldom an appropriate climate for rapid economic expansion, certainly not within the urgent time schedules of a war. In a region where normally business talent had shied away from industry because of the high returns on trading and real estate,[13] and at a time when black market hawkers could earn a generous life pension from the sale of one set of tires,[14] excessive haggling over prices and profits with local producers could easily jeopardize Army and M.E.S.C. negotiations on military contracts or the promotion of a new plant for the output of import substitutes. Nor were low prices a good companion for cereal collection schemes or an effective argument with governments determined to hold on to cereal reserves.

If inflation in some cases stimulated the appetite for overseas goods, there were other cases when it did just the opposite, mainly where high prices lapped up excessive purchasing power so that not enough was left for extravagance. Indeed, some Anglo-American advisers urged a free market for all but the most essential consumer goods on these grounds. They pointed to the example of Britain, where foods were controlled while much of the rest was left to be sold at what the traffic would bear, with the middleman's profit largely absorbed by high taxes.[15]

As an organization committed at one and the same time to the reduction of sea-borne imports and the stimulation of local production and the distribution of local surplusses within the region, the Middle East Supply Centre could not take a rigid position on the question of high prices. It was not that the policy of the Centre, among various alternatives, preferred the way of inflation; it was simply that the Centre refused to defer slavishly to the fear of inflation when vital objectives were at stake.[16]

This position was not always clearly understood or appreciated in London or by British officials on the scene. The fight against inflation was led by two powerful champions in the Middle East. One was the office of the Economic Adviser to the Minister of State, headed successively by R. F. Kahn (1941–1942), the famed Cambridge University economist and a close associate of Keynes, and E. M. H. Lloyd (1943–1944), an internationally recognized authority on rationing and food administration, whose book *Experiments in State Control at the War Office and the Ministry of Food,* published in 1924, still is recognized as a classic in the field.[17] The other was the British Treasury which had a large delegation in the Middle East (headed in the later stages by W. A. B. Iliff) and which was the parent agency of the u.k.c.c.[18] Although both the Economic Adviser and the Treasury men worked in general harmony with the Centre they did not succumb to the general Allied disposition in the Middle East to delegate responsibility for economic matters to m.e.s.c. They kept the realm of financial policy firmly in their collective hands (which does not mean they always agreed with each other) and often made their influence felt on local authorities independently of the Centre.[19] (Significantly, m.e.s.c., despite its octopus-like appropriation of new responsibilities, never established a division for financial matters but relied on the Ministry of State and the Treasury delegations for policy guidance, information and the supply to territorial governments of technical assistance in public finance and monetary management. This, then, was one of the few realms in which the Minister of State did not abdicate his prerogatives in economic affairs to the Centre.) [20]

Although they were in full accord with the drive to make the region self-sufficient and less dependent on shipping, Kahn and particularly Lloyd, in their positions as advisers to Britain's principal political authority in the Middle East, tended to lay greater stress on the prerequisites of internal stability than the more impatient Director General of the Supply Centre who was willing to take more chances in whipping the region into a state of economic mobilization and more rapid economic forward motion. The views of the two treasury delegations were influenced by the foreseeable effects of Middle East inflation on the pocketbooks of their countries and on Allied economic policy after the war.[21] During the war, inflation meant a greater Allied outlay for offshore procurement; there were frequent hints by certain experts that inflation-ridden countries of the Middle East should be persuaded to devalue their currencies—a prospect of particular fearfulness to these governments.[22] The agents of the British Treasury were also concerned about the accumulation of large Middle Eastern balances in the Sterling Area Pool which, at the end of the war, was bound to haunt a financially and productively weakened Britain with massive demands for dollar allocations; Middle East members of the Pool were known to be anxious to release the pentup demand for consumer goods in the only country capable of supplying them—the United States.[23] Meanwhile the Americans took umbrage at the profiteering which inflation enabled Middle Eastern traders to practice with lend-lease goods.[24] Both Treasuries exhibited apprehension on what the soaring price levels might do to the ability of Middle Eastern countries to sell their principal exports after the war and the calls that these countries might be induced to make for economic help should their exports stall.[25]

Among the special initiatives originating with these dispatchers of anti-inflationary drives were, in the individual territories, the insistent promotion of point rationing, consumption taxes, and the issue of savings bonds.[26] On the regional level, a noteworthy deed was the convocation of regional conferences on inflation (1942), distribution and rationing (1943), and general financial problems (1944), all held in Cairo. The outstanding regionwide maneuver was the sale of gold on the open market from August 1943 to June 1944.

This novel and ingenious experiment was conceived by Kahn after he had witnessed an abortive attempt by Allied authorities in Syria and Lebanon after liberation to bring down prices and break the rings of speculators by throwing on the market at deliberately low prices more than 100,000 tons of wheat brought in under great difficulty from overseas.[27] Convinced that neither force nor dumping actions could bring hoarders, speculators, and prices to their knees, he presented the following argument to the Anti-Inflation Conference of 1942 in Cairo:

In order to save shipping it was vital to see that the towns were fed to the maximum possible extent on home-produced cereals; but cutting down imports of consumer goods made it difficult to provide the producer with an incentive to sell his grain. The villagers were having to reduce their consumption of sugar, tea, textiles, hardware, tools, and utensils. Experience in Persia and Syria had shown that the problem of inducing landowners and peasants to part with their grain in exchange for rapidly depreciating paper money was a real one. Gold in the form of coins or jewelry was an article that from time immemorial had appealed to the acquisitive and hoarding instincts of the people, and was traditionally used both as a form of savings and for personal display. In good times, when prices were high, producers bought necklaces of gold coins, bangles, and other jewelry of solid gold to adorn their womenfolk; and in bad times they would sell these to meet the claims of the moneylender.

There was no tradition of hoarding paper money and still less of investing in government bonds. A gold sovereign could indeed be regarded as the Middle East equivalent of a British war-savings certificate. Owing to its high intrinsic value gold could be shipped to the Middle East with the minimum call on transport. At prices ruling in Syria a ton of wheat was worth about two fine ounces of gold. At this rate, 50 tons of gold (nine-tenths fine) would be equal in value to 672,000 tons of wheat, which was greater than the total tonnage of cereals imported into the Middle East in 1942. There was thus a prospect of making a major economy of tonnage, if gold could be shipped to the Middle East to extract home-produced wheat for feeding the towns instead of having to divert shipping for imported wheat.[28]

The scheme was accepted by London, and later by Washington;[29] a total of 1.2 million ounces of gold, in the form of coins and jewelry, was disposed of through banks in all parts of the Middle East at whatever prices the market would yield. The demand was heavy as indicated by an average of $57 paid per ounce (compared with the official rate of $35). During the first five months, these sales absorbed about 38 per cent of the total increase in note circulation during that period; they also lightened the financial burden of Allied off-shore purchases. They were, according to an official report, more effective as an antidote in Iraq in five months than all other deflationary measures taken by the Iraqi government in a full year. In Syria and Lebanon, gold sales for a short time actually exceeded the main inflationary ferment—military expenditures—and circulation of notes declined.[30]

The paucity of British gold reserves and the reluctance of the United States to use any major part of its large gold hoard limited the duration and overall effectiveness of the program. And unfortunately there were no other programs in which the objectives of shipping economy, savings to the public purse, and price restraint could be combined so simply and on so broad a front, and with so little need for stepping on the sensitive toes of individual governments in the Middle East. In general, economic and financial policy-making for the region had to choose between painful alternatives, and the choice did not always gain unanimous consent among the policy-makers, sometimes not even among Allied officials.

Several cases of such disagreement pitted the Middle East Supply Centre against its faithful handyman, the u.k.c.c., and through it, the British Treasury. These cases were reminiscent of the campaign Jackson and his aides conducted in favor of all-out production and rigid superintendence in the Middle East economy against the cautious orthodoxy or some of their countrymen in high places.[31] This time, the dispute arose from the refusal of u.k.c.c., with the express approval of the Chancellor of the Exchequer, to carry out bulk purchases of cereals on behalf of the Centre in Egypt, Iraq and Syria. The grounds given by u.k.c.c. were that prices were too high and that haggling was in order in the interest of checking inflation and avoiding a loss to the Company, since it had to distribute the cereals in low-price parts of the region. In each case m.e.s.c. protested to London that the acceptance of prices above the world market was a necessity if one was to encourage production, secure surpluses for distribution to deficit areas and ease the drain on Allied shipping. In each case m.e.s.c. won out. Subsequent events then demonstrated that by winning, the Centre had averted a fatal slowdown in urgently needed grain deliveries to Cyprus, Palestine, Iran, and the armed services; through distribution of the grain thus purchased as well as by the encouragement given to cultivators in the surplus countries, it also had forestalled a much grimmer price eruption than the one visualized by the u.k.c.c. and London.[32]

To toe the line of monetary stability in the innumerable crises it had to confront was a purpose but not always a possibility for the Centre. Almost every time the region was urged or compelled to make its purchases from local rather than overseas sources, the result was higher prices. Almost every time a local entrepreneur was assisted in the establishment or expansion of a factory or service facility, the key incentive was a promise of lucrative army contracts or civilian sellers' markets on the horizon. Every time surpluses of food were wrenched from one country to feed another it had to be done through higher than world or peacetime prices. But all this did save shipping space.

On the other hand, every time the Middle East Supply Centre persuaded the supply captains of America and Britain to grant export licenses and shipping permits for the benefit of the Middle East it won a skirmish *against* the forces of inflation. When new products and services finally rolled off the new or expanded facilities vitalized by M.E.S.C. pump-priming, the inflationary imbalance of demand and supply was redressed a bit in favor of supply; the same happened every time the cereal collection schemes, with their flexible yet circumscribed price-fixing provisions, their subsidization of retail prices and their growing reserve stocks, completed a cycle—they brought comfort to the consumer and frustration to the hoarder. Every time M.E.S.C. exacted commitments on price limitations from traders, manufacturers and service purveyors whose import licences it approved, the galloping of prices was slowed. Every time it insisted on distributing American and British supplies at landed cost and not at the tempting quotations of the free market, and whenever it ensured their flow past the black market, a blow was struck for sound money.

Compared with the success of price containment in Britain and the United States, the results obtained in the Middle East appear hardly impressive, except in the Sudan where the cost of living rose but 60 per cent thanks largely to the heavy subsidization of essential consumer goods financed from equally heavy taxes on exports.[33] In Iran, where conditions were worst, the consumer price index reached a level of 756 in 1944 (1939 = 100); Egypt, Palestine, and Cyprus registered rises between 100 and 200 per cent, while the indices for Syria-Lebanon and Iraq soared to 540 and 611 respectively.[34] By comparison, the cost of living index in the United States went up only 30 per cent during the war. The flourishing black markets where prices naturally were far above the official indices must also be taken into account. Nevertheless, what could easily have developed into a runaway inflation, post-World War I German or Hungarian style, did not materialize; the social and economic structure of the region held firm, in the sense that there was no calamitous increase in its long-endured infirmities; [35] and prices of bread and very basic essentials were apparently held sufficiently in check—by rationing, ceilings, or subsidies—to avert the shame of a famine due to prices rather than shortages. Like the Axis, inflation won battles in the Middle East but it did not win the war.

Viewed in this light a measure of success can be claimed for the anti-inflation effort made in the Middle East. What relative share M.E.S.C. and the other participants had in this accomplishment cannot be determined; successful measures credited to certain agencies could have been inspired or initiated by others. Most incisive measures like those adopted in Egypt, Palestine, and the Sudan were taken in a local framework but the timetable indicates a regional coincidence between a tightening of controls, the appearance of the Middle East Supply Centre and the actions of Kahn and Lloyd and of the gentlemen from the British and American Treasuries.

However, the Middle East Supply Centre received this tribute from Lloyd:

That inflation was kept in check, as much as it was, was in no small measure due to the fact that all over the Middle East, through careful planning of imports and organized collection of bread grains at fixed prices, the food supply of the towns was maintained.[36]

Facing the Future

Gold sales and the many other facets of financial policy in the Middle East keynoted the proceedings of the 1944 Financial Conference. From these discussions came many valuable insights into the economic complexities of the region and the many pitfalls to be faced by any large-scale effort to bend this large, unruly subcontinent to a common purpose. In 1944, on the eve of the landing in Normandy, it was inevitable that the experience thus gained would be evaluated in terms of common purposes in the dawning era of postwar reconstruction.

Statements at the Conference by representatives of independent Middle Eastern governments spelled this perspective out in the clearest possible terms. Behind the whole question of prices, said the Deputy Prime Minister of Lebanon, Habib Bey Abi Chahla, lay the political anarchy of the Middle East: Egypt, Palestine, Syria, Lebanon, and Iraq ought to form an economic union to pool their resources and share according to their needs.[37]

For nearly three years, this economic union had existed *de facto* because of the policy of economic regionalism practiced by the Middle East Supply Centre. The pooling of resources and the sharing in accordance with need had been the guiding formula of its food, materials, transport, and medical administration. The work had been crowned by the steady pressure of the Program (Trade Relations) Division aimed at making regional cooperation something more than merely a case-by-case improvisation. In drafting the shipping programs that were to be sent to the loading areas overseas a balance sheet of Middle Eastern resources and needs was constructed that offered an unprecedented view of the strength that union offered to the region.

Each month, the chancelleries and government houses received from the Division a unique document drafted from such data: This was the M.E.S.C. "Commodity Index" which told its readers in detail where within the borders of the M.E.S.C. jurisdiction they could obtain needed supplies, most of which had formerly been considered as irreplaceable imports from overseas; the index gradually became the master working sheet from which individual governments drew up their trade and import licensing program. It directed their attention to available stocks of tire retreads in Iran, aspirin in Cairo, dentures in Palestine, leather boots in the Sudan, leopard skins in Ethiopia, pyrites in Cyprus, pandermite in Turkey, lignite in Eritrea, sodium sulphide in Iraq, newly grown jute in Egypt, millet in Libya, glass in Lebanon, and orange marmalade in Syria.[38]

Every month also, Allied officials in each Middle Eastern territory received a copy of the monthly *Middle East Economic and Statistical Bulletin,* a secret, comprehensive situation report issued by the Information and Intelligence Section of M.E.S.C. in cooperation with the Ministry of State. From it information could be gleaned on trade and production statistics, as well as information on crop prospects, ship departures in overseas ports, the commencement of new industrial projects, an abstract of new discoveries at local research institutes, the opening of new road connections, a new process to convert nightsoil into fertilizers, new licensing procedures in the territories, the latest Allied supply dispositions, warnings of impending shipping strictures, the arrival of fumigation experts from Canada, and organizational and staff changes in the supply departments of various governments. As far as military security permitted it, the regional trends and prospects reported in this "club circular" were shared with local officials.[39]

The Program Division also turned itself into purveyors of marketing and promotion initiatives. One result was the first Palestine Industry Exhibition ever held in Egypt; there Arab and Jewish industry from the Mandate territory displayed in fraternal association the results of their industrial stature.[40]

One historic result of "economic unification" under M.E.S.C. auspices was the new pattern in which goods moved into and across the region: trade among the "core" countries of the Middle East had constituted 7 per cent of total trade before the war; it accounted for 33 per cent in 1943.[41] Another result was the increased traffic of persons and ideas.

The Financial Conference of 1944 with its colorful conglomeration of Arab, Jewish, Turkish, Persian, Cypriot, British, and American government delegates would have been a milestone even if no meaningful word had been spoken. Just by meeting, the delegates made history, for between World War I and World War II not a single regional conference on economic affairs had taken place in the Middle East with the possible exception of a small hydrographic convention in 1921 and a meeting of delegates from Muslim countries to discuss an abortive project to reconstruct the Hejaz Railway; this solitary link between Medina and Jordan was destroyed by the British and Arabs in World War I and never repaired despite its importance to the pilgrim traffic. Now, in the course of three years (1942–1945) through the instrumentality of the Middle East Supply Centre and the Minister of State, no less than eight important regional assemblies of government officials and experts were called together to deal with questions of finance, agriculture, statistics, locusts, transport, rationing, and cereal collections.[42] Like the Financial Conference the other meetings looked not only to the past but the future. The Agricultural Conference resolved to propose the establishment of a Middle East Council of Agriculture to "formulate and recommend measures for individual and joint action by any or all of the member Governments for the coordination of agricultural development projects and policies."[43] The Middle East Statistical Conference recommended support for the project of creating a permanent Middle East Statistical Bureau.[44] The Financial Conference, noting the progress made in the floating of internal loans for anti-inflationary purposes, agreed that "the development of a capital market in Middle Eastern countries . . . [and] the habit of saving and investment . . . should prove of lasting benefit to the economy of Middle Eastern countries." [45] And Habib Bey spoke hopefully of "economic union."

The bey also decried the "political difficulties" that such a scheme would encounter, [46] but in fact the political climate had never been more favorable; because of it, talk of economic union was raised above the realm of mere conference congeniality. Political federation had been a theme song in the Middle East since 1941. In 1943, Nuri al-Said took his Fertile Crescent scheme for the unification of Iraq, Syria, Lebanon, Palestine, and Jordan (with autonomy held out for the Jewish sector) to the Minister of State, James Landis, and his Arab *confrères*. In 1944 this and other proposals were overshadowed by the preparations for the Alexandria Conference at which the League of Arab States was born. [47]

This was the culmination of the growth of an idea—Arab Unity —hastened by British endorsement, the elimination of French and Italian footholds in the area, and the more intense intra-regional traffic of schemes and persons owing to isolation from the rest of the world; it was also, as Fayez Sayegh affirms, a sort of reflex reaction to the "unmistakable trend toward regional organization in the world at large." [48] This "unmistakable trend" as seen from the Middle East was first of all political—closely connected with the search for new formulas of collective security in the world. It was also a matter of economic policy; however: "Plans for the economic reconstruction of the Middle East [after World War II] cannot ignore the worldwide tendency towards unification of small states within the larger unit of a union," said Alfred Bonné, the economic adviser of the Jewish Agency for Palestine, in 1945. [49] Both the political and the economic aspirations of regionalism in the Middle East recognized that treaties and understandings were not enough to make unification a reality: there was a need for "institutions" able and ready to "overcome the inevitable discontinuousness of planning and action resulting from the lack of a permanent organization with permanent agencies and staff." [50]

With British help, the Arab States now were creating the political institutions that would, it was hoped, push the dream of regional unity over the threshold of significance. In the economic sphere, Britain (and America) had in effect presented the Middle East with a ready-made institution which, though originally of limited military orientation, had so expanded its scope and influence that it could be offered as part of a dowry to the union to be consummated at Alexandria. This was the Middle East Supply Centre.[51]

Already, the Centre had drawn Arab attention to an aspect of regional unification largely neglected by the makers of manifestos, and deemed chimerical by experts before the war because of an alleged "non-complementarity" of the constituent economies.[52] Beginning in 1943 the calls for economic reconstruction and development on a regional basis after the war multiplied.[53] Economics was extolled not only as a pacemaker of Arab unity but possibly as a peacemaker between Arabs and Jews in strategic Palestine.[54]

The Middle East Supply Centre was ready to adjust to this new turn of events, just as it had in other situation changes. A year earlier, in June 1943, a new perspective had arisen when, upon conclusion of the North African campaign, the Mediterranean was reopened to Allied merchant shipping. The most critical factors in the shipping crisis of the Middle East, namely the long haul around the Cape which had added six or seven weeks to the voyage of each convoy, and much of the U-boat menace, disappeared.[55] The original *raison d'être* for the M.E.S.C.'s existence, the shortage of shipping, was fading. Yet so close had been the involvement of the agency in the economic welfare of its ward area that a disengagement was unthinkable as long as other threats to that welfare existed. Without fanfare or change in procedure the workload and the policy-making were shifted to the problem of *supply* shortage—the threat that amid the rapacious demands of giant Anglo-American and Soviet operations, to which now were added the urgent requisitions for liberated lands, the cries of the Middle East might go unheard. M.E.S.C. became the guardian against wastage of Allied supplies and, simultaneously an effective petitioner on behalf of the civilian population of the Middle East. Now, in the middle of 1944, with final victory in sight, the agency turned its eyes to the imminence of postwar reconstruction.

It did so "with the greatest pleasure." At the Middle East Agricultural Conference, in February 1944, the Director General, in his closing address, contrasted the spirit of the Conference with the early days of the Centre. Then, he said:

Our work was mainly restrictive in that we were telling you how little you could live on. That was not a pleasant task. Of course we were playing a part in the military strategy of the North African campaign. . . . That campaign is won, and it is with the greatest pleasure that we can turn to more constructive work. The time has come to turn swords into plowshares.[56]

The eager embrace of new responsibilities was not simply the agitated search for new tasks of an agency anxious to survive. The truth was that every new task assumed was inextricably linked to tasks of the past. Shipping was mixed up with supply, and supply was mixed up with the return to a peacetime economy under conditions marked by the incapacity of most of the traditional supplier countries (notably England, France, Germany, Italy, and Japan) and a disarray of international monetary relationships. Caring for the basic needs of civilian populations during an immediate emergency could not be isolated from concern over the long pull of an economy so feeble in its service to the masses in food, shelter, jobs, roads, power, housing, and hope for a better life. Even if humanitarian considerations were ignored—and they were not ignored at the Centre—it was clear that prosperity and stability in the Middle East would be as important to Anglo-American objectives in times of peace as it was in times of war—particularly in view of the wartime drain on Western oil resources. For an organization such as M.E.S.C. to bow out before at least some seeds of continuity had been sown from the safety and development measures of the war, would have been against the national interest of Britain and the United States. It also would have disavowed Allied pronouncements on the postwar fight for freedom from want.

As early as June 1943, the United Nations Conference on Food and Agriculture at Hot Springs, Virginia, had warmly endorsed the principle of regional consultation and coordination for the solution of the world's food and agricultural difficulties in the months preceding and following the end of the war.[57] An extended tenure for M.E.S.C. as the only regional organization extant in the Middle East, at least while the war lasted, was in direct conformity with the official policy of the Allies. It was proudly noted at the Middle East Agricultural Conference, that this was the first meeting held anywhere in the world in compliance with the Hot Springs resolution.[58]

The attention to postwar detail in the Middle East Supply Centre, incidentally, was not confined to application of Allied postwar policy in its own ward area. The experience gained in the Middle East was communicated to other areas of the world. The Centre's Director of Food and Agriculture visited Italy after the expulsion of the enemy to render assistance to the reorganization of food supply and distribution in that badly disrupted nation.[59] The North African Economic Board set up after the Allied landings in Morocco and Algeria to deal with that area's rehabilitation called on the Centre for advice and assistance.[60] Early in 1944, Landis started a series of consultations concerning the post-liberation establishment of a Balkan Supply Centre, intended to extend the methods and plans of M.E.S.C. both to the immediate economic rehabilitation of Greece and of Southeastern Europe, and to the long-range realization of the old dream of Balkanic integration.[61] As early as July 1942 M.E.S.C. carried out the British initiative which created the Middle East Relief and Refugee Administration (MERRA) under the aegis of the Minister of State, "the first substantial effort to deal with the problem of displaced persons in its new form"; [62] the "new form" was cooperation among the major powers pooling both their resources and information on need. MERRA served as model for the organization of the United Nations Relief and Rehabilitation Administration which not only absorbed MERRA but also in 1945 appointed Commander Jackson its Senior Deputy Director General for a tenure again studded with notable personal achievements.[63] Representations also were made to various Allied organs and committees working on the charter of the new world organization to remind them of the useful lessons of wartime regionalism in the Middle East.[64]

Commander Jackson's speech at the Middle East Agricultural Conference listed three paramount prerequisites for applying these very lessons to the economic destiny of the Middle East, after the day of final victory.

> First, there must be common action and mutual trust. We see already that machinery to achieve this is being set up, and we see examples, of which this Conference is a notable one, of common consultation and action. Second, all that consultation and trust is useless unless there is some definite plan of action, unless we know what we wish to achieve. Third, there must be leadership.[65]

The first prerequisite, common action and mutual trust, was in the realm of political relationships. Regional economic cooperation, Jackson implied, was impossible without a political entente among the nations planning to cooperate. A political consensus had to exist among the political units of the region, the independent states, Arab or otherwise, and the dependencies now ruled exclusively by British colonial, mandatory or occupation authorities. This was the crux of all schemes, but its handling was beyond the pale of M.E.S.C. jurisdiction and competence. Jackson hopefully referred to the nascent League of Arab States born under the sign of Arab-British friendship as the "machinery" that might bring about "mutual trust" among the Arab States, and between them and the Western nations interested in promoting regionalism in the Middle East.[66]

However, the second point, elaboration of a program or a list of desiderata, was very much in the province of the Centre; it was, after all, at this juncture, the foremost repository of data, knowledge, and administrative experience in Middle Eastern economics. The Centre never published a comprehensive blueprint or plan presenting in systematic fashion its vision of its future, one reason being unresolved differences of opinions among its leaders on questions like that of the sterling area links of large parts of the region.[67]

But plans and proposals there were, in abundance. To summarize them one must go to many sources: The recollections of the men who guided the operations of M.E.S.C., such as Jackson, Landis, Woodbridge, Murray, Nicholson, Lloyd, Macduffie, Winant, Dawson, E. E. Bailey, and others. One must plow through the avalanche of technical reports drafted in the wake of the numerous field missions and surveys conducted by divisional teams of the Centre.[68] One must study in detail the views of the Scientific Advisory Mission attached to M.E.S.C., and composed of three distinguished British and American men of science and technology: Dr. B. A. Keen, then Assistant Director of the Rothhamsted Agricultural Experiment Station in England and member of numerous survey missions and study teams in many parts of the world; Dr. E. B. Worthington, then Director of the Freshwater Biological Association in England and author of the most authoritative study in its field up to that time, *Science in Africa;* and Dr. H. B. Allen, then Director of Research of the Near East Foundation in New York, and a recognized pioneer in rural community work in Iran. Their findings— concerned mostly with agriculture, social conditions, and rural life —were published shortly after the war. They were hailed then as the first scholarly and comprehensive region-wide studies of economic problems in the Middle East to appear before the public, and the "most lasting and fruitful legacy" of the Middle East Supply Centre.[69] Jackson and Murray revealed some of their thoughts to a wider public in July 1945 when they addressed a meeting of the Royal Central Asian Society in London.[70] Murray gave further elaborations in January 1947 in an article published by *International Affairs*.[71] Landis divulged another spectrum of plans in a 1944 speech before the Economic Section of the Fuad I Society in Cairo and in two statements made in the United States.[72]

Finally, there are the proceedings of the regional conferences brought together by the Minister of State and the Centre. Only those of the Middle East Agricultural Conference were published on a limited scale; the others have to be hunted down in private collections and a few libraries across the world. For the fortunate student who gains access to all of them, they are a unique source of data and impressions on a vast panorama of problems, practices, attitudes, and visions prior to the period when the committees and commissions of the Economic and Social Council of the United Nations began to offer similar forums to the spokesmen of Middle Eastern countries.[73]

The blueprint for action of the Middle East Supply Centre sketched out in all these sources did not focus around grandiose master plans like those formulated in various parts of the world, particularly Eastern and Central Europe.[74] Nor did M.E.S.C. identify itself with some overly enthusiastic proposals for the Middle East such as the perpetuation of centralized regional control over overseas trade and agricultural surpluses or an "ever-full granary" scheme, to ban famine from the Middle East.[75]

At the same time, a belief in the utility and feasibility of far-reaching economic cooperation among the countries of the Middle East was firmly upheld. Brushed aside was the question of economic complementarity, the apparent absence of which had convinced experts before the war that the Middle East was not susceptible to treatment as an economic unit.[76] The three reports of the Scientific Advisory Mission took great pains to stress the *sameness* of economic deficiencies and structures in the countries observed as justification for the practice of economic regionalism.[77] Dr. Keen strongly echoed this sentiment at the Middle East Agricultural Conference when he spoke of the "realization that there are many common difficulties facing the Middle East countries and that common methods of solution to some of these difficulties are likely to be the only possible way of improving the general condition in this part of the world." [78]

If one looks for a term to characterize the general tenor of the M.E.S.C. approach to postwar reconstruction and development, the answer will not be found in the contemporary vocabulary of economic development policies. The plan of the Centre, if such it can be called, bore all the marks of the pragmatism which had marked policy-making at the top from the beginning.

What the Centre proposed, in numerous direct and inferential approaches to responsible circles in the Middle East, in England, and the United States, was a gradual saturation of the region with coordinating interstate arrangements with regard to economic tasks and problems where the presence of multistate interests was manifest (as in the case of multinational rivers) or where there was an obvious similarity and simultaneity of condition in several or all parts of the region. This network of regional arrangements would have been exemplified by interstate consultations on the control of rivers; arrangements for meeting locust attacks; containment of epidemics; the development of training institutions financed and patronized by all nations of the region; the development of laboratories and research institutes; river valley development; interstate highways and railroads; port development; improvement of official statistics and economic research; the development of agricultural industries; agricultural credit; plant and animal selection and breeding; improvement and standardization of produce quality; organization of marketing; food processing; land reform; housing; communications; taxation; power development; the use of oil revenues; price maintenance for agricultural commodities; industrialization; conservation; land utilization; irrigation techniques; the promotion of more nutritional food habits and standards; the search for capital and monetary stability.[79]

Essentially, then, M.E.S.C. proposed a program which would represent a *first step* in the drive toward regional economic integration of the area. It recognized the fact that unlike areas such as Europe for which the Allies were contemplating very advanced schemes of integration, the Middle East in its recent history, despite many bonds created by history, culture and commerce, had known only the vaguest traffic of ideas and information on economic and social problems across the borders and only a minimal level of scientific and governmental exchanges; thus both the experience of regional coordination and the knowledge of common problems, apart from what World War II had brought to the area, were in their infancy. At such a stage advanced notions such as customs unions, centralized economic planning, regional exchange controls, and the like, would fatally stumble over the lack of knowledge and trained personnel. Moreover, with most of the independent nations having but recently acquired the attributes of full sovereignty, an incisive curtailment of their economic sovereignty would encounter psychological resistance. Also, some of the newly independent nations were bound to object that immediate full regional integration of the area might freeze the economic structures they had inherited from their erstwhile suzerains without providing them with an opportunity to promote such changes as industrialization, the departure from mono-cultural status in farming, and a reduction of the hold of foreign nationalities on key occupations and industries.

In short, the M.E.S.C. idea was directed toward what may be called an economic "get acquainted" program in the area, combining a stimulation of various social and economic programs in each country and territory and promoting interstate consultation and cooperation for each of the programs. In this functional manner each nation would broaden its knowledge of its own economic and social condition while at the same time learning of similar problems and remedial techniques among a host of friendly neighbors. Out of this, it was expected, the concept of a common regional economy would take substance and shape, a corps of regionally minded officials, experts and administrators would form, a tradition of seeking help within the region for internal projects, of arbitrating conflicts among the region's membership, and of closing ranks in solidarity in dealings with extra-regional powers, would evolve organically and lay the foundations for ultimate unity. Seen from a historical perspective, this program appears to anticipate strikingly the approach and work pattern developed by the regional commissions of the United Nations.

Amid all the flexibility and maneuverability, amid all the de-emphasis of compulsion and contractual strait-jackets, there was one stern and unconditional demand: There must be machinery, machinery to generate initiatives, to implement plans, and to provide assistance. As to its nature, M.E.S.C. recommendations were hesitant and fragmentary, partly because of the uncertainty of Anglo-American intentions regarding the Middle East after the war and partly because of the hope that the United Nations would in due course set up agencies and procedures for international assistance to the economic development of regions like the Middle East. However, Commander Jackson and many of his aides were firmly convinced that a prime need after the war would be a regional bureau operated jointly by the United States, Britain, the independent countries of the Middle East, and possibly other powers such as the Soviet Union and France. Such a bureau would have several functions. It would constantly remind all countries concerned of the developmental and improvement needs of the peoples and nations of the region, armed with the facts and intelligence provided by an economic intelligence staff in constant observation of the area. It would serve as a clearing house and source for technical advice and technical experts. It would organize and service the growing practice of consultation among the various states and administer whatever coordination arrangement might result from such exchanges. And it would keep alive the interest of the Great Powers in the development of the Middle East after the end of hostilities, contrary to what happened after the last war when powers like the United States studiously avoided the assumption of peacetime responsibilities in the area. The permanent Middle East Statistical Bureau proposed by the Middle East Statistical Conference, and the central Institute of Agricultural Development proposed by the Agricultural Conference "to supplement the work now being carried on in individual countries and to serve the Middle East as a whole by enabling fullest use to be made of such trained personnel and facilities as are now available," would be part of this "Centre." [80]

M.E.S.C. officials furthermore believed in the need to set up regionwide councils of government representatives for the major group of identifiable economic and social problems of the Middle East. An example was the projected Middle East Council of Agriculture recommended in the resolutions adopted by the Agricultural Conference; this idea originated with the Supply Centre, which had called the conference. In its Resolution No. 4, the conference suggested that this council "might be composed of representatives of the constituent governments, to provide a forum for a discussion of common agricultural problems through periodic meetings and through the publication of a journal on Middle East agriculture, and to disseminate agricultural knowledge through exhibitions."

The councils and the central bureau were the key proposals of M.E.S.C. regarding regional postwar machinery. Of course, schemes and ideas sprang up in abundance among the many imaginative and enthusiastic men that crowded the M.E.S.C. roster. M.E.S.C. chiefs at one time had serious discussions in Washington and London concerning sponsorship of a Middle Eastern Investment Bank nourished by contributions from the Great Powers and from part of the region's oil revenues. The project never got beyond the discussion stage, mostly because of the expectations connected with the International Bank for Reconstruction and Development born at the Bretton Woods Conference.[81]

This, then, was M.E.S.C.'s design for the postwar era of the Middle East. Together with various programs for helping the Middle East through the anticipated supply and reconversion difficulties that might arise after the end of hostilities and persist for some time while the world recovered, it was a testimony to the degree in which the Centre had identified itself with the long-term interest and needs of the Middle East. Nothing could show better the amazing evolution of the Centre since it had started operations in two small rooms of General Wavell's Middle East Command in 1941 as an advisory unit for civilian shipping for the Middle Eastern area, than its succinct recommendations on land reform.[82]

The design was there; how was it to become reality? In the latter half of 1944, officials of the Middle East Supply Centre, above all Jackson and Landis, journeyed around the Middle East and across the Atlantic to acquaint and impress governments with their proposals.[83] In the capitals of countries encompassed by the M.E.S.C. jurisdiction, there was general assent to the principle, although not necessarily to the details on machinery or the roster of nations to sponsor it. In Britain, agreement was a foregone conclusion. The key decision, however, had to be made in Washington. (French and Soviet approval, while desired, were not deemed essential.) Direct participation by major powers outside the region was considered important because of the long period during which their experts and funds would be needed to supplement the meager resources of the Middle East; it was also deemed essential as a means to preserve the goodwill and political tractability of the region. For Britain to be the sole sponsor or to align herself exclusively with France and Russia would inevitably taint the whole venture with imperialism in the eyes of Middle Eastern leaders; as during the war, United States cooperation was needed as a psychological counterweight. The importance of oil production as a source of wealth and economic development in the Middle East also made agreement between the two principal concessionaires imperative before associating themselves jointly with the M.E.S.C. program. And for some time after the war, the United States would have to be the principal purveyor of funds, considering the time it would take before England, France, or the Soviet Union regained their capacity to help others. And funds were needed in considerable amount as the element which would justify and legitimize "foreign" participation in a scheme of primary concern to the Middle East.

Because of the constant growth of United States interest in the operation of the Centre—as expressed for example by the rapid increase in the number of American staff members—there was hope that Washington would accept without great difficulty the idea of some continuity for this fruitful association. Jackson and Landis also hoped that because it provided a tested and confirmed framework for such continuity, agreement would be reached on entrusting to the Middle East Supply Centre in an appropriately revamped form the role of the "regional bureau" that was meant to bring the wartime seeds of regional cooperation to a permanent flowering for betterment and peace in the Middle East.

In all this, they were to be sadly disappointed.

10

Conclusion

The Dissolution of M.E.S.C.

ON 1 November 1945, the United Kingdom and the United States officially dissolved the Middle East Supply Centre. The effort to give the Centre permanency and the Middle East a chance to preserve the élan and the elation of economic development achieved during the war had failed.

For this effort to succeed, one of several alternatives should have been endorsed by interested governments. These were alternatives to what until then had been the fountainhead of justification and authority of the Centre in the Middle East: the shortage of shipping and supplies. Such stringencies were rapidly coming to an end and could no longer legitimize the continued existence of the Centre on an "unreconstructed" basis. The alternatives were these:

1. The joint espousal by the United States and Britain, perhaps in association with other countries, of a vast program of economic aid and technical assistance for the Middle East. This would have made plausible the maintenance of a regional organization now aimed at long-term economic growth projects and using the disbursement of funds and technical counsel as a leverage for inducing local action.

2. An agreement between the United Kingdom and the independent Middle Eastern states, particularly the members of the Arab League, to operate a reorganized Centre along lines mutually agreed upon and with substantial British financial and technical help. (This was to be done on the assumption that the United States in rejecting the first alternative also would reject the call to a Middle Eastern aid program on its own terms.)

3. Agreement among the Middle Eastern states, particularly the Arab League nations, to "appropriate" the Centre and operate it

without outside management although not necessarily without outside help.

4. Incorporation of the Centre into the United Nations structure.

None of these alternatives could sprout to life in the political environment of the early postwar period.

The policy of the United States to conduct an independent economic policy in the Middle East was already well rooted when the American decision not to participate in a postwar continuation of the work of the Middle East Supply Centre was taken. Its first manifestation took place shortly after the German threat to the Middle East had been overcome. On 25 May 1943, Secretary of State Cordell Hull wrote to Admiral William D. Leahy, the President's Chief of Staff, proposing that the policy of the United States should be "to welcome direct inquiries from officials . . . of independent Middle East countries except Turkey . . . regarding the availability of American military supplies to meet their needs. . . ." The British Government, explained Hull, had in the past insisted to these Governments that all requests for Allied military assistance he chanelled through the British. "It is considered that it would be highly damaging to American prestige throughout the Arab world and prejudicial to the maintenance of good relations with the countries of that region, and consequently prejudicial to vital American economic interests, to permit this. . . ." Leahy agreed with the Secretary, and steps were taken to inform the Governments of the Middle East of American policy on lend-lease.[1]

The appointment of James Landis as American Director of Economic Operations in the Middle East had been made with an eye on postwar economic opportunities. Landis had established the American Economic Mission in the Middle East, the A.E.M.M.E., shortly after his arrival in Cairo, and one of its prime tasks was to see that wartime economic controls would not adversely affect American commercial enterprise after the war. The Roosevelt letter of March 1944 had also been very specific on this point.[2] This underlying suspicion of the possible role M.E.S.C. would play in British commercial and economic planning for the postwar Middle East became overt in the Culbertson Report of the following Fall. William S. Culbertson, a prominent American businessman, was sent to the Middle East and North Africa as chairman of a Special Economic Mission "for the restoration of trade to commercial channels." [3] On 28 September 1944, the Department of State had already suggested in an *aide-mémoire* to the British Embassy that the "extensive system of import controls developed by the Middle East Supply Center" was no longer necessary since the supply of civilian goods had improved enormously and the shipping situation also had eased with the production of new ships and the decline of the submarine menace. It was suggested that controls be maintained only for a "select list of commodities in very short supply." The *aide-mémoire* then went on to state that the United States in fact had decided to implement its own proposals and in effect would not be bound by decisions of M.E.S.C. except for commodities in short supply. The Department proposed that talks be held to work out the details of the new American program. Landis went to London and on 18 October an agreement to relax controls was reached.[4]

In the meantime Culbertson and his mission had been touring the Middle East and on 15 November 1944, submitted his Report.[5] It consisted of a 32-page summary of general observations and seven bulky annexes dealing with specific problems. One of these annexes was devoted to M.E.S.C. Commenting on American participation in M.E.S.C., the Annex stated that while collaboration had been real and in many respects effective "it has not at any time transformed M.E.S.C. into a genuine joint undertaking." Here in a nutshell was a clear statement of an opinion that had been steadily growing among Americans outside M.E.S.C. ranks since the defeat of Rommel. The Annex went on to add that the underlying cause of the different national approaches to the work of M.E.S.C. was the different value each country placed on the Middle East. To the British the area was vital; the Americans had never thought so even when the Mediterranean had been closed to shipping in 1941, though perhaps this attitude was in the process of changing.[6] In short, M.E.S.C. was a British agency and its policies reflected primarily, though not exclusively, British interests.

The years 1944 and 1945 also saw the growth of conflicts between the United States and Britain on specific economic interests, particularly oil,[7] but also including such interests as postwar aviation rights [8] as well as general commercial access to the Middle East; all of the Arab states, except for Syria and Lebanon, were a part of the Sterling area.[9] In Saudi Arabia, the sole Middle Eastern country where American oil interests were paramount, competition between the two countries for influence grew at times into bitter struggles between the men on the spot. The issue, of course, was complex. Britain had been for a hundred years and more the chief and latterly the only foreign influence in Saudi Arabia. Now the Americans were seeking to establish their own presence in the Arabian Peninsula to protect their only major source of oil outside the Western Hemisphere, except for the minority interest held in Iraqi oil. This American policy in Saudi Arabia received its ultimate sanction when President Roosevelt made a point of meeting King Abdul Aziz al-Saud on an American cruiser in the Suez Canal in February 1945, on the return from the Yalta Conference.[10]

With the end of the War in Europe, the development of American postwar policies accelerated. Memoranda were written, meetings held, telegrams sent, decisions made. The common theme running through all these discussions was suspicion of British policy and present influence in the area.[11] In August 1945 the Minister in Egypt reported to Washington that the American "spokesmen" at M.E.S.C. had pressed their British counterparts for the dissolution of the Centre at the earliest possible moment, "in view of declared United States policy of eliminating wartime controls," and had suggested 1 October as the date of dissolution. The British countered with 31 December. The Department of State replied on 20 August, instructing the Legation to press for the earliest liquidation of the Centre in view of the end of the war with Japan. A compromise was reached and on 26 September 1945 the two Governments issued a joint statement announcing the end of M.E.S.C. on 1 November 1945.[12]

The degree to which the hopes of those who saw M.E.S.C. playing a significant role in the Middle East after the War were built on sand is nowhere demonstrated better than in the record of a Conference between President Truman and the Ministers to Egypt, Saudi Arabia, Syria and Lebanon, and the Consul General in Jerusalem, on 10 November, in the wake of the dissolution of M.E.S.C. The four Chiefs of Mission had asked for the interview to get assurances from the President that the United States would continue its policies of encouraging independence of the Middle Eastern states, encouraging close relations with the United States and the "Western democracies," and supporting the Open Door. George Wadsworth, Minister to Syria and Lebanon, spoke for the group, and his comments, while they should not be taken as representing the opinion of the State Department, or his colleagues in the Foreign Service generally, did reflect a pattern of thinking about the Middle East that had a direct effect on the fate of the Middle East Supply Centre. He said to the President, in the course of a lengthy presentation of his views, that the Governments of the Middle East wanted to know "most of all" whether the United States was going to "follow through" with its wartime policies or revert to the policies followed after World War I. "In the latter event," said Wadsworth, "the Governments to which we are accredited know from bitter experience and present trends that Britain and France will make every effort to consolidate their prewar spheres of influence; they look especially to us to support them in their efforts to block any such development. If the United States fails them, they will turn to Russia and will be lost to our civilization; of that we feel certain. On the other hand, there need be no conflict between us and Russia in that area. On the contrary, Russian policy has thus far paralleled our own. . . ." [13]

The rapidly developing tension over the British presence in Egypt, the Suez Canal, and Palestine made a close economic partnership between Middle Eastern states and Britain alone an impossibility. Sponsorship of M.E.S.C. by the states of the region themselves proved equally unfeasible: the populations and their governments were as eager to dismantle wartime restrictions—which M.E.S.C. had symbolized *par excellence;* pivotal sectors like Iran and Jewish Palestine were either lukewarm about regional unification or undesirable to some as partners; and the Arab League preferred to serve the purposes of a postwar M.E.S.C. by its own creations so as to owe no debt of gratitude to foreign powers. The United Nations was not ready until 1948 to accept the principle of economic regionalism and to accommodate strong regional bodies in its structure. So, the Middle East Supply Centre was allowed to be plowed under by the frantic demobilization of the Allied war machine. But a legacy remained.

The Middle East Supply Centre had been the main instrument through which Britain and the United States had preserved the civilian populations of the Middle East from hunger and general economic collapse; in this process the Centre had been not a mere executor of orders from above but often an initiator of the very commands it received. Because of wartime prosperity, the newly independent nations of the Middle East could make their entrance on the scene of world affairs with their feet planted on an economy that was freer from destruction than many other parts of the globe. The Middle East Supply Centre had been a part of those developments which hastened the identification of the Middle East as a regional entity recognized as such on the inside and the outside. It had demonstrated to what an extent economic coordination among the territories of the region could be carried if the political environment was favorable. In doing so it had considerably expanded the horizon of problems held susceptible to regional cooperation. Instead of thinking only in terms of mere "accommodations" such as the control of international rivers, railroad traffic or arrangements for free port facilities, the promoters of regional cooperation now took agriculture, health, currency, banking and economic development in general unto their purview. This was the way in which the regional economic commissions of the United Nations were to conduct their deliberations.

Notes

Introduction

1. Keith A. H. Murray, "Feeding the Middle East in War-time," *Royal Central Asian Journal* 33 (July–October 1945): 233–247.

Chapter 1

1. S. McKee Rosen, *The Combined Boards of the Second World War* (New York: Columbia University Press, 1951), p. 272.

2. William Y. Elliott, *The British Commonwealth at War* (New York: Alfred A. Knopf, 1943), pp. 4–18; Henry Chalmers, "Economic Pooling and Lend-Lease Operations Among the Belligerent Allies," *Foreign Commerce Weekly*, 10 (13 March 1943): 3; Heather J. Harvey, *Consultation and Cooperation in the Commonwealth* (London: Oxford University Press, 1952), pp. 353, 388.

Prominent examples of wartime cooperation of this type among the allies in the Mediterranean area were the following organizations:

Eastern Group Supply Council—Composed of representatives of the United Kingdom and all Commonwealth nations and territories "East of Suez," including spokesmen of Allied theater commanders. Organized in December 1940 as a result of a conference in New Delhi, the Council represented one of the first steps by which Great Britain encouraged the outlying lands and military establishments of the Empire to have recourse to local and regional rather than overseas resources in the procurement of defense supplies. The Council brought about the formation of such agencies as the Middle East Provisions Office which coordinated and encouraged military procurement for the Middle East Command in the Middle East area.

The Middle East, East African, and West African Supply Centres—Civilian agencies set up by the British government alongside the Middle East, East African, and West African Commands. Within the areas entrusted to these Commands it was the function of the supply centers to determine, for the benefit of British and American shipping authorities, the minimum of goods which the areas must import from overseas for the civilian population. Another function was the encouragement of local production and a greater exchange within the regions of local surpluses so that the need for seaborne imports could be further reduced.

East African Governors' Conference—Backed up by a permanent secretariat, the Conference provided a channel of consultation and coordination for the handling of economic problems in the British colonies of East Africa arising from the war. It guided and supervised the activities of the East African Supply Centre.

North African Economic Board—Established after the Allied invasion of French North Africa, the Board brought together American, British, and French officials dealing with the control of civilian imports, the organization of food supply, the rehabilitation of transportation, and the encouragement of local production for military and civilian use, as well as the exchange of surpluses among the separate territories comprising the French Colonial Empire in North Africa.

3. George Kirk, *The Middle East in the War* (London: Oxford University Press, 1952), pp. 160–173.

4. Ibid., pp. 168–169.

5. For the effect of this wartime experience on British foreign service operations after the war, see U.K., British Information Service, *The Organization of the British Foreign Service* (New York, September 1949), p. 2. This document attributes to wartime lessons the greater emphasis which is placed on economics in the training and briefing of British diplomatic officials of all ranks now.

6. Interview with James M. Landis, 9 February 1953.

7. Relations with Turkey (which was not under Allied control) were extremely touchy. A wholly separate system of civilian supply was set up in Washington and London, and Turkey was included in the m.e.s.c. program of grain shipments only. John P. Dawson to Norman S. Mangouni, 30 December 1970.

8. "Review of the Work of the Middle East Supply Center," U.S., Department of State, *Bulletin* 13 (30 September 1945): 493.

9. Ibid., p. 494.

10. See United Nations, Economic and Social Council, *Report of the Adhoc Committee for the Middle East*, Suppl. 4 (E/1360-E/AC. 26/16), p. 7. Committee members included Egypt, France, Iran, Iraq, Lebanon, Turkey, the U.S.S.R., the U.K., and the U.S.

11. Speech by Sir Francis Joseph, acting chairman, u.k.c.c., *New York Times*, 18 December 1943.

12. "An International Example," *Economist* 145 (4 September 1943): 300–302.

13. (New York: W. W. Norton & Co., 1948), pp. 209–212.

14. Kirk, *The Middle East in the War*, p. 162.

15. See chap. 9, infra; see also Kirk, *Middle East in the War*, p. 160.

16. Fayez A. Sayegh, "Recent Trends Toward Arab Unity," *Lands East* 3 (April 1958): 9.

17. Najla Izzedin, *The Arab World* (Chicago: Henry Regnery Co., 1953), p. 321.

18. Memorandum, "Israeli Opinion on the M.E.S.C.," Yaakov Shimoni, Counselor, Embassy of Israel, Washington, to the author, 1 September 1953.

19. Judah L. Magnes, "Toward Peace in Palestine," *Foreign Affairs* 21 (January 1943): 239–249.

Chapter 2

1. T. Vail Motter, *The Persian Corridor and Aid to Russia*, U.S., Department of the Army, the United States Army in World War II: The Middle East Theater (Washington, D.C.: Government Printing Office, 1953), p. 5.

2. "Dissolution of the Middle East Supply Center," U.S., Department of State, *Bulletin* 13 (30 September 1945): 493; see also Lord Altrincham, "Les Problèmes du Moyen-Orient," *Politique Etrangère*, 12 (July 1947): 261–274, and Kirk, *Middle East in the War*, pp. 169–193.

3. Eric H. Biddle, *Manpower: A Summary of the British Experience* (Chicago: Public Administration Service, 1942), passim.

4. R. W. B. Clarke, *The Economic Effort of War* (London: Allen & Unwin, 1940), pp. 203, 212–213; W. K. Hancock and M. M. Gowing, *British War Economy* (London: H.M.S.O., 1949), chap. 3 and pp. 120–135, 137, 149, 176; Donald F. Heatherington, "Great Britain's Wartime Exports," *Foreign Commerce Weekly* 17 (16 December 1944): 4; E. L. Hargreaves and M. M. Gowing, *Civil Industry and Trade* (London: H.M.S.O., 1952), pp. 17, 119.

5. International Labour Office, *The Exploitation of Foreign Labour by Germany*, Studies and Reports, Series C, no. 25 (Montreal, 1945), p. 12.

6. Clarke, *Economic Effort*, passim; Alan R. Prest, *War Economics of Primary Producing Countries* (Cambridge: At the University Press, 1948), pp. 284–286.

7. Hancock and Gowing, *War Economy*, p. 281.

8. Prest, *War Economics*, pp. 79–86. See also Mordecai Ezekiel, ed., *Towards World Prosperity* (New York: Harper and Brothers, 1947), pp. 267–268.

9. Hargreaves and Gowing, *Civil Industry and Trade*, pp. 51, 58–59, 68, 71, 137–139; Heatherington, "Wartime Exports," p. 42; Memorandum, "Palestine Import Licensing Policy," U.S., Consulate General, Jerusalem, to Culbertson Mission, 1944 (Private Papers of William S. Culbertson);

"Growth of the U.K.C.C.," *Economist* 145 (13 November 1943): 651–652; Clarke, *Economic Effort*, p. 132; H. Duncan Hall and C. C. Wrigley, *Studies of Overseas Supply*, History of the Second World War, United Kingdom Civil Series, chap. 9; U.K., Board of Trade, *Aims and Plan of Work of the Export Council* (London: H.M.S.O., 1940), passim.

10. U.K., *Parliamentary Debates* (Commons), 5th ser., 365 (1940): 2070–2071 and 2039–2099, and 367 (1940): 559–570; Earl Winterton, "The Mobilization of the British Commonwealth," *Quarterly Review* 278 (April 1941): 157–170; Earl Winterton, "Imperial Strategic Reserves," *Royal Central Asian Journal* 26 (January 1942): 30–34.

11. Speech by the Viceroy of India at the Eastern Group Supply Conference, Delhi, India, 25 October 1940. Mimeographed. [Copy of text seen at British Information Service, New York].

12. U.K., Mesopotamia Commission, *Report of the Commission Appointed by Act of Parliament to Enquire into the Operations of War in Mesopotamia* (London: H.M.S.O., 1917), p. 105. See also T. E. Lawrence, *Seven Pillars of Wisdom* (Garden City, N.Y.: Doubleday, Doran & Co., 1926), p. 59.

13. Royal Institute of International Affairs, *The World in March 1939* (London, 1952), p. 93.

14. Centre d'études de politique étrangère, Bibliothèque genérale de l'Ecole pratique des hautes etudes, *Industrialisation de l'Afrique du Nord* (Paris: Librairie Armand Colin, 1952), pp. 9, 140.

15. David J. Dallin, *Soviet Russia's Foreign Policy* (New Haven: Yale University Press, 1942), passim; R. J. Collins, *Lord Wavell (1883–1941)* (London: Stoughton, 1948), pp. 207, 212, 243.

16. U.K., *Parliamentary Debates* (Commons), 5th ser., 361 (1940): 838; *Bulletin of International News* 18 (22 March 1941): 324–328; Jewish Agency for Palestine, *Economic Research Institute Bulletin* 3 (November–December 1939): 176, 4 (September 1940): 60, 6 (1942): 54; Esco Foundation for Palestine, *Palestine, A Study of Jewish, Arab and British Policies* (New Haven: Yale University Press, 1947), vol. 2, pp. 1022, 1051; Palestine News Service, *Palnews*, Mid-September 1945, p. 4; U.K., Colonial Office, *Annual Report on Aden and Aden Protectorate, 1946* (London: H.M.S.O., 1948), p. 3.

17. Sir Douglas G. Harris, "The War Supply Board," *Palnews*, 10 March 1941, pp. 1–2.

18. National Bank of Egypt, *Report of the Ordinary General Meeting* (Cairo, 1940), pp. 1–2.

19. Winston S. Churchill, *Their Finest Hour* (Boston: Houghton Mifflin Co., 1949), pp. 426, 506; idem, *The Grand Alliance* (Boston: Houghton Mifflin Co., 1950), pp. 753, 757, 764, 798; Robert E. Sherwood, *Roosevelt and Hopkins*, rev. ed. (Harper and Brothers, 1950), p. 301; William L. Langer and S. Everett Gleason, *The Undeclared War, 1940–1941* (New York, Harper and Brothers for Council on Foreign Relations, 1953), pp.

397–401, 417, 590, 780; Collins, *Lord Wavell*, passim; U.S., Department of State, *Foreign Relations of the United States, 1941*, vol. 3, pp. 292–295.

20. Churchill, *Finest Hour*, p. 706; Hancock and Gowing, *British War Economy*, pp. 250–253, 434; *Foreign Commerce Weekly* 7 (18 April 1942): 19.

21. Royal Institute of International Affairs, *The Middle East: A Political and Economic Survey* (London: R.I.I.A., 1951), p. 3.

22. Churchill, *Grand Alliance*, p. 5; Collins, *Lord Wavell*, p. 220.

23. Winston S. Churchill, *The Hinge of Fate* (Boston: Houghton Mifflin Co., 1950), pp. 6–9, 11, 42; idem, *Grand Alliance*, pp. 411–420, 465, 491, 540–541; Sherwood, *Roosevelt and Hopkins*, pp. 182, 314–316, 594–599; Langer and Gleason, *Undeclared War*, pp. 589–592.

24. Churchill, *Finest Hour*, p. 446.

25. Memorandum, President Roosevelt to Harry Hopkins, General Marshall, and Admiral King (see Sherwood, *Roosevelt and Hopkins*, pp. 604–605); U.S., Department of State, *Foreign Relations, 1941*, vol. 3, pp. 264 ff.

26. Hancock and Gowing, *War Economy*, p. 214.

27. Churchill, *Grand Alliance*, p. 783; Langer and Gleason, *Undeclared War*, p. 102.

28. Churchill, *Hinge of Fate*, pp. 6–11; idem, *Grand Alliance*, pp. 411–418.

29. Royal Institute of International Affairs, *World in March 1939*, p. 128; James L. Barton, *The Story of Near East Relief* (New York: Macmillan Co., 1930), p. 77.

30. Churchill, *Grand Alliance*, pp. 555, 576–577; idem, *Hinge of Fate*, p. 296.

31. W. Gordon East, "The Mediterranean: Pivot of Peace and War," *Foreign Affairs* 31 (July 1953): 623; U.K., Ministry of Information, *The Work of the Middle East Supply Centre During the European War* (Cairo: Nile Press, 1945), p. 4.

32. Royal Institute of International Affairs, *Middle East*, p. 78; "Harbours of the Mediterranean," *Egyptian Gazette* (Cairo), 10 April 1939.

33. George Kirk, *The Middle East in the War*, p. 200; Esco Foundation for Palestine, 2:992; Halford L. Hoskins, "The Guardianship of the Suez Canal," *Middle East Journal* 4 (April 1950): 148; *Oriente Moderno* 20 (September 1940): 441.

34. Hancock and Gowing, *War Economy*, passim; Charles Issawi, *Egypt: An Economic and Social Analysis* (London and New York: Oxford University Press, 1947), p. 105. Later in the war Allied military and civilian constructions were to multiply port capacity by the creation of new harbors, the expansion of old ones, and the establishment of inland links, in Iran, the Levant, Iraq, and the Red Sea coast.

35. Kirk, *Middle East in the War*, p. 171.

36. Churchill, *Grand Alliance*, p. 863; Frederick G. Winant, "The

Combined Middle East Supply Program," U.S., Department of State, *Bulletin* 10 (26 February 1944): 199–203.

37. Kirk, *Middle East in the War*, pp. 175, 179; Prest, *War Economics*, p. 153; M.E.S.C., "Organization and Policy Handbook"; interview with E. Lewis Jones, 15 August 1951.

38. Winant, "Supply Program," p. 200.

39. Ibid.

40. W. N. Medlicott, *The Economic Blockade*, U.K., Civil Series, History of the Second World War, vol. 1 (London: H.M.S.O., 1952), p. 612; Sir Oliver Mance, "The Future of British Trade with Turkey," *Royal Central Asian Journal* 27 (January 1943): 17.

41. U.S., Department of State, *Mandate for Palestine* (Washington, D.C.: Government Printing Office, 1931), p. 4; Barton, *Near East Relief*, pp. 71, 96–97, 343; Faith Jessup Kahrl, "September Incident in Lebanon," *Arab World* 1 (Summer 1944): 51; Albert H. Hourani, *Syria and Lebanon: A Political Essay* (London: Oxford University Press, 1946), pp. 230–231.

42. Kirk, *Middle East*, p. 171; *Report of the Director-General to the Regional Meeting for the Near and Middle East of the International Labour Organisation, Cairo, November 1947* (Istanbul: I.L.O., November 1947), passim; *Palnews*, 25 February 1942, p. 5.

43. Francis Boardman, "Civilian Requirements from War to Peace: The Middle East Supply Center," U.S., Department of State, *Bulletin* 13 (23 December 1945): 994–999.

44. *Foreign Commerce Weekly* 2 (8 March 1941): 419; Robert J. Barr, "Iraq Today," *Foreign Commerce Weekly* 10 (20 February 1943): 6; U.K., *Overseas Economic Surveys, Iraq, June 1949* (London: H.M.S.O., 1949), p. 7; *International Labour Review* 43 (January 1943): 67; Kirk, *Middle East in the War*, pp. 170, 179; M.E.S.C., "Handbook," p. 51; I.L.O., *Report of the Director-General*, passim; *Al-Ahram* (Cairo), 9 February 1941; *Palnews*, 12 February 1942, p. 9; Interview with Sir Geoffrey Prior, 28 March 1953; Frederick G. Winant and John P. Dawson, "The Middle East Supply Program," *Foreign Commerce Weekly* 15 (1 April 1944), pp. 3 ff.

Chapter 3

1. For a description of the navycert system see W. N. Medlicott, *The Economic Blockade*, passim.

2. *Eurygaster integriceps* Puton (Hemiptera: Scutelleridae). This pentatomid is one of the most destructive pests of grain in the Near East. Main damage to the grain is two-fold—adults feed on stems of young plants and later adults and nymphs attack the kernels. The former damage often amounts to loss of over 25 per cent of stand in non-irrigated fields while attack on kernels, by no more than two to three insects per square yard, can cause total loss of crop. Another type of damage is caused by intro-

duction of enzymes into the grain which lower the baking quality of the flour. Although losses caused by this insect vary over the region, they are seldom less than 25 per cent of the crop. It has been said that the pest causes more damage than grasshoppers in Iraq in some seasons. In Iran, during the periods when the entire wheat crop was destroyed, the inhabitants were forced by famine to move from one part of the country to another. "Senn Pest," U.S., Department of Agriculture, Plant Pest Control Division, *Cooperative Economic Insect Report*, vol. 7, no. 5 (1 February 1957): 88; "The Senn Pest," idem, PA-582, August 1963.

    3. "The Middle East I: Food and Politics," *Economist* 144 (20 February 1943): 230.

    4. Donald F. Heatherington, "Sterling Balances and Britain's External Debt, Part II," *Foreign Commerce Weekly* 17 (4 November 1944): 13; Alan R. Prest, *War Economics of Primary Producing Countries*, pp. 91, 163; Royal Institute of International Affairs, *The Middle East: A Political and Economic Survey*, p. 69.

    5. Royal Institute of International Affairs, *The Middle East*, p. 224; Mordecai Ezekiel, ed., *Towards World Prosperity*, p. 251; Harold and Doreen Ingrams, "The Hadhramaut in Times of War," *Geographic Journal* 105 (January–February 1945): 1–29; Prest, *War Economics*, p. 120; Robert Shaffer, *Tents and Towers of Arabia* (New York: Dodd, Mead and Co, 1952), pp. 7–8; Philip W. Ireland, "The Near East and the European War," *Foreign Policy Reports* 16 (15 March 1940): 1–4; Raymond F. Mikesell and Hollis B. Chenery, *Arabian Oil: America's Stake in the Middle East* (Chapel Hill, N.C.: University of North Carolina Press, 1949), passim.

    6. Albert J. Dorra, "L'industrie Egyptienne et ses possibilités de développement," *L'Egypte Contemporaine* 34 (November 1943): 452; Ezekiel, *World Prosperity*, p. 251; *Foreign Commerce Weekly* 19 (23 June 1945): 26; *Oriente Moderno* 20 (March 1940): 134 and 22 (October 1942): 427; U.K., Ministry of Information, Overseas Publicity Telegram, "British Army Brings Development to the Middle East," Factual Background no. 143 (London, 3 December 1942); E. B. Worthington, *Middle East Science: A Survey of Subjects Other Than Agriculture* (London: H.M.S.O., 1946), pp. 10–11; George Kirk, *The Middle East in the War*, passim; T. Vail Motter, *The Persian Corridor and Aid to Russia*, passim; Royal Institute of International Affairs, *The Middle East*, p. 78; Minister Alexander Kirk, U.S. Legation, Cairo, to Secretary of State, "Wheat Supply Situation," mimeographed, 11 June 1942 (file no. 861.31).

    7. *Foreign Commerce Weekly* 2 (1 February 1941): 187 and 11 (6 June 1943): 27; *Oriente Moderno* 21 (April 1940): 197; Prest, *War Economics*, pp. 7, 92, 99, 108, 129, 222; International Labour Office, *Report of the Director-General to the Regional Meeting for the Near and Middle East of the International Labour Organisation, Cairo, November 1947*, passim; interview with Macduffie, 20 January 1953.

    8. Ephraim G. Erickson, "Protest Society: Social Irrationality in the Ex-

tra-Territorial One-Sex Company Town," Ph.D. dissertation, University of Chicago, August 1947, passim.

9. Lewis V. Thomas and Richard N. Frye, *The United States and Turkey and Iran* (Cambridge: Harvard University Press, 1951), passim; *Foreign Commerce Weekly* 2 (8 March 1941): 419. On the pre-emptive buying of Turkish chromium, see U.S., Department of State, *Foreign Relations of the United States, 1941*, vol. 3, pp. 936–974.

10. *Foreign Commerce Weekly* 3 (5 April 1941): 6; Prest, *War Economics*, p. 207; Kirk, *Middle East in the War*, pp. 35–36; "Annual Meeting of Ottoman Bank," *Times* (London), 24 December 1942.

11. Prest, *War Economics*, p. 129; "Middle East I," *Economist*, p. 231.

12. Gaston Leduc, "L'évolution économique du Moyen-Orient," *Politique Etrangère*, 12 (July 1947): 288; Samuel Goldberg, "Syria Before the Clash," *Foreign Commerce Weekly* 3 (28 June 1941): 533.

13. Motter, *Persian Corridor*, passim.

14. J. D. Lotz, "Problems and Proposals: The Iranian Seven Year Plan," *Middle East Journal* 4 (Winter 1950): 102–105.

15. Lord Rennel of Rodd, *British Military Administration of Occupied Territories in Africa During 1941–1947* (London: H.M.S.O., 1948), pp. 86–93.
This was not the only headache plaguing liberation or occupation authorities in the Italian colonies. One of the most vexatious habits—almost impossible to control—was that of the local populations to celebrate their deliverance from the enemy by a joyous destruction of many useful works of the Italian colonization. Thus, when the Eighth Army arrived in Libya, they found (on top of the demolition effected by the enemy) that the desert Arabs were feting the event by cutting down a million trees which the Italians had planted. The cycle was completed six years later when the United Nations announced the independence of the new Kingdom of Libya: By way of celebration the same Arabs tore up the green shoots the British had carefully planted in the meantime (Ritchie Calder, *Men Against the Desert* [London, 1951], quoted in *Middle Eastern Affairs* 3 [October 1952]: 293–294).

16. *Foreign Commerce Weekly* 1 (2 November 1940): 229.

17. Interview with E. Lewis Jones, 15 August 1951.

18. Interview with R. W. Bailey, 27 August 1952.

19. Ömer Celâl Sarc, "Economic Policy of the New Turkey," *Middle East Journal* 2 (October 1948): 440.

20. Interview with Bailey.

21. Winston S. Churchill, *The Hinge of Fate* and *The Grand Alliance*, passim; Robert E. Sherwood, *Roosevelt and Hopkins*, passim.

22. Kirk, *Middle East in the War*, p. 356; *Foreign Commerce Weekly* 1 (12 October 1940): 57, 2 (8 February 1941): 258.

23. *Foreign Commerce Weekly* 2 (29 March 1941): 529, 3 (21 June 1941): 500, and 8 (4 July 1942): 17.

24. F. Lawrence Babcock, "The Explosive Middle East," *Fortune* 30

(September 1944): 116; *Oriente Moderno* 22 (January 1942): 23, 23 (July 1942): 290; Esco Foundation for Palestine, *Palestine, A Study of Jewish, Arab and British Policies* (New Haven: Yale University Press), vol. 2, p. 962; "The Middle East I," *Economist* 144 (20 February 1943): 230–231; interview with Hassan S. Kekhia, 27 August 1953; Cyrus L. Sulzberger, "German Preparations in the Middle East," *Foreign Affairs* 20 (July 1942): 663–678.

25. Olaf Caroe, *Wells of Power: The Oilfields of South-Western Asia* (London: Macmillan & Co., 1951), p. 56; Albert H. Hourani, *Syria and Lebanon: A Political Essay*, pp. 234–236; *Oriente Moderno* 22 (July 1942): 281; U.S., Department of State, *Foreign Relations, 1942*, vol. 4, pp. 67–71.

26. Interviews with Macduffie and Jones.

27. Prest, *War Economics*, p. 9.

28. Kirk, *Middle East in the War*, p. 211; Australian Institute of International Affairs, *The Middle East: Australia's Frontline*, World Affairs Paper no. 3 (Sydney, January 1941), p. 13; interview with Macduffie.

29. *Oriente Moderno* 23 (February 1943): 76–77; *Nabard-i Imruz* (Teheran), 18 April 1943.

30. *Foreign Commerce Weekly* 1 (11 December 1940): 280.

31. Interview with Macduffie.

32. Alford Carleton, "The Syrian Coup d'Etat of 1949," *Middle East Journal* 4 (Winter 1949): 1–11.

33. T. Hodgkin, *Nationalism in Colonial Africa* (London: F. Muller, 1956), passim.

34. Interviews with Jackson (1 June 1954), and Macduffie and Landis (9 February 1953); K. D. D. Henderson, *The Making of the Modern Sudan* (London: Faber & Faber, 1953), passim; E. M. H. Lloyd, *Food and Inflation in the Middle East, 1940–1945* (Palo Alto: Stanford University Press, 1956), pts. 3 to 5.

35. Prest, *War Economics*, passim; Robert J. Barr, "Palestine's New Economic Controls," *Foreign Commerce Weekly* 10 (13 February 1943): 11, 29; Jean Godard, "Le problème du blé en Syrie et au Liban pendant la Guerre," *L'Egypte Contemporaine* 35 (March–April 1944): 309–344; Muhammad Ali al-Ghatit, "L'agriculture en Egypte et l'aprés-guerre," *L'Egypte Contemporaine* 35 (January–February 1944): 59; Jean Ahoury, "Les répercussions de la guerre sur l'agriculture égyptienne," *L'Egypte Contemporaine* 38 (March–April 1947): 234–235; Edwin Samuel, "The Government of Israel and its Problems," *Middle East Journal* 3 (January 1949): 10; *Economic Research Institute Bulletin* (Jerusalem) 6 (1942): 52–53.

36. H. Duncan Hall and C. C. Wrigley, *Studies of Overseas Supply*, chaps. 2, 9.

37. *Foreign Commerce Weekly* 2 (11 January 1941): 77; Australian Institute of International Affairs, *Australia's Frontline*, p. 25; Prest, *War Economics*, p. 200; *Palnews*, 21 January 1942, p. 8.

38. E. L. Hargreaves and M. M. Gowing, *Civil Industry and Trade*, passim; see also chap. 5, infra.

39. Churchill, *Hinge of Fate*, passim, and *Grand Alliance*, pp. 66, 337, 405. Churchill lists dissatisfaction with the unloading, refitting, and battle-readying of tanks as one of the principal reasons for relieving General Wavell from command (idem, *Grand Alliance*, p. 338).

40. R. J. Collins, *Lord Wavell (1883–1941)*, passim.

41. Kirk, *Middle East in the War*, p. 172.

42. Louis E. Frechtling, "Allied Strategy in the Near East," *Foreign Policy Reports* 17 (1 February 1942): 274–283, passim; *Times* (London), 13 August 1941 and 23 September 1941; British Information Service, New York, to the author, 15 December 1953.

43. Churchill, *Grand Alliance*, p. 113.

Chapter 4

1. E. M. H. Lloyd, *Food and Inflation in the Middle East, 1940–1945*, pp. 76–78.

2. R. J. Collins, *Lord Wavell (1883–1941)*, pp. 271–272.

3. Lloyd, *Food and Inflation*, pp. 76–77; interviews with Charles Empson, 15 November 1956, and Eric H. Biddle, 14 January 1953.

4. Lloyd, *Food and Inflation*, pp. 76–77.

5. Ibid.; Collins, *Lord Wavell*, pp. 271–272.

6. Lloyd, *Food and Inflation*, pp. 76–77. The u.k.c.c. had been created by the Treasury to undertake economic warfare purchases in the Balkans and Turkey (ibid.).

7. Ibid.

8. Like the War Shipping Administration later established in the U.S., the British Ministry of Shipping—absorbed by a new Ministry of War Transport in April 1941—acted as dispatcher for the national merchant fleet and all Free Europe vessels in British ports.

9. Lloyd, *Food and Inflation*, pp. 76–77; interview with Biddle; Francis Boardman, "Civilian Requirements from War to Peace: The Middle East Supply Center," U.S., Department of State, *Bulletin* 13 (23 December 1945): 994–999.

10. Interview with Biddle; E. M. Nicholson to the author, 16 September 1952.

11. Winston S. Churchill, *The Grand Alliance*, pp. 783–785.

12. Ibid.; see also chaps. 6, 7, infra.

13. There was no consultation with non-British authorities in the Middle East on the project.

14. George Kirk, *The Middle East in the War*, p. 172; Lloyd, *Food and Inflation*, p. 79.

15. Except where American sources are directly quoted, the British spelling of Centre has been used throughout this study.

16. E. M. Nicholson to the author.

17. At the first session, on 24 April 1941, there were present representatives of the Embassy, the U.K.C.C., the Ministry of Shipping, G.H.Q., the Administration of Occupied Enemy Territories (former Italian colonies in East Africa), the East African War Supplies Board, and the governments of Palestine, Malta, Cyprus, and the Sudan (Lloyd, *Food and Inflation*, p. 79).

18. *Times* (London), 13 August 1940 and 23 September 1940; Heather J. Harvey, *Consultation and Cooperation in the Commonwealth* (London: Oxford University Press, 1952), pp. 365–367; see chap. 3, supra.

19. Harvey, *Consultation and Cooperation*, pp. 365–367.

20. Lloyd, *Food and Inflation*, p. 77.

21. Churchill, *Grand Alliance*, p. 64. By an ominous twist of fate, the arrival in Cairo of the two British dignitaries coincided with the landing, on an airfield near Tripoli, Libya, of one Erwin Römmel, carrying with him the Führer's commission as newly appointed commander of the Italo-German forces in North Africa (ibid., p. 199); Sir Llewellyn Woodward, *British Foreign Policy in the Second World War* (London: H.M.S.O., 1962), pp. 132–136; U.S., Department of State, *Foreign Relations of the United States, 1941*, vol. 3, pp. 690, 826–827, 833–844.

22. Churchill, *Grand Alliance*, pp. 64–68.

23. Ibid., pp. 347–350, 396.

24. Ibid., p. 793.

25. Ibid. The unusual title given to Haining appears to go back to Cromwellian days.

26. Kirk, *Middle East in the War*, p. 159; Churchill, *Grand Alliance*, pp. 347, 793; Lloyd, *Food and Inflation*, p. 83.

27. Collins, *Lord Wavell*, p. 431. Haining had the additional misfortune to arrive as the Prime Minister's personal watchdog and troubleshooter at a time when the Middle East Command was highly sensitive to interference from "politicians." Churchill was blamed for having pushed Wavell against his will into the Greek disaster and then having fired him when the adventure went wrong. "I cannot doubt," writes Churchill, "that in these circles of the Staff there was a strong feeling that the new Commander [Auchinleck] should not let himself be pressed into hazardous adventures, but should take his time and work on certainties. Such a mood might well have been imparted to General Auchinleck" (Churchill, *Grand Alliance*, pp. 404–405).

28. Cecil B. Brown, *Suez to Singapore* (New York: Random House, 1942), pp. 83–84.

29. Kirk, *Middle East in the War*, p. 161.

30. Collins, *Lord Wavell*, p. 431. Haining even made a futile effort to enlist the help of American representatives in Cairo in his search for authority, pointing to his official responsibility for the processing of American supplies; interview with General Russell L. Maxwell, 2 October 1952.

31. Kirk, *Middle East in the War*, p. 161; Collins, *Lord Wavell*, p. 431.

32. The melancholy fate of the Intendancy illustrated clearly the pit-falls awaiting an agency expected to operate outside both the military and the normal diplomatic establishment of Britain in the Middle East yet assigned to duties which vitally affected both. First, there was the Com-mander-in-Chief, representing the "men who do the fighting," always su-preme; antagonizing him or his officers meant rebuff without recourse, as General Haining had found out to his dismay. Then, the Foreign Office, the Colonial Office, and other ministries active in the area and jealous of their traditional prerogatives. Conscious of this, London could seldom provide "interlopers," however legitimate their business, with clear direc-tives and incontrovertible authority, but resorted to the time-honored de-vice of hedging its prescripts with "you will consults" and "you will coor-dinates," those dreaded leashes which from time immemorial have plagued governmental expediters and troubleshooters. The success of the latter then depended on their ability to make *ad hoc* "arrangements" based on mutual accommodations and personal congeniality rather than clear directives. At that, such arrangements could be disturbed or shat-tered momentarily by the uncoordinated action of a single Ministry or military unit, by a change in personnel, or by one of the many impetuous interventions of the Prime Minister who could not possibly be aware of the many fine webs of accommodation through which previous directives had been integrated into the complex administrative life of a large and active theater. (For example, there is no evidence that Churchill was aware of the creation of M.E.S.C. when he appointed an "Intendant General" to take charge of military and civilian supply matters; indeed, there is no reference to the Centre in any of his writings about the war.) Thus, the fate of unorthodox creations such as the "Intendant General," the "Minister of State," the "Middle East Provisions Office," the "Eastern Group Supply Council," and the "Middle East Supply Centre" hinged largely on personal leadership—skill, connections in high places, bravado, and luck being the most important ingredients. By all accounts, General Haining was deficient in skill, luck, and bravado, during his Cairo tenure.

33. "The position of the Minister of State was thus one of considerable difficulty, as he found himself dealing with a number of matters for which other ministers had parliamentary responsibilities at home. The fact that in addition it was desirable, whenever possible, to send to the Cabinet *agreed* recommendations from the three Services and the various Departments of State represented in the Middle East added to the diffi-culties" (Kirk, *Middle East in the War*, p. 160, 167). [Author's italics.]

34. Ibid., p. 173.

35. See chap. 3, supra.

36. Lloyd, *Food and Inflation*, p. 81.

37. Alan R. Prest, *War Economics of Primary Producing Countries*, passim.

38. Lloyd, *Food and Inflation*, pp. 81, 84–85.

39. Ibid., pp. 85–86; interview with Biddle.

40. Ibid.

41. Ibid.; Kirk, *Middle East in the War*, pp. 167–168.

42. See chap. 5, infra.

43. George Woodbridge, *UNRRA: The History of the United Nations Relief and Rehabilitation Administration* (New York: Columbia University Press, 1950), passim; interview with George Woodbridge, 18 August 1952; Charles P. Taft to the author, 14 September 1952.

44. Winston S. Churchill, *the Hinge of Fate*, pp. 85–86.

45. Interview with Sir Geoffrey Prior, 21 May 1953.

46. Lloyd, *Food and Inflation*, pp. 86–87; interviews with Jackson, Biddle, and Prior.

47. Ibid. In mapping out a campaign for economic mobilization and trade controls and preparing proposals for meeting the specific difficulties of individual countries, Jackson had as his closest adviser a recognized authority, Professor R. F. (now Lord) Kahn who had studied under Keynes at Cambridge University. Keynes himself was economic adviser to the Churchill government and had captured the public imagination with his sweeping and often unorthodox proposals for financing the war and mobilizing the country's resources while keeping inflation in check. The characteristic boldness of Keynesian views was reflected in the economic programs which Jackson under Kahn's guidance drafted for various Middle Eastern countries (Lloyd, *Food and Inflation*, pp. 88, 208).

48. Ibid., pp. 99–100.

49. Ibid., pp. 86–88, 92.

50. Ibid., pp. 99–101. During the life of m.e.s.c. there were to be other comprehensive British and American studies of a similar nature. Like the Baliol-Scott report, they were never made public. The most detailed analysis was prepared for the U.S. Bureau of the Budget, in order to document a proposed appropriation toward the upkeep of the Centre. Special Mission of the Bureau of the Budget, "Regional Organization in the Middle East" [by Eric H. Biddle], 2 vols. (London, 28 May 1943). The author was granted access to vol. 1.

51. Egypt, Ethiopia, Saudi Arabia, Iraq, Iran, Turkey, Aden, Cyprus, Malta, the Somalilands, the Persian Gulf Sheikhdoms, the Sudan, Eritrea, Palestine, Transjordan, Syria, Lebanon, and Yemen. Malta's inclusion was temporary, Yemen's indirect. Turkey participated in the m.e.s.c. scheme only for grain imports; for other items an Anglo-American Coordinating Committee (a.a.c.c.) in Ankara performed functions similar to those of m.e.s.c. After the defeat of Rommel, Tripolitania and Cyrenaica were added to m.e.s.c.'s responsibilities.

52. An American observer of m.e.s.c. was moved to remark on this point: "I cannot think of a more complex political and economic group

for servicing in the matter of civilian supplies under war conditions" (Frederick G. Winant and John P. Dawson, "The Middle East Supply Program," p. 1).

53. Lloyd, *Food and Inflation,* pp. 99–101.

54. Ibid.

55. Ibid., p. 101 and passim.

56. U.K., Ministry of Information, "Broadcast on Middle East Supply Centre," press release (London, 30 October 1942).

57. "Il Centro per i Rifornimenti del Medio Oriento," *Oriente Moderno* 22 (11 December 1942): 506.

58. Several desperation convoys to Malta were virtually destroyed by air and sea attacks.

59. Lloyd, *Food and Inflation,* p. 91.

60. Kirk, *Middle East in the War,* pp. 218–220.

Chapter 5

1. The history of the first contacts between the U.S. and M.E.S.C. is based on information and documents released to the author during interviews with Winant, Maxwell, Jones, and Boardman, in Washington, 21 August 1952. See also Winant and John P. Dawson, "The Middle East Supply Program," passim.

2. T. Vail Motter, *The Persian Corridor and Aid to Russia,* p. 11; Sir Llewellyn Woodward, *British Foreign Policy in the Second World War,* pp. 161–163; U.S., Department of State, *Foreign Relations of the United States, 1941,* vol. 3, pp. 383–477.

3. Government controls over exports had been instituted in the U.S. in July 1940 under the direction of Col. (later General) Russell L. Maxwell. The principal purpose had been to block the export of materials essential to national defense to Axis destinations. Maxwell has stated that his office started very early to cooperate with British schemes of curbing pre-emption of overseas shipping space by civilian luxury items; it also, according to Maxwell, took pains to strike a rough regional balance in certifying exports to areas such as the Middle East (interview with Maxwell); "Controls of Exports from the United States of Munitions, Materials, and Machinery Essential to National Defense," U.S., Department of State, *Bulletin* 3 (6 July 1940): 11–12.

4. R. M. Leighton and R. W. Coakley, *Global Logistics and Strategy, 1940–1943,* U.S., Department of the Army (Washington, D.C.: Government Printing Office, 1955), pp. 143 ff.; Robert E. Sherwood, *Roosevelt and Hopkins,* p. 440.

5. William L. Langer and J. Everett Gleason, *The Undeclared War, 1940–1941,* pp. 589–592; Winston S. Churchill, *The Grand Alliance,* pp. 424–425.

6. Ibid. Only President Roosevelt's concordance with Churchill's pleas had prevented this view from prevailing in American strategy before and after Pearl Harbor (cf. supra, p. 25).

7. U.S., General Services Administration, *Federal Records of World War II*, vol. 2 (Washington, D.C.: Government Printing Office, 1951), pp. 792–793.

8. William H. McNeill, *America, Britain and Russia, Their Cooperation and Conflict, 1941–1946* (London: Oxford University Press, 1953), p. 267.

9. This one event was to Churchill "one of the heaviest blows I can recall during the war" (idem, *The Hinge of Fate*, p. 382); see also U.S., Department of State, *Foreign Relations, 1942*, vol. 4, pp. 71–87.

10. Churchill, *Hinge of Fate*, p. 521; E. M. H. Lloyd, *Food and Inflation in the Middle East, 1940–1945*, p. 88.

11. K. D. D. Henderson, *The Making of the Modern Sudan*, pp. 250–251.

12. See Frank E. Manuel, *The Realities of American-Palestine Relations* (Washington, D.C.: Public Affairs Press, 1949); Laurence Evans, *United States Policy and the Partition of Turkey, 1914–1924* (Baltimore, Md.: Johns Hopkins Press, 1965); John A. DeNovo, *American Interests and Policies in the Middle East, 1900–1939* (Minneapolis, Minn.: University of Minnesota Press, 1964); Benjamin Shwadran, *The Middle East, Oil, and the Great Powers* (New York: Frederick A. Praeger, 1955); E. A. Speiser, *The United States and the Near East*, rev. ed. (Cambridge: Harvard University Press, 1950).

13. See Cecil B. Brown, *Suez to Singapore*, passim; Frank Gervasi, *War Has Seven Faces* (Garden City, N.Y.: Doubleday, Doran & Co., 1942), passim.

14. U.S., Department of State, *Foreign Relations, 1933*, vol. 2, pp. 320–326.

15. Motter, *Persian Corridor*, p. 7.

16. William A. Eddy, *F.D.R. Meets Ibn Saud* (New York: American Friends of the Middle East, 1954), p. 43; U.S., Department of State, *Foreign Relations, 1941*, vol. 3, pp. 624–651. On 18 July 1941, President Roosevelt noted on a memorandum sent to him by Jesse Jones, Federal Loan Administrator, outlining a program of aid to Saudi Arabia, that he, the President, hoped the British would "take care of" the King of Saudi Arabia. "This is a little far afield for us," was the President's comment (ibid., pp. 642–643).

17. Assistant Director of Naval History, U.S., Department of the Navy, Washington, D.C., to the author, 9 July 1959.

18. Motter, *Persian Corridor*, p. 7.

19. U.S., Foreign Economic Administration, "The Middle East Supply Center," mimeographed (Washington, May 1944), pp. 3–4; Lloyd, *Food and Inflation*, pp. 92–93.

20. H. Duncan Hall, *North American Supplies,* Great Britain, Civil Series, History of the Second World War (London: H.M.S.O., 1955), p. 83.

21. Ibid., pp. 83–85; W. N. Medlicott, *The Economic Blockade,* pp. 352 ff.

22. W. K. Hancock and M. M. Gowing, *British War Economy,* passim; Hall, *North American Supplies,* chaps. 7–9, 11.

23. McNeill, *America, Britain and Russia,* pp. 171–174; Robert E. Sherwood, *Roosevelt and Hopkins,* chaps. 20, 25.

24. Motter, *Persian Corridor,* pp. 4–7, 488, 494, 498–501.

25. Hall, *North American Supplies,* pp. 319–320; Raymond Clapper, "Sky Trail Across Africa," *Palestine Post* (Jerusalem), 12 December 1942, p. 1; Ephraim Gordon Erickson, "Protest Society: Social Irrationality in the Extra-Territorial One-Sex Company Town," passim.

26. Grace A. Witherow, "Cash Foreign Trade of the United States During the War Years," *Foreign Commerce Weekly* 19 (19 May 1945): 7; U.S., Department of State, "Official History of Lend-Lease, Middle East, Part 2: Civilian Lend-Lease" [by Letitia Lewis]. (Washington, D.C.: n.d.), p. 52.

27. U.S., General Services Administration, *Federal Records of World War II,* vol. 2, pp. 792–794.

28. Motter, *Persian Corridor,* pp. 163–164, 449; Memorandum, "American Missions in Iran," prepared by Culbertson Mission (n.d.); U.S. Army, Persian Gulf Command, Office of the Fiscal Adviser, "Irrigation in Iran," (Teheran, March 1944) (Private Papers of William S. Culbertson); U.S., Department of State, *Foreign Relations, 1942,* vol. 4, pp. 222–263.

29. Motter, *Persian Corridor,* pp. 165, 449.

30. On the appointment of a Minister Resident in Saudi Arabia and the opening of a Consulate in Dhahran see U.S., Department of State, *Foreign Relations, 1943,* vol. 4, pp. 830–840; on the appointment by the U.S. of a Diplomatic Agent accredited to Syria and Lebanon and the general question of the recognition of the two states see idem, *Foreign Relations, 1941,* vol. 3, pp. 785 ff. and *Foreign Relations, 1942,* vol. 4, pp. 641 ff.

31. U.S., Office of War Information, *American Handbook* (Washington, D.C.: Public Affairs Press, 1945), pp. 16–66; Motter, *Persian Corridor,* p. 447 ff.; U.S., Department of State, *Bulletin* 6 (28 March 1942): 261; ibid., 13 (27 December 1945): 339; U.S., Foreign Economic Administration, "Middle East Supply Center," passim; George Lenczowski, *Russia and the West in Iran* (Ithaca, N.Y.: Cornell University Press, 1949), p. 271; M.E.S.C., "Organization and Policy Handbook," pp. 1–3.

32. The paramount role of American equipment in the battle that made Montgomery's reputation is amply documented by numerous chroniclers (including Montgomery himself). Of special interest is the book by Capt. B. H. Liddell Hart, *The Tanks: The History of the Royal Tank Regiment,* 2 vols. (New York: Frederick A. Praeger, 1959). As cited by Gordon Harrison in his book review (*New York Times Book Review,* 12 April 1959, p. 36), Capt. Hart, one of Britain's best-known writers on mil-

itary affairs, argues vigorously that Montgomery (who has written a fore-word to the book) became the victor of El Alamein chiefly by the grace of timing in the arrival of supplies. According to Hart, Auchinleck after set-ting the stage for victory in North Africa, was sacrificed to the political demand for a change, just before the tanks he needed to win could arrive. See also Sir Arthur Bryant, *The Turn of the Tide, 1939–1943: A Study Based on the Diaries and Autobiographical Notes of Field Marshal the Viscount Alanbrooke* (London: William Collins Sons & Co., 1957), chaps. 9–10.

33. Lloyd, *Food and Inflation,* p. 81; interview with Orchard.

34. "The Middle East I: Food and Politics," *Economist* 144 (20 February 1943): 231. [Author's italics.]

35. Michael Straight, *Make This the Last War: The Future of the United Nations* (New York: Harcourt, Brace Co., 1943), p. 78.

36. E. L. Hargreaves and M. M. Gowing, *Civil Industry and Trade,* p. 172.

37. McNeill, *America, Britain and Russia,* p. 150.

38. H. Duncan Hall and C. C. Wrigley, *Studies of Overseas Supply,* passim; Hargreaves and Gowing, *Civil Industry and Trade,* passim; S. McKee Rosen, *The Combined Boards of the Second World War: An Ex-periment in International Administration,* passim; McNeill, *America, Britain and Russia,* pp. 749–750.

39. Ibid.

40. Langer and Gleason, *Undeclared War,* pp. 433–435; Churchill, *Grand Alliance,* p. 417; Lloyd, *Food and Inflation,* p. 91.

41. Langer and Gleason, *Undeclared War,* pp. 397–401; Churchill, *Grand Alliance,* p. 110.

42. Churchill, *Grand Alliance,* p. 282. An important byproduct of the Donovan visit was an intensification of U.S. exertions in Turkey. These in-cluded not only the accelerated shipment of arms and grains to the An-kara Government, but various economic warfare interventions at a time when the British were running short of adequate means to counteract the unrestrained German campaign of political bribery through commerce (David J. Dallin, *Soviet Russia's Foreign Policy,* p. 406).

43. Churchill, *Grand Alliance,* p. 754.

44. Edward R. Stettinius, Jr., *Lend-Lease: Weapon for Victory* (New York: Macmillan & Co., 1944), p. 94.

45. Sherwood, *Roosevelt and Hopkins,* p. 301; Churchill, *Grand Alli-ance,* pp. 351, 764–765, 794; Brown, *Suez to Singapore,* p. 36; Langer and Gleason, *Undeclared War,* p. 780.

46. See fn. supra; Lloyd, *Food and Inflation,* p. 91.

47. Motter, *Persian Corridor,* pp. 7–27; Sherwood, *Roosevelt and Hop-kins,* p. 301.

48. Motter, *Persian Corridor,* chaps. 1–3; idem, pp. 73, 140–145, 276.

49. Ibid., p. 16. In addition to Harriman, James Roosevelt, who also

had toured the Middle East in 1941, and Harry Hopkins, who adopted the aid to Russia program as his special province, had a hand in framing this document (ibid., chaps. 1, 2).

50. Ibid.

51. Motter, *Persian Corridor,* passim.

Chapter 6

1. E. M. H. Lloyd, *Food and Inflation in the Middle East,* 1940–1945, p. 93.

2. M.E.S.C., "Organization and Policy Handbook," p. 3. The regular spokesman for the Minister was Sir Arthur Rucker, his Secretary.

3. U.S., Bureau of the Budget, Special Mission, U.S. Embassy, London, "Regional Organization in the Middle East" [by Eric H. Biddle], vol. 1, pp. 84 ff.; Francis Boardman, "Civilian Requirements from War to Peace: The Middle East Supply Center," p. 994; Frederick G. Winant and John P. Dawson, "The Middle East Supply Program," p. 3 ff.

4. Interview with Moffat, New York, 24 October 1952.

5. Winant and Dawson, "Supply Program," p. 9; interview with Winant. As early as May 1942, the Chief of the Division of Near Eastern Affairs in the Department of State had urged, in the light of the critical situation in the Western Desert in the Spring of 1942, that the U.S. appoint an overall political representative in the Middle East, equal in rank and function to the British Minister of State, with a high-ranking military advisor. This proposal, though endorsed by the Secretary of State, was rejected by the War Department because the Middle East "theater of activity was allocated to the British" (U.S., Department of State, *Foreign Relations of the United States, 1942,* vol. 4, pp. 76–78).

6. See announcements in U.S., Department of State, *Bulletin* 9 (11 September 1943): 167 and *New York Times,* 11 September 1943, p. 1.

7. Interview with Winant, Washington, D.C., 29 August 1952; Don Lohbeck, *Patrick J. Hurley, an American* (Chicago: Henry Regnery Co., 1956), p. 189.

8. U.S., Department of State, *Bulletin* 9 (11 September 1943): 167; *New York Times,* 11 September 1943. As noted infra, Landis arrived in Cairo in December 1943. After having familiarized himself with conditions in the Middle East and the operations of the M.E.S.C., Landis in February 1944 wrote a draft letter for the signature of President Roosevelt describing Landis' responsibilities and authority and outlining the goals of American policy as they might be implemented through the association of the U.S. with M.E.S.C. This draft letter was rewritten by Harry Hopkins and submitted to the President. It laid very heavy emphasis on encouraging vigorous and independent policies by the indigenous governments of the Middle East and a strong American stand against any form of discrimination. On 12 February the President sent the draft to Stettin-

ius, then Acting Secretary of State, saying that though he liked the general ideas presented in the draft, he wanted the State Department to submit a redraft because he thought the Landis-Hopkins version "emphasizes too much our economic interests and looks too much as though we were trying to steal the economic position away from the other nations" (U.S., National Archives, Department of State, 800.24/1541). The final version as signed by the President and transmitted to Landis on 6 March 1944, while retaining the fundamental principles of Landis and Hopkins, modified their expression considerably and defined the major task of Landis as "primarily the conduct of economic activities relating to the war" in the course of which he would "put first the strengthening in every way the warm and cooperative relations with our Allies, upon which our success in the war, and thereafter, so largely depend" (U.S., Department of State, *Foreign Relations, 1944*, vol. 5, pp. 1–2).

9. Interview with Landis; F. Lawrence Babcock, "The Explosive Middle East," *Fortune* 30 (September 1944): 116 ff.

10. U.S., Foreign Economic Administration, "The Middle East Supply Center," passim.

11. Boardman, "Civilian Requirements," passim; Dawson to Mangouni, 30 December 1970. Colonel Hoskins, a man with wide experience in the Middle East, had been sent on a mission to the Governments of the Middle East in the Fall of 1942 to explain the position of the U.S. Government on questions affecting the interests of Middle East states. The mission had been organized with the full support of the President during the previous Summer when Allied fortunes in the area were at their lowest and before the British victory at El Alamein. The most important subject that the Hoskins Mission discussed was the question of the future of Palestine (U.S., Department of State, *Foreign Relations, 1942*, vol. 5, pp. 24–36).

12. Interview with Woodbridge.

13. Note, for example, the general inability of the "Combined" (Anglo-American) Boards for Production and Resources, for Food, for Shipping Adjustment, and for Munitions Assignments to progress beyond the stage of across-the-table bargaining of national positions (William H. McNeill, *America, Britain and Russia, Their Co-operation and Conflict, 1941–1946*, pp. 112–137; S. McKee Rosen, *The Combined Boards of the Second World War: An Experiment in International Administration*, passim).

14. James M. Landis, "Anglo-American Cooperation in the Middle East," *Annals* 240 (July 1945): 64–72. Interview with Livingston L. Short, New York, 21 September 1951. On the change in American attitude towards economic cooperation with Britain after the German threat to the Middle East had been defeated, see infra, chap. 10. See also n. 8, supra, for letter from Roosevelt to Landis in March 1944 outlining American economic policy in the Middle East.

15. Interviews with Macduffie, Winant, Woodbridge, and Levison.

16. Interviews with Jackson, Winant, and Macduffie; Lloyd, *Food and Inflation*, p. 98.

17. Interview, 14 August 1952.

18. Interview with Douglas M. Moffat, New York, 24 October 1952.

19. Lloyd, *Food and Inflation*, p. 98.

20. Ibid., p. 94. Among the Americans who served on this committee at various times were W. Averell Harriman, U.S. lend-lease coordinator; James W. Riddleberger, and Winthrop J. Brown.

21. Ibid., p. 95; Winant and Dawson, "Supply Program," p. 7 ff.; *New York Times*, 16 October 1944. Under U.S. law, the Foreign Economic Administration, created in 1943 from an amalgamation of several agencies, licensed most non-military exports and authorized non-military Lendlease shipments. For Middle Eastern purposes, F.E.A. delegated its powers to CAMES as its "certifying agency." For this purpose F.E.A. issued to CAMES every six months a "program license" stating maximum totals for various commodities that were expected to be available for Middle Eastern use in the six months ahead; CAMES then "certified" individual shipments, guided by M.E.S.C. listings. The six-month "programs" were worked out by the Middle East Division of F.E.A. from data submitted by M.E.S.C. and reviewed by the Policy Committee of CAMES (Leo T. Crowley, "The Foreign Economic Administration," *Foreign Commerce Weekly* 14 [5 February 1944], passim; Winant and Dawson, "Supply Program," passim; Philip Young, "F.E.A. Functions in the Export Field," *Foreign Commerce Weekly*, 15 [15 April 1944]: 8; "Program License Authorizing Exportations to the Middle East," *Foreign Commerce Weekly* 13 [16 October 1943]: 36). No other area of the world receiving U.S. nonmilitary supplies was given a preferential regime of this nature (interview with Orchard).

22. H. Duncan Hall, *North American Supplies*, passim; T. Vail Motter, *The Persian Corridor and Aid to Russia*, p. 450 ff.

23. It was also a tribute to the tact and diplomacy of Britain's representatives in CAMES who, like the American spokesmen in the Middle East Supplies Committee in London, made but sparing use of their prerogatives (interviews with Winant, Cristelow, Winthrop Brown, and James W. Riddleberger, Washington, D.C., 22 August 1952).

24. Interview with Winant; Lloyd, *Food and Inflation*, pp. 94–95.

25. Interviews with Winant, Woodbridge, and Rex A. Anderson, Washington, 14 July 1951; U.S., Foreign Economic Administration, "The Middle East Supply Center," p. 23; Winant and Dawson, "Supply Program," pp. 8–9. American sources had special praise for the assistance received from Paul A. Wilson and David Greenhill, of the British Treasury Mission; Allan Cristelow, of the British Supply Council; and F. J. Brown, manager of the New York office of the U.K.C.C. Cristelow and Brown served longest in their respective assignments and became part of the

British contingent of CAMES—Cristelow as member of the executive committee and Brown as manager of its New York office (CAMES absorbed the U.K.C.C. office in New York early in 1944).

26. Interview with Winant; Lloyd, *Food and Inflation*, pp. 94–95.

27. George Kirk, *The Middle East in the War*, pp. 344–368.

28. "Exchange of Correspondence between Col. J. J. Llewellin, Minister Resident in Washington for Supply, United Kingdom, and Thomas K. Finletter, Special Assistant to the Secretary of State, United States, Aug. 5, 1943 to Oct. 15, 1943," furnished to the author during interview with Winant.

29. See chap. 7; also memorandum, U.K., British Ministry of Supply Mission, New York, "The Flow of Civilian Requirements to the Middle East-Persian Gulf Area," 30 April 1943. A very helpful factor was the experience which the predominately British staff of the CAMES office had accumulated between 1940 and 1941 in the Port of New York while allocating space on British vessels on behalf of the British Ministry of War Transport and the U.K.C.C.

30. Lloyd, *Food and Inflation*, p. 107.

31. In other words, the question had to be settled whether at a particular time a certain commodity or shipping convoy should come from an American or British-controlled source, so as to minimize the strain on the total facilities of the Allies.

32. U.S., Department of State, *Foreign Relations, 1943*, vol. 14, pp. 1–5.

33. Interview with Orchard.

34. Interview with Cristelow.

35. Interview with Dr. Mohammed A. Rifaat, Cairo, 20 July 1954.

36. Interview with Cristelow.

37. Interviews with Winant and Anderson.

38. Ibid.; U.S., Department of State, "Official History of Lend-Lease, Middle East, Part II: Civilian Lend-Lease" [by Letitia Lewis], p. 44 ff.

39. Lloyd, *Food and Inflation*, p. 81.

40. M.E.S.C., "Handbook," p. 3.

41. Interviews with Cristelow.

42. Interview with Biddle.

43. In other words, the threat to recommend against allocation of shipping space to a local area. See p. 76, infra.

44. Lloyd, *Food and Inflation*, pp. 90–91.

45. Grace A. Witherow, "Cash Foreign Trade of the United States During the War Years," p. 7; U.S., Department of Commerce, *International Transactions of the United States During the War, 1940–1945* (Washington, D.C.: Government Printing Office, 1948), passim.

46. In April also Rashid Ali al-Kaylani launched his putsch against the Regent of Iraq and the Anglo-Iraqi alliance, with reverberations throughout the Arab world (Kirk, *Middle East,* pp. 56–77; interview with Nathir Akram Umari, New York, 15 February 1954).

47. See chap. 4, supra.

48. Lloyd, *Food and Inflation*, p. 114.

49. Palestine, War Supply Board, miscellaneous files from 1940–1945, seen at Archives of State of Israel, Hakirya; Lloyd, *Food and Inflation*, passim.

50. How governments occasionally did call M.E.S.C.'s hand is exemplified by the following incident reported by Marshall Macduffie: At one point, the Egyptian authorities were asked by the Centre to buy water disinfectants in Palestine instead of the U.S., to save shipping. The Egyptians demurred on the grounds that the substitutes were several times as costly as the American product. When M.E.S.C. tried to persist, the Egyptian representative dared the agency to shoulder the responsibility for an outbreak of epidemic diseases in his country, and won his point.

51. William R. Polk and W. Jack Butler, "What the Arabs Think," *Headline Series of the Foreign Policy Association* 96 (November–December 1952), passim.

52. William H. McNeill, *America, Britain and Russia, Their Co-operation and Conflict, 1941–1946*, pp. 40–41, 99, 462; Kirk, *Middle East*, pp. 24–25, 361, 433; Charles O. van der Plas, "Some Aspects of Postwar Problems in the Netherlands East Indies," *Agenda* 1 (October 1942): 329–338.

53. Lohbeck, *Patrick J. Hurley*, p. 119.

54. Lloyd, *Food and Inflation*, p. 97.

55. E. A. Speiser, *The United States and the Near East*, pp. 238–239; James L. Barton, *The Story of Near East Relief*, passim; Frederick G. Winant, "United States Economic Policy in the Middle East" (Washington, 12 September 1944) (Private Papers of William S. Culbertson).

56. This was clearly demonstrated in Iran where the British occupation army, the British Embassy, U.K.C.C., and the Minister of State urged numerous steps for the management of food supply, the control of inflation, and the firming of internal security on the Teheran government, but saw them fully implemented only after American advisers and experts were consulted by the Iranians or placed in charge of specific programs by them (Motter, *Persian Corridor*, chap. 20; Lloyd, *Food and Inflation*, chaps. 18, 25, 28).

57. Interviews with Winant, Macduffie, and Landis. Americans were not the only beneficiaries of this strategy. In Syria and Lebanon, Maj. Gen. Sir Edward Spears, representing Britain, had far less trouble in instituting a system of compulsory grain collection than did agents of the Free French "Delegation" speaking for the French overlord after the expulsion of Vichy forces (Lloyd, *Food and Inflation*, chap. 17; F. Lawrence Babcock, "The Explosive Middle East," p. 103 ff.).

58. Interview with Landis.

59. M.E.S.C., *The Proceedings of the Conference on Middle East Agricultural Development, Cairo, February 7th-10th, 1944*, Agricultural

Reports, no. 6 (Cairo: M.E.F. Printing and Stationery Services, 1944), passim; Kirk, *Middle East*, p. 255.

60. See chap. 2; interviews with Landis, Jackson, and Woodbridge.

61. Times *(London)*, 10 April 1945.

62. Ibid.; "An International Example," passim; Kirk, *Middle East*, p. 189.

63. Among all former officials of M.E.S.C. questioned on this aspect, there is unanimity that the American refusal to go along killed the plan for a permanent Supply Centre in the Middle East. See chap. 10, supra.

64. Lloyd, *Food and Inflation*, chaps. 13–15.

65. Interview with Winant.

66. Lloyd, *Food and Inflation*, passim.

67. Contrary to American practice, the British government constantly stresses the importance of keeping its foreign-based personnel fully informed of all world-wide developments that may have even remote relevance to their assignments. Thus it happened that Britons in Cairo knew ahead of their American friends of an impending visit of the Truman Committee investigating the U.S. war effort on behalf of the United States Congress (interviews with Macduffie and Maxwell).

68. Lloyd, *Food and Inflation*, pp. 149, 171.

69. Motter, *Persian Corridor*, passim.

70. Lloyd, *Food and Inflation*, passim.

71. Interviews with Macduffie and Mills.

72. See chap. 6.

73. Interview with Macduffie.

74. Lloyd, *Food and Inflation*, p. 88.

75. Ibid., p. 164; Kirk, *Middle East in the War*, p. 184.

76. Motter, Persian Corridor, chap. 20. This was but one of many wartime examples of the fundamental objection of U.S. generals to consider the political aspect of their strategy (McNeill, *America, Britain and Russia*, p. 750). See also U.S., Department of State, *Foreign Relations, 1943*, vol. 4, pp. 384 ff., passim.

77. M.E.S.C., *Proceedings*, passim.

78. Interviews with Boardman, Winant, and Frechtling.

79. See chap. 4.

80. His reticence was undoubtedly made easier by the fact that both Jackson and Casey were Australians and found it easy to establish a personal relationship which ignored prerogatives of rank and title.

81. Lloyd, *Food and Inflation*, p. 85; interview with Jackson.

Chapter 7

1. The information detailed in this chapter on the structure and procedures of M.E.S.C. has been drawn in the main from the following

sources: M.E.S.C., "Organization and Policy Handbook"; Palestine, War Supply Board, miscellaneous files; Private Papers of Marshall Macduffie and William S. Culbertson; Frederick G. Winant and John P. Dawson, "The Middle East Supply Program"; M.E.S.C., "The M.E.S.C. Story"; E. M. H. Lloyd, *Food and Inflation in the Middle East, 1940*–1945, pts. 2, 3, 5; E. M. Nicholson to the author, New York, 16 September 1952; R. W. Bailey to the author, Washington, D.C., 14 November 1952; James M. Landis to the author, New York, 12 July 1951; John P. Dawson to the author, Ann Arbor, Mich., 18 October 1951; interviews with Winant, Jackson, Macduffie, Rifaat, Empson, Cristelow, Jones, Landis, Prior, Woodbridge, R. W. Bailey, Dr. E. E. Bailey (London, 7 September 1954), Francis Kettaneh (New York, 31 January 1953), Sir Reader Bullard (New York, 15 January 1953), N. Lardicos (Cairo, 19 July 1954), John McCloud (New York, 25 December 1954), R. C. Thompson (New York, 12 December 1954), A. H. Hamdy (Cairo, 10 July 1954), and Thomas J. Higgins (New York, 31 May 1956); U.S., Office of War Information; "The Middle East Supply Center," *Foreign Commerce Weekly* 11 (5 June 1943): 8 ff.; "The Middle East Supply Center," *Bulletin of International News* 21 (5 August 1944): 619–625, 21 (2 September 1944): 707–712; "Middle East Supply Centre," *Economist* 141 (15 November 1941): 604; and "F.E.A. Licensing Policy for Shipments to the Middle East (Current Export Bulletin no. 242)," *Foreign Commerce Weekly* 19 (12 May 1945): 54. The following documents of M.E.S.C. also were consulted: "Note on the Food Situation in Central and North East Saudi Arabia" (Cairo, November 1943); "Circular Letter PS/90"; "Memorandum Regarding Proposed Scheme for Centralised Purchase of Cotton Piecegoods in India" (Cairo, June 1943); "Plan of Organization" (June 1943); "supplies from North America" (Cairo, n.d.); "Territorial Papers Submitted to the Middle East Financial Conference, Cairo, April 1944" (Cairo, 1944). A further list of other documents and reports bearing upon the Middle East economy, developed by M.E.S.C. and the Spears Mission and other agencies, is included in Appendix B.

2. Like most civilian establishments of the U.K. in military operations areas, M.E.S.C. at this point was administered and stratified on military lines. Its staff had army ranks and pay and wore appropriate uniforms. This arrangement was continued during the initial phase of U.S. co-sponsorship. The new American staff members donned British uniforms and enjoyed all the office privileges and personal conveniences available to British officers of their rank in the Middle East Command area; only the pay came from the U.S. purse. Jackson, as Director General, was one of the few exceptions to the uniform policy: as a commander in the Royal Australian Navy, he was outranked by several subordinate to him in the M.E.S.C. structure, and, although given the simulated rank of Major General, wore mufti.

3. The procurement overseas of certain equipment and commodity items was effected outside the normal private trade channels and therefore outside the scope of local import licenses. Certain staple goods fell under the "bulk indent" system described elsewhere in this chapter. The needs of public utility plants and certain manufacturing and servicing facilities performing mainly for the Middle East Provisions Office of the Middle East Command were reported to the Centre separately under the label of "requirements of sponsored undertakings." The demands of the petroleum companies were collected and screened by the Middle East Petroleum Committee and, like the "sponsored" items, were placed without changes into M.E.S.C.'s monthly program. For a considerable period the railroads of the region were supervised by the British forces which also looked after their equipment needs.

4. It was the policy of the Centre to avoid as much as possible a rupture in the traditional trading patterns of the Middle East. It was considered not only fair but expedient to keep alive long established connections between Middle Eastern importers and their old overseas exporters. One compelling reason for this was the matter of servicing and spare parts for imported equipment; for example, to shift truck parts procurement from British to American sources would give rise to serious maintenance problems. Therefore, in designating the "loading area" for individual licenses the original preference of the importer was respected whenever feasible. Often, however, inter-Allied decisions to concentrate the production of certain commodities in one particular area blocked such endeavor.

5. The mounting of a new Allied offensive, a heavy convoy calamity, or the liberation of a famished area could cut suddenly and deeply into the shipping pool. For example, the preparations for the North Africa landing imposed a 50 per cent cut in the original shipping allocation for the Middle East.

6. The close cooperation between shipping authorities and expediters for Middle Eastern cargoes in British and American ports occasionally produced an unexpected bonus. Production or inland transport delays sometimes prevented a cargo from being delivered aboard within the stipulated time. Rather than have the ship leave partially empty the maritime dispatchers would agree to fill the space with items that had not been cleared through the various control states. In this case, CAMES or S.S.M.E. could stage a last-minute roundup of goods stranded in port warehouses or resting in dealers' stocks. Thus, an occasional shipment of long-absent luxuries or semi-luxuries would legally slip into the Middle East and bring delight to a merchant and his customers.

7. Reimbursable lend-lease shipments were handled in the same manner as regular lend-lease shipments, particularly as far as procurement, priorities, transportation, and delivery were concerned; however, instead

of being posted to the balance sheet of lend-lease and reverse lend-lease, these shipments must be settled at regular intervals by dollar transfers to the U.S. By the fall of 1943 lend-lease was administered by the F.E.A. Dawson to Mangouni, 30 December 1970.

8. M.E.S.C., "The M.E.S.C. Story," p. 12.

9. Such requests were frequent, and difficult to reject, even though past evidence showed that the cars invariably went to the black market.

10. Walter Diamond to Harvey H. Hall, Washington, D.C., 27 February 1952.

11. Helen Kitchen, *"Al-Ahram:* The *Times* of the Arab World," *Middle East Journal* 4 (Spring 1950): 155–169.

Chapter 8

1. Data and background material for this case history were obtained by the author during visits to Omdourman, Khartoum, and Cairo in 1954. Research included interviews in Khartoum with N. Seroussi and Hassan Abdul Aziz, as well as officials of the Ministry of Commerce, Industry, and Supply of the Government of the Sudan, and in London with L. Eisinger (13 September 1954).

2. See chaps. 2, 3, supra; also Zionist Organization of America, *Palestine Yearbook, Volume 2: 5707 (1945–1946)* (New York, 1946), pp. 106, 376.

3. Ibid.

4. United Nations, Secretariat, Department of Economic Affairs, *Review of Economic Conditions in the Middle East* (New York, March 1951), pp. 15–16, 52–57.

5. Ibid., p. 16.

6. Ibid.; Zionist Organization of America, *Palestine Yearbook,* pp. 169–187; Government of Palestine, *Statistical Abstract of Palestine, 1944–1945* (Jerusalem, 1945), p. 51.

7. See U.K., Board of Trade, *Overseas Economic Surveys for Egypt* (1947–48), *Palestine* (1945), *Iraq* (1948), *Iran* (1948), and *Turkey* (1947) (London: H.M.S.O.); "Syria and Lebanon: Economic Conditions," *Foreign Commerce Weekly* 15 (29 April 1944): 17 ff. Gaston Leduc, *L'Evolution économique du Moyen-Orient,* pp. 284–300; U.K., Colonial Office, *Annual Report on Aden and Aden Protectorate, 1946,* passim; Republic of Lebanon, *The Economic Development of Lebanon,* Report to the Government of Lebanon by Sir Alexander Gibb and Partners (London, 1948), passim.

8. Nahum Goldmann, "An Eye-Witness Report on Jewish Palestine," *Free World* 9 (January 1945): 47 ff.

9. Interviews with Dr. Alfred Michaelis (New York, 14 October 1953), S. Mizrachi (Beirut, 2 July 1954), S. Lackany Bey (Cairo, 10 July 1954), and E. Witcon (Jerusalem, 2 September 1954).

10. U.K., Ministry of Information, Overseas Publicity Telegram, "British Army Brings Development to the Middle East" (London, 3 December 1942); Zionist Organization of America, *Palestine Yearbook*, pp. 376–378.

11. Joel Sayre, *Persian Gulf Command* (New York: Random House, 1945), p. 78; interview with Hamdy; Zionist Organization of America, *Palestine Yearbook*, pp. 378–379.

12. R. J. Collins, *Lord Wavell (1883–1941)*, passim; George Kirk, *The Middle East in the War*, p. 168; Memorandum, Jewish Agency for Palestine, Economic Research Institute, "Economic War Policy in Palestine" [by D. Horowitz] (Jerusalem, 17 February 1941), passim; "Repercussions Economiques de l'Occupation de la Syrie et du Liban par les Forces Alliées," *Commerce du Levant* (Beirut), 5 December 1941; R. el-Mallakh, "The Effects of the Second World War on the Economic Development of Egypt," Ph.D. dissertation, Rutgers University, Department of Economics, 1954, passim; René Francis, *Egypt and Industry* (Cairo, 1949), p. 16; Sayre, *Persian Gulf Command*, passim.

13. See chap. 2, supra.

14. Ibid.

15. Memorandum, "Economic War Policy in Palestine," passim; interviews with Witcon and Bonné, and Ettan Ezrachi (New York, 6 February 1953).

16. See chap. 9, infra.

17. Zionist Organization of America, *Palestine Yearbook*, pp. 101–125.

18. H. Duncan Hall and C. C. Wrigley, *Studies of Overseas Supply*, passim.

19. The following information on the activity of the Materials Division is based, unless otherwise stated, on these sources: M.E.S.C., "Organization and Policy Handbook," pp. 65–75; M.E.S.C., "The M.E.S.C. Story," pt. 3; E. M. H. Lloyd, *Food and Inflation in the Middle East, 1940–1945*, chaps. 11–13; interviews with Macduffie, Eisinger, Jackson, and Gordon. See also M.E.S.C., "Plan of Organization," chart on pp. 204–205, infra.

20. The U.S.C.C. was formed in 1943 by the U.S. Government as a counterpart to the U.K.C.C. It never attained the scope of the U.K.C.C. Its activities were principally directed at purchases of scarce raw materials in all parts of the world not under Axis control (see Leo T. Crowley, "The United States Commercial Company," *Foreign Commerce Weekly* 15 [24 June 1944]); interview with Arthur D. Schulte, New York, 20 March 1956.

21. Interview with Woodbridge.

22. M.E.S.C., "Handbook," pp. 74–75.

23. Interviews with Hamdy, Michaels, Kamil Azmi (Cairo, 15 July 1954), and George Phares (Damascus, 7 July 1954).

24. Lloyd, *Food and Inflation*, p. 87.

25. Government of Palestine, *Palestine War Supply Board* (Jerusalem, June 1942), p. 6.

26. Ibid. The influence of M.E.S.C. is shown both in the timing and the type of industrial growth.

27. United Nations, Department of Economic Affairs, *Review of Economic Conditions in the Middle East*, pp. 70–71; M.E.S.C., Secretariat, "Handbook," p. 1.

28. See chap. 2, supra.

29. M.E.S.C., "Handbook," pp. 10, 12, 14.

30. Lloyd, *Food and Inflation*, passim; Keith A. H. Murray, "Feeding the Middle East in War-time," pp. 233–247.

31. Lloyd, *Food and Inflation*, pp. 130–131; Kirk, *Middle East*, p. 180; U.S., Department of State, *Foreign Relations of the United States, 1942* vol. 4, pp. 120–222.

32. The following information on the activities of the Food and Agriculture Division was derived, unless otherwise noted, from Lloyd, *Food and Inflation*, passim; Murray, "Feeding the Middle East," passim; "The Middle East I: Food and Politics," *Economist* 144 (20 February 1943): 230–231; M.E.S.C., "Handbook," pp. 14–17, 51–64; M.E.S.C., "The M.E.S.C. Story," pt. 2; Kirk, *Middle East in the War*, pp. 169–192; "The Middle East Supply Center," *Bulletin of International News*, passim; U.K., British Military Mission in the Levant, "Memorandum on Rationing in Syria and Lebanon" (Beirut, 3 August 1943). The following publications and documents of the M.E.S.C. also were consulted: *M.E.S.C.: "Some Facts About the Middle East Supply Centre* (Cairo: Nile Press, 1944), passim; "Notes on Middle East Cereals Position, 1942–1943," mimeographed (Cairo, 11 May 1942); *The Proceedings of the Conference on Middle East Agricultural Development, Cairo, February 7th–10th, 1944*, passim.

33. Lloyd, *Food and Inflation*, pp. 110–112. See also Appendix A, Table 1.

34. M.E.S.C. sent several agricultural survey missions through the Middle East between 1942 and 1944. Many of their reports are included in the Bibliography, infra.

35. See M.E.S.C. in Appendix B, infra.

36. Lloyd, *Food and Inflation*, chaps. 17, 31.

37. Ibid., chap. 31.

38. See Appendix A, Table 2.

39. See Appendix A, Table 3.

40. Lloyd, *Food and Inflation*, p. 324.

41. Ibid., pp. 327–328.

42. Ibid., pp. 3–4, chap. 34.

43. Information on the transport situation in the Middle East during World War II, and the activities of the M.E.S.C. Division of Transport, was derived from the following sources, unless otherwise noted: M.E.S.C., "Handbook," pp. 19–20, 76–131; M.E.S.C., "M.E.S.C. Story," pp. 52–54; M.E.S.C., *M.E.S.C.: Some Facts*, passim; M.E.S.C., "Report on Visit to Palestine" [by R. H. Court] (Cairo, 10 December 1944) and "Report on a Visit to Ethiopia" [by A. F. Anderson] (Cairo, 1944); interviews with

John F. Coneybear (New York, 12 December 1952), William A. Gordon, Francis H. Kettaneh (New York, 6 February 1953), and George A. Apelian, owner, Fabrique Nationale de Chaussures en Caoutchouc, Bourj Hammoud, Lebanon (Bois de Boulogne, Lebanon, 5 August 1970); F. H. Kettaneh, "From Chariots to Tanks," *Rotarian* 60 (May 1942): 16–20; Chester Wardlow, *The Transportation Corps: Responsibilities, Organization, and Operations*, U.S. Army (Washington, D.C.: Government Printing Office, 1951), pp. 4, 11, 22; T. Vail Motter, *The Persian Corridor and Aid to Russia*, passim.

44. See end of chap. 6.

45. Interview with Sir Reader Bullard; William H. McNeill, *America, Britain and Russia, Their Co-operation and Conflict, 1941–1946*, pp. 56–60.

46. This was not always a one-way street. On a number of occasions tires and parts of various sizes were interchanged between army and civilian stocks. This helped military transport officers eliminate "misfits" between vehicles and parts owing to lags in collateral procurement, unexpected rates of losses in certain vehicle types and mingling of U.S. and British equipment.

47. Note the following pronouncement of the Palestine War Supply Board: "Petrol is rationed (although ample supplies are available, petrol being a byproduct of the refinement of the crude oil which is brought in by the pipe line from Iraq to Haifa) so as to keep non-essential vehicles in gentle [*sic*] use" (Government of Palestine, *Palestine War Supply Board*, p. 5).

48. The effects on imports and use of vehicles can be seen from the following examples: During 1943 only 333 automobiles, trucks, and chassis were imported into Egypt as compared with 6,969 in 1938 (Egyptian Ministry of Finance trade statistics). In Palestine only 31 private automobiles and taxis were newly registered as compared with 532 in 1939 (*Statistical Abstract of Palestine, 1944–1945*, p. 251).

49. Unless otherwise noted, the following description of its work is based on the following sources: M.E.S.C., "Handbook," pp. 20–21, 82–84; M.E.S.C., "M.E.S.C. Story," chap. 11; Lloyd, *Food and Inflation*, pp. 8, 316, 336; interviews with Henry Van Zile Hyde, M.D. (Washington, 15 August 1951), E. B. Worthington (New York, 23 March 1953), Filippo Pansera, M.D. (Cairo, 18 July 1954), B. Mavromichalis (New York, 12 January 1953), and Jackson; Doreen Warriner, *Land and Poverty in the Middle East* (London: R.I.I.A., 1948), passim; E. B. Worthington, *Middle East Science: A Survey of Subjects Other Than Agriculture*, chaps. 12–14; Royal Institute of International Affairs, *The Middle East: A Political and Economic Survey* (London, 1951) passim.

50. M.E.S.C., "Handbook," p. 12.

51. Alfred Bonné, *The Economic Development of the Middle East* (New York: Oxford University Press, 1945), pp. 30–32.

52. See Lloyd, *Food and Inflation*, p. 336, and *Statistical Abstract for*

Palestine, 1944–1945, pp. 26–29. Lloyd cites declines in infant mortality in Palestine, Cyprus, and Egypt during the war years. The Palestine *Abstract* further shows the following data for average life expectancy in the two principal ethnic census groups:

	1936–38	*1942–44*
Muslims		
Male	46.70	49.35
Female	48.53	50.40
Jews		
Male	60.79	64.13
Female	64.47	65.87

53. Worthington, *Middle East Science*, chap. 12.

Chapter 9

1. See April 1944 issues of *Egyptian Gazette* (Cairo), *Egyptian Mail* (Cairo), *Palestine Post* (Jerusalem), *Commerce du Levant* (Beirut), and *Journal de Teheran*.

2. M.E.S.C., "Proceedings of the Middle East Financial Conference, April 24–29, 1944" (Cairo, 1944).

3. Ibid.

4. Interviews with Macduffie.

5. Ibid.; interviews with Apelian, Kettaneh, Azmi, Mavromichalis, Michaelis, Ezrachi, and Mizrachi.

6. Interview with Jackson.

7. E. M. H. Lloyd, *Food and Inflation in the Middle East, 1940–1945*, pt. 4; M.E.S.C., "The M.E.S.C. Story," ch. 13; R. S. Sayers, *Financial Policy, 1939–45*, United Kingdom Series, History of the Second World War (London: H.M.S.O., 1956), passim; M.E.S.C., "Proceedings," passim.

8. F. Lawrence Babcock, "The Explosive Middle East," pp. 113 ff.; interview with Moffat.

9. Interview with Bullard.

10. Lord Moyne, the Deputy Minister of State, in his opening remarks as chairman of the Financial Conference, specifically referred to this interpretation. He understood, he said, that in the French language the word "inflation" meant expansion of currency base on government borrowing from the bank of issue. He then, tactfully, added that a "less restricted" (and more practical) definition implied any increase of prices accompanied by an increase of money in circulation. During a later session, a French financial adviser to the Syrian and Lebanese governments, Professor Gaston Leduc, rallied to the defense of his country's honor by insisting again that "inflation did not exist in the Middle East in the strict sense" (Lloyd, *Food and Inflation*, p. 196).

11. "I hope," the governor of the National Bank of Iran stated, "that

the Conference will find some other terminology to describe the present situation in the Middle East. I have seen the harm caused in Iran by the use of the word 'inflation' " (ibid.).

12. Ibid.

13. Royal Institute of International Affairs, *The Middle East: A Political and Economic Survey*, p. 77.

14. See chap. 8, supra.

15. Lloyd, *Food and Inflation*, p. 199. The fact that this system worked well in Great Britain did not mean, of course, that it would succeed in the highly stratified and multicultural society of the Middle East. Consumer concepts of what was essential varied widely, not only from country to country but among the many ethnic divisions within countries and communities: In Palestine, Jews were heavier consumers of meat, Arabs demanded more bread; in Ethiopia, the substitution of gray for white sheeting was unacceptable to certain tradition-bound groups, while immaterial to others. Serious questions of racial and social equality would be raised. Rural dwellers might also be incensed at being forced to sell their cereal output at compulsory prices while "semi-luxuries" they wished to buy in the cities were going sky-high.

16. For an illustration of this attitude, see pp. 147–149, infra.

17. See Introduction by M. K. Bennett, Director of the Food Research Institute of Stanford University, to Lloyd, *Food and Inflation*.

18. In 1944, a third champion was added with the arrival of Dean Landis and a group of advisers from the U.S. headed by Raymond F. Mikesell.

19. Interviews with John W. Gunter (Washington, D.C., 2 August 1952), William A. B. Iliff (Washington, D.C., 18 August 1952), Raymond F. Mikesell (Washington, D.C., 30 December 1953), and Dero A. Saunders (New York, 20 September 1951).

20. M.E.S.C., "Handbook," pp. 87–88.

21. See n. 19. Note by contrast the statement in M.E.S.C., "Handbook," p. 10, that the Centre is not concerned "with the furtherance of particular trade policies."

22. Lloyd, *Food and Inflation*, p. 201; M.E.S.C., "Proceedings," passim.

23. Interviews with Iliff and Saunders.

24. Babcock, "Explosive Middle East," p. 113 ff.

25. Lloyd, *Food and Inflation*, p. 201.

26. In 1943, the U.S. provided direct financial aid to Iran and to Saudi Arabia. The U.S. Treasury agreed to buy up to $30,000,000 of Iranian Rials for dollars to stabilize the currency and to check inflation (U.S., Department of State, *Foreign Relations of the United States, 1943*, vol. 4, pp. 561–600). Lend-lease was utilized to provide Saudi Arabia with silver bullion coined into replicas of Maria Theresa Thalers (an Eighteenth Century Austrian coin which had attained great popularity in Ethiopia and Saudi Arabia) to take the place of the normal supply of currency reduced by the decline of pilgrim traffic. (U.S., State Department, *Foreign Relations, 1943*, vol. 4, pp. 888–920; George Kirk, *The Middle East in the*

War, pp. 354–369; T. Vail Motter, *The Persian Corridor and Aid to Russia*, chap. 20; Lloyd, *Food and Inflation*, pp. 187–188; interview with Landis).

27. Lloyd, *Food and Inflation*, pp. 208–209.

28. Ibid., p. 211.

29. Among those consulted in London were Kahn's old mentor, Lord Keynes, who expressed himself in favor of a vastly increased scope for the gold sale program, and with this in mind advocated that the U.S. should throw its large gold reserves into the fray. He added in one of his typical sallies that it might be the last chance that the U.S. would ever have of finding any use for its treasure (ibid., pp. 209–210).

30. Ibid., pp. 211–217.

31. Chaps. 4, 8, supra.

32. Lloyd, pp. 113–116.

33. Ibid., pp. 181–182; interview with M. E. Wordsworth, Beirut, 13 July 1954.

34. Lloyd, *Food and Inflation*, chap. 20. See also Appendix A, Table 4.

35. Indeed, the impact of inflation was cushioned by particular social factors and in some cases even became a blessing. Being rural and with farming concentrated on subsistence crops during the war, a large segment of the population was sheltered from the excesses of the market sector by the relative self-sufficiency of the subsistence sector. Inflation also helped many farmers free themselves from their debt burden, if their commitments were payable in money rather than kind (interview with E. R. Raymond, Washington, D.C., 15 August 1951).

36. Lloyd, *Food and Inflation*, p. 331.

37. Ibid., p. 206.

38. M.E.S.C., "Handbook," p. 38; M.E.S.C., "Circular Letter PS/90: M.E.S.C. Standard Commodity List, Amendment Schedule no. 3," mimeographed (Cairo, 7 December 1944).

39. Ibid., pp. 87–88; M.E.S.C., "Middle East Economic and Statistical Bulletin," 3 vols. (1943–1945), mimeographed, issued monthly in Cairo.

40. Government of Palestine, *Catalogue of the Palestine Government Industrial Exhibition, Cairo, 1941* (Jerusalem, 1941).

41. See Appendix, Table 3.

42. Lloyd, *Food and Inflation*, pp. 290–292, 368.

43. Ibid., pp. 348–351.

44. Ibid., p. 316.

45. Ibid., p. 342.

46. Ibid., p. 206.

47. Fayez A. Sayegh, *Arab Unity*, chap. 9. For an account of American attitudes on and relations to the Alexandria Conference and the League of Arab States, with a summary of events leading up to the signing of the Pact of the League, see U.S., Department of State, *Bulletin*, 18 May 1947, pp. 963 ff.

48. Sayegh, *Arab Unity*, p. 115; idem, "Recent Trends Toward Arab Unity," p. 9.

49. Alfred Bonné, *The Economic Development of the Middle East* (London: Oxford University Press, 1945), p. 122.

50. Sayegh, *Arab Unity*, p. 115.

51. Jackson relates that during the Alexandria meeting he was told by Arab statesmen that his Centre had done "its share" in promoting the creation of the Arab League (interview with Jackson).

52. Alfred Michaelis, "Trade Relations Between the Countries of the Near East in 1938," *Palnews Economic Annual of Palestine, 1939* (Tel-Aviv, 1939), pp. 118 ff.

53. Bonné, *Economic Development*, p. 112.

54. Judah L. Magnes, "Toward Peace in Palestine," pp. 239–249.

55. Lloyd, *Food and Inflation*, p. 138.

56. M.E.S.C., *The Proceedings of the Middle East Agricultural Development Conference, Cairo, November 7th–10th, 1944*, p. 204.

57. Ibid.

58. Ibid.

59. M.E.S.C., "Cereal Collection in Italy" [by K. A. H. Murray], Agricultural Reports, no. 11 (Cairo, July 1944).

60. M.E.S.C., "Handbook," p. 38.

61. Interview with Landis.

62. Arnold and Veronica Toynbee, eds., *The Realignment of Europe* (London: R.I.I.A., 1955), p. 65.

63. Ibid., p. 120.

64. Interview with Jackson.

65. M.E.S.C., *Agricultural Development Conference*, p. 205.

66. Interview with Jackson.

67. Interview with Woodbridge.

68. A partial list of these reports will be found in the Bibliography.

69. Lloyd, *Food and Inflation*, p. 104; Kirk, *Middle East in the War*, p. 183, The titles of the three reports follow: H. B. Allen, *Rural Education and Welfare in the Middle East* (London: H.M.S.O., 1946), B. A. Keen, *The Agricultural Development of the Middle East* (London: H.M.S.O., 1946), and Worthington, *Middle East Science*.

70. Robert G. A. Jackson, "Some Aspects of the War and its Aftermath in the Middle East," *Royal Central Asian Journal* 32 (July–October 1945): 258–268; Keith A. H. Murray, "Feeding the Middle East in Wartime," pp. 233–247.

71. Keith A. H. Murray, "Some Regional Problems of the Middle East," *International Affairs* 23 (January 1947): 11–19.

72. James M. Landis, "Economic Relationships Between the United States and Egypt," *L'Egypte Contemporaine* 36 (March 1945), 217–227; idem, "Middle East Challenge," *Fortune* 32 (September 1945): 160–164; idem, "Anglo-American Co-operation in the Middle East," *Annals of the*

American Academy of Political and Social Science 240 (July 1945): 64–72.

73. M.E.S.C.: "Proceedings of the Middle East Anti-Inflation Conference, Cairo, September 1942;" "Proceedings of the Middle East Conference on Control of Distribution and Rationing, Cairo, August 21–23, 1943"; "Proceedings of the Conference on Cereals Policy, Damascus, April 4–6, 1944," Agricultural Reports, no. 9 (Cairo, May 1944); see also proceedings of Financial and Agricultural and Development conferences cited supra.

74. Feliks Gross, "Peace Planning for Central and Eastern Europe," *Annals* 171 (March 1944): 169–176; Lawrence L. Barrell, "The Middle European Blueprint," Ph.D. dissertation, New York University, Department of Government, June 1957.

75. Such proposals are discussed in "The Middle East I: Food and Politics," *Economist* 144 (20 February 1943): 230–231.

76. Michaelis, "Trade Relations," pp. 118 ff.

77. See reports cited in n. 69.

78. M.E.S.C., Agricultural Development Conference, p. 195.

79. Ibid., pp. 195–203.

80. Ibid., pp. 205–208.

81. Interviews with Landis and Winant.

82. Lloyd, *Food and Inflation,* pp. 305–306.

83. Interviews with Jackson and Landis.

Chapter 10

1. U.S., Department of State, *Foreign Relations of the United States, 1943,* vol. 4, pp. 1–5.

2. See chap. 6, fn. 8, *supra.*

3. The Culbertson Mission was sent with the full approval of President Roosevelt. In a memorandum from Secretary of State Hull to the President dated 12 July 1944, Hull asked that Culbertson be given the temporary rank of Ambassador for the term of his Mission. He added that the specific objectives of the Missions were to review problems relating to the return of trade to normal channels as soon as conditions permitted and to recommend procedures to assure the fullest participation possible of private interests in government transactions. Commented Hull: "The Department attaches considerable importance to the Mission. . . ." (U.S., National Archives, Department of State, 033.1151 R/7–2144).

4. U.S., Department of State, *Foreign Relations, 1944,* vol. 5, pp. 41–42. In the covering memorandum sent to Secretary Hull by Wallace Murray, director of the Office of Near Eastern and African Affairs, with a draft of this *aide-mémoire,* Murray referred to the recent conversation between the Secretary and Landis when the Secretary had approved in principle the content of the *aide-mémoire.* The enclosed draft had been prepared by Landis and was now being submitted for the Secretary's approval. The draft was returned with the notation: "OK/CH" (U.S., National Archives, Department of State, 800.24/9–2844).

5. For the covering letter accompanying the Report to the Secretary of State, together with correspondence relating to the Mission, see U.S., Department of State, *Foreign Relations, 1944*, vol. 5, pp. 38–40. The Report itself with the Annexes is not printed. The Annexes to the Report covered such topics as the M.E.S.C., lend-lease, finance and currency exchange, oil, and sea and air communications.

6. U.S., National Archives, Department of State, 033.1151 R/11–1544 (Culbertson Report).

7. U.S., Department of State, *Foreign Relations, 1944*, vol. 5, pp. 8–37; *Foreign Relations, 1945*, vol. 8, pp. 49–63.

8. U.S., Department of State, *Foreign Relations, 1945*, vol. 8, pp. 64–81.

9. *Ibid.*, pp. 33–48. Woodward, *British Foreign Policy*, gives an account of these Anglo-American differences on the Middle East from the British point of view in ch. 8, passim.

10. The underlying conflict of interests between the U.S. and Great Britain in the Middle East came out into the open in Saudi Arabia as early as 1943. Gen. Patrick Hurley, sent as the President's Personal Representative to observe conditions in the Middle East in the Spring of 1943, had reported that the British were attempting to maneuver the United States out of Saudi Arabia; he was also extremely critical of British policies in Iran; U.S., Department of State, *Foreign Relations, 1943*, vol. 4, pp. 361–426, passim. His reports to the President are at pp. 363–370 and 420–426. The tension increased throughout 1944 and 1945; U.S., Department of State, *Foreign Relations, 1944*, vol. 5, pp. 8–37, 658–773, passim, and Woodward, *British Foreign Policy*, pp. 395–401. Oil and military assistance to Saudi Arabia were prominent topics at the conference between British and American officials on Middle Eastern questions held during the visit of Under Secretary of State Edward R. Stettinius Jr., to London in April 1944, particularly in the meeting of 12 April (U.S., National Archives, Department of State, 740.0011 Stettinius Mission/130).

11. No small contribution to this mood was made by the Truman Committee of the Senate which toured the Middle East in 1943 investigating American military operations. The Committee Report, made public in the *Congressional Record*, was highly critical of the British.

12. U.S., Department of State, *Foreign Relations, 1945*, vol. 8, pp. 85–87.

13. *Ibid.*, pp. 10–18.

Middle East Supply Centre
Plan of Organisation
June 1943

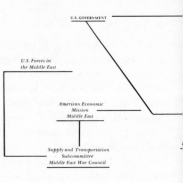

- U.S. GOVERNMENT
- U.S. Forces in the Middle East
- American Economic Mission Middle East
- Supply and Transportation Subcommittee Middle East War Council

---

Distribution & Rationing Specialists → Assistant Executives → Clerks

Director of Materials
P.A.

Assistant Director Materials Supplies
P.A.

- Engineering Materials
- Machinery, Timber & Building Materials
- Glass, Pottery, Matches
- Chemicals, Tanning
- Materials, Insecticides
- Hides, Skins, Leather
- Textiles, Jute Sacks, Cordage
- Paper, Newsprint, Cardboard
- Miscellaneous
- Tobacco
- Coal & Petroleum Products, Oil Company Requirements
- Lubricating Oil
  - Automobile Spare Parts
  - Textile
  - Leather, Hides & Skins
  - Rubber Technologist
  - Paint
  - Paper
  - Engineering Products
  - Pottery & Ceramics
  - Chemical Products
  - Heat Engineer
  - Industrial Investigator "A"
  - Industrial Investigator "B"
  - Industrial Investigator "C"

Pool of Technical Specialists — Varying Grades Employed as Available

Assistant Director Industrial Production
P.A.

- General Development Manager "A"
- General Development Manager "B"
- Production Statistician
  - Laboratory Assistants
- Mining Development Manager
- Chemical Development Manager
- Engineering Development Manager
- Salvage

Director of Medical Requirements
P.A.

- Supply & Distribution
- Organisation
- Production
- Bacteriologist

Director of Transport
P.A.

- Vehicle Supplies & Control
- Transport Rationalisation
- Spare Part Supplies & Control
- Tyre Supplies & Control
  - Assistant Executives → Clerks

Secretary
P.A.

- Organisation & Methods Officer
- Establishment Officer
  - Superintendent Female Staff → Typists
  - Travel & Accommodation
  - Assistant Establishment Officer & Records
- Accounts Officer
  - Assistant Accountant & Equipment & Servicing Officer
- Chief Clerk
  - Telegrams
  - Registry & Archivist → Clerks; Orderlies

LONDON	C.A.M.E.S.	Middle East Supplies Committee

IRAQ		
Commercial Secretary		
Executive	1	In Charge
Executive	1	Assistant
Executive	1	Supplies
Executive	1	Industrial Surveys
Executive	1	Engineering Surveys
Typists		Agricultural Adviser
Clerks		

PERSIA-IRAQ COMMAND		
Executive (Liaison)	1	
Assistant Executive	1	
Clerk	1	

PERSIA		
Director or Assistant Director	1	In Charge
Executive	1	Assistant
Executives	1	Supplies
Executives	1	Transport
Executives	2	Road, Rail & Port Movement
Executives	2	Industrial Surveys
Executive	4	Chemical Surveys
Executive	1	Textile Surveys
Executive	1	Agricultural Adviser
Typists	1	Administration
Clerks		

ARAB SHEIKDOMS		

TRIPOLITANIA		
Assistant Director	1	Civil Affairs Branch General Headquarters
Executive	1	
Clerk	1	

CYRENAICA		
Assistant Director	1	Civil Affairs Branch General Headquarters
General Headquarters		

MALTA		
Representative in Middle East		

EAST AFRICA		
Assistant Director	1	War Supply Board

Assistant Director, Clerk } If Required

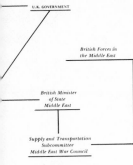
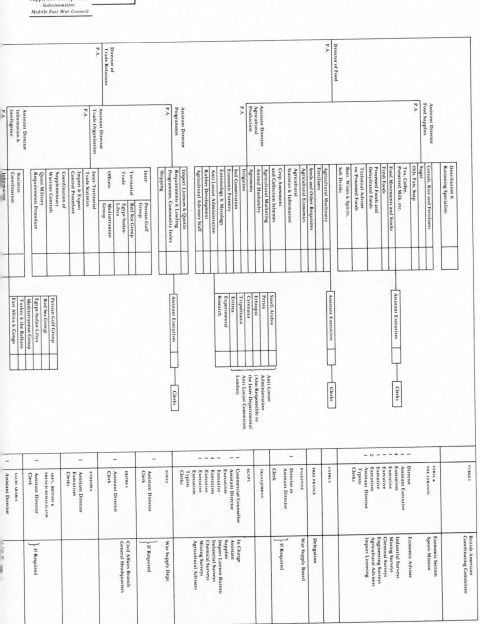

Appendix A

TABLE 1
Overseas Shipments of Cereals
Received in Middle East, 1942–1943
(in thousand long tons)

Period	Civilian	Armed forces	Total
January-June 1942	400.6	115.7	516.3
July-December 1942	65.1	61.5	126.6
Total 1942	465.7	177.2	642.9
January-June 1943	63.6	28.9	92.5
July-December 1943	105.4	141.3	246.7
Total 1943	169.0	170.2	339.2

Source: Middle East Supply Centre. Middle East defined as the area under m.e.s.c. jurisdiction. Included in shipments are consignments of rice from India.

TABLE 2

TONNAGE OF SHIPS IN EXTERNAL TRADE
ENTERING HARBORS OF CERTAIN
MIDDLE EASTERN COUNTRIES,
1939, 1943, AND 1945 TO 1949
(IN MILLIONS OF TONS)

Country	1939	1943	1945	1946	1947	1948	1949
Egypt[a]	30.1	12.6	18.3	37.0	. .	. .	. .
Iran[b]	7.1	3.4	7.5	8.6	15.0	. .	. .
Iraq[c]	0.7	0.4	0.4	0.5	0.7	1.0	. .
Israel/ Palestine	4.4	2.2	3.3	4.5	5.4	0.8[d]	2.1[e]
Lebanon[f]	2.6	0.6	0.3	1.0	1.6	1.9	2.3[g]
Turkey[h]	5.9	0.2	2.0	2.9	4.2	. .	. .

Source: U.N., *Review of Economic Conditions in Middle East* (1951); figures refer to net registered tonnage.

[a] Including ships passing through Suez Canal; including entrances into all Egyptian ports, even when more than one port is entered during one voyage.

[b] Including ships in ballast; figures refer to year beginning 21 March.

[c] Port of Basra only.

[d] June to December, Israel only.

[e] 1950: 2.4 million tons.

[f] Port of Beirut only; including ships in ballast and coastal shipping.

[g] 1950: 2.6 million tons.

[h] Foreign ships only.

TABLE 3

DIRECTION OF TRADE OF SELECTED
MIDDLE EASTERN COUNTRIES, 1938–1949
(IN PERCENTAGE OF TOTAL VALUE)

Trade with	Egypt		Iran [a]		Iraq [b]		Israel/Palestine [c]		Lebanon and Syria		Turkey	
	Imports	Exports	Imports	Exports	Imports	Exports	Imports	Exports	Imports	Exports	Imports	Exports
Belgium, France, Luxembourg, Netherlands:												
1938	12.8	10.7	7.3	7.9	5.5	2.1	6.9	14.2	19.0	20.0	4.1	6.6
1943	—	—	0.1	—	—	—	—	—	—	—	0.8	1.1
1946	7.1	9.9	1.9	7.8	1.3	14.0	3.0	3.6	7.9	20.7	2.8	8.3
1948	13.5	13.1	8.3	7.6	6.7	3.6	6.7	5.4	17.4	12.1	8.5	8.5
1949	12.9	11.1	4.9	5.9	...	...	6.6	7.6	17.1	8.4	9.7	9.8
United Kingdom:												
1938	22.5	31.8	8.1	6.3	30.1	24.4	13.2	49.2	13.4	6.1	11.2	3.4
1943	17.3	29.8	5.4	6.0	10.9	3.8	6.7	8.0	8.1	19.6	15.9	10.8
1946	29.2	15.7	17.9	12.5	44.1	9.6	20.2	17.9	17.6	2.7	19.3	17.5
1948	20.7	28.5	27.4	21.8	43.5	16.6	19.7	31.9	19.6	1.8	24.3	14.7
1949	21.1	16.8	24.4	24.8	...	...	9.3	53.8	20.9	8.7	17.2	12.3
Rest of Europe:												
1938	35.2	33.3	64.1	67.9	16.9	6.5	43.3	19.4	25.0	15.7	68.3	72.6
1943	1.6	0.6	23.4	17.1	1.8	—	0.5	1.6	1.0	6.8	61.5	51.1
1946	12.5	25.0	30.5	24.1	2.7	0.2	9.3	9.9	5.5	3.1	26.3	31.7
1948	25.4	23.0	17.0	15.1	11.7	6.0	16.7	20.0	10.7	4.0	28.8	38.2
1949	20.3	31.3	11.0	24.7	...	...	24.9	19.7	10.6	13.9	32.9	47.2

United States:												
1938	6.5	2.3	8.6	8.2	9.1	15.2	8.5	2.2	7.1	6.0	10.5	12.3
1943	10.5	8.6	7.7	22.3	6.2	1.6	6.9	18.3	5.7	2.4	2.4	20.5
1946	10.7	7.9	23.2	18.5	7.9	9.1	8.2	20.8	17.9	17.5	31.3	20.3
1948	7.0	3.1	30.0	15.2	7.9	12.1	8.8	2.6	18.9	4.4	23.3	21.7
1949	8.2	2.7	42.1	8.5	.	.	31.3	15.6	23.1	3.4	20.2	14.3
Middle East countries:												
1938	7.1	7.3	0.3	4.4	8.4	23.0	16.6	11.8	15.8	44.8	1.5	1.9
1943	42.8	21.7	21.8	21.7	21.8	49.5	61.0	67.8	51.3	71.0	5.3	16.2
1946	20.7	13.8	2.0	22.7	20.2	33.6	39.6	40.4	18.7	48.0	8.2	19.1
1948	11.7	5.3	3.9	21.5	9.4	39.5	32.4	31.8	12.8	74.6	4.9	14.6
1949	10.1	5.9	4.0	23.7	.	.	4.8	0.3	13.3	56.6	6.5	9.8
India, Pakistan, Ceylon:												
1938	3.1	5.1	8.4	4.9	6.9	8.2	2.4	0.6	3.4	—	1.6	0.1
1943	10.2	31.5	38.3	15.3	55.9	2.1	6.1	1.7	20.4	—	10.0	—
1946	3.9	19.3	15.2	10.3	15.7	22.0	2.6	3.4	3.4	—	4.4	0.2
1948	6.4	17.7	9.7	17.7	7.9	18.2	1.4	2.5	0.9	—	2.5	0.1
1949	5.7	22.5	9.0	10.6	.	.	0.5	0.3	2.2	0.1	1.6	0.4
Other countries:												
1938	12.8	9.5	5.0	6.2	21.3	14.8	9.1	2.6	16.3	7.4	2.8	3.1
1943	17.6	7.8	3.3	17.6	3.4	43.0[d]	18.8	2.6	13.5	0.2	4.1	0.3
1946	15.9	8.4	9.3	4.1	8.1	11.5	17.1	4.0	29.0	8.0	7.7	2.9
1948	15.3	9.3	3.7	1.1	12.9	4.0	14.3	5.8	19.7	3.1	7.7	3.2
1949	21.7	9.7	4.5	1.8	.	.	22.6	2.7	12.8	8.9	11.9	6.2

Source: United Nations, *Review of Economic Conditions in the Middle East, 1949–50.*

[a] Data are for twelve months beginning 21 March of the year indicated; 1938 figures are for the period between 22 June 1937 and 21 June 1938; imports and exports by concessionaires are excluded.

[b] Including imports by petroleum companies and excluding exports of petroleum products.

[c] Figures for 1947 have been used instead of 1948 figures.

[d] Exports by the British Army accounted for practically the whole of this percentage.

TABLE 4

INDICES OF COST OF LIVING AND WHOLESALE PRICES IN SELECTED MIDDLE EASTERN COUNTRIES, 1939–1950 (1939 = 100)

Year	Egypt		Iran[a]		Iraq[b]		Israel/Palestine[c]		Lebanon[d]		Turkey[e]	
	Cost of living[f]	Wholesale prices	Cost of living	Wholesale prices	Cost of living	Wholesale prices	Cost of living	Wholesale prices	Cost of living	Wholesale prices	Cost of living	Wholesale prices
1940	113	124	110	113	··	138	118	124	110	156	111	125
1941	138	156	152	143	··	179	141	170	··	309	136	173
1942	184	200	269	251	··	383	194	248	287	626	229	335
1943	242	254	649	460	··	590	232	302	441	835	343	583
1944	279	300	756	499	584	534	237	319	560	953	334	453
1945	293	318	643	468	567	503	253	319	607	1,038	350	439
1946	287	308	576	451	601	482	267	332	553	889	338	422
1947	279	292	583	483	673	527	271	342	500	797	340	427
1948	281	316	639	525	··	558	338	453	492	777	341	460
1949	278	298	697	490	540	463	347	438	461	641	374	497
First half	278	302	709	521	573	481	364	479	492	722	371	509
Second half	277	294	684	459	506	445	329	396	430	561	376	485
1950	293	··	570	414	491	475	321	375	426	108[g]	356	446[g]
First half	287	316[h]	596	402	487	462	319	376	419	99[g]	370	456
Second half	300	334[h]	545	425	495	488	322	373	433	118[g]	344	437[g]

Source: U.N., Review of Economic Conditions in the Middle East, 1949–50.

[a] Wholesale prices in Teheran.

[b] Baghdad; wholesale prices, December 1938 to August 1939 = 100.

[c] Cost of living, August 1939 = 100. Wholesale prices, Tel Aviv, Haifa, Jaffa and Jerusalem, 1939 to January 1948; Tel Aviv, February 1948 to June 1949; Tel Aviv, Haifa and Jerusalem, beginning July 1949.

[d] Cost of living, Beirut; June to August 1939 = 100. Wholesale prices, June 1939 = 100.

[e] Istanbul.

[f] Cairo; June to August 1939 = 100.

[g] New index; base, January 1950 = 100.

[h] July to October.

Appendix B

M.E.S.C. Publications

Beirut. B.M.E.O. M.E.S.C. "Circular Letters." M.E.S.C.,
Program Division. Mimeographed [distributed to field offices of M.E.S.C.
and territorial governments]. Cairo, n.d.

Beirut. B.M.E.O. M.E.S.C. "Middle East Economic and Statistical Bulletin."
M.E.S.C., Program Division. Mimeographed [issued monthly for distribution to field offices of M.E.S.C. and territorial governments]. Cairo,
1942–1945.

Beirut. B.M.E.O. M.E.S.C. "Organization and Policy Handbook."
M.E.S.C., Secretariat. Mimeographed. Cairo, [January 1944].

Beirut. B.M.E.O. M.E.S.C. "Plan of Organization." M.E.S.C.,
Secretariat. Chart. Cairo, 1943.

Beirut. B.M.E.O. M.E.S.C. "Questionnaire for Industrial Investigation Reports." M.E.S.C., Materials Division. Cairo, n.d.

M.E.S.C.: Some Facts About the Middle East Supply Centre. Cairo: Nile
Press, 1944.

Beirut. B.M.E.O. M.E.S.C. "Supplies from North America."
M.E.S.C., Secretariat. Mimeographed. [Cairo], n.d.

Beirut. B.M.E.O. M.E.S.C. "The M.E.S.C. Story."
M.E.S.C., Secretariat. Mimeographed. [Cairo], n.d.

M.E.S.C. and Other Reports and Documents

GENERAL

Beirut. B.M.E.O. M.E.S.C. "Consumer Goods and Grain Extraction: Draft
Report on a Survey Undertaken Between November 1943 and May
1944" [by P. A. Wilson]. M.E.S.C., Food Division, Agricultural Reports,
no. 12. Cairo, July 1944.

Beirut. B.M.E.O. MS. 1/1/1. M.E.S.C. "Crops and Livestock Report in the
Middle East During 1945." M.E.S.C. Cairo, February 1945.

Beirut. B.M.E.O. M.E.S.C. "Memorandum on Monetary and Banking Statistics." M.E.S.C., Program Division, Territorial Papers Submitted to the

Middle East Financial Conference, Cairo, April 1944, no. E-1. Cairo, 1944.

Beirut. B.M.E.O. MS. 15/1/3. "Middle East Rationing and Distribution Conference Held in Cairo 1943" [by G. M. Dreosti]. N.p., 1 February 1944.

Beirut. B.M.E.O. MS. 1/1/10. M.E.S.C. "Minutes of Cereals Control Conference, Cairo, 12th and 13th November, 1942." [Cairo], n.d.

Beirut. B.M.E.O. MS. 55/1/8. "Note on Industrial Development of the Middle East" [by L. Eisinger]. N.p., 12 July 1944.

Beirut. B.M.E.O. M.E.S.C. "Note on Middle East Cereals Position 1942–43." M.E.S.C., Food Division. Cairo, 11 May 1942.

Beirut. B.M.E.O. M.E.S.C "Notes and Statistics Relating to Inflation in the Middle East." M.E.S.C., Program Division, Territorial Papers Submitted to the Middle East Financial Conference, Cairo, April 1944, no. A-1. Cairo, 1944.

Beirut. B.M.E.O. MS. 1/7/9. "Notes on the Cost of Planting and Producing Hemp" [by Najib Alam ad-Din]. N.p., 2 February 1943.

Beirut. B.M.E.O. M.E.S.C. "Outline of Principal Middle East Industries." M.E.S.C., Materials Division. Cairo, December 1944.

Beirut. B.M.E.O. MS. 55/1/7. "Outline of the Probable Trend of Industrial Development in the Middle East" [by L. Eisinger]. N.p., 12 July 1944.

Beirut. B.M.E.O. MS 55/1/6. M.E.S.C. "Possibilities for Post-War Development of Middle East Industries" [by L. Eisinger]. M.E.S.C. Cairo, 27 November 1943.

Beirut. B.M.E.O. MS. 54/2/8. "Post-war Development, Mining" [by J. D. Boyd]. N.p., 21 may 1944.

Beirut. B.M.E.O. MS. 1/1/13. M.E.S.C. "Proceedings of the Conference on Cereals Policy held in Damascus, April 4th–6th, 1944." M.E.S.C., Food Division, Agricultural Reports, no. 9. Cairo, May 1944.

Beirut. B.M.E.O. MS. 0/1/4. M.E.S.C. "Proceedings of the Second Agricultural Conference Held at the British Embassy, Cairo, January 21st and 22nd, 1943." M.E.S.C. Cairo, n.d.

Beirut. B.M.E.O. MS. 1/1/11. "Report on Cereals Supply and Cereals Control Scheme in the Middle East, July 1942 to December 1943" [by R. F. Birch]. Cairo, December 1945.

Beirut. B.M.E.O. M.E.S.C. "Report on Factors Concerning Canning Factory Production" [by B. Fleming]. M.E.S.C., Food Division. Cairo, October 1942.

Beirut. B.M.E.O. M.E.S.C. "Resolutions of the Statistical and Rationing Conference." M.E.S.C., Program Division, Territorial Papers Submitted to the Middle East Financial Conference, Cairo, April 1944, no. F-1. Cairo, 1944.

Beirut. B.M.E.O. MS. 5/1/1. M.E.S.C. "The Agricultural Machinery Situation in the Middle East in 1943" [by Keith A. H. Murray and B. H. Thibodeaux]. M.E.S.C., Food Division, Agricultural Reports, no. 1. Cairo, February 1943.

Beirut. B.M.E.O. M.E.S.C. "The Effect of Control of Distribution on Inflation: Memorandum by the Middle East Supply Centre." M.E.S.C., Program Division, Territorial Papers Submitted to the Middle East Financial Conference, Cairo, April 1944, no. D–1. Cairo, 1944.

The Proceedings of the Conference on Middle East Agricultural Development, Cairo, February 7th–10th, 1944. M.E.S.C., Food Division, Agricultural Reports, no. 6. Cairo: M.E.F. Printing and Stationery Services, 1944.

Beirut. B.M.E.O. MS. 62/1/5. "Trade in the Middle East" [by A. W. Richardson]. N.p., 1 May 1944.

EGYPT

Beirut. B.M.E.O. M.E.S.C. "The Foreign Trade of Egypt During 1943." M.E.S.C., Program Division. Cairo, n.d.

Beirut. B.M.E.O. M.E.S.C. "The Future Development of the State Farms at El Kharg[a]" [by Wing Comdr. Dunstan Skilbeck, R.A.F.]. M.E.S.C., Food Division. Cairo, March 1944.

Beirut. B.M.E.O. MS. 55/2/28. "General Survey of the Production of Matches in Egypt." N.p., 31 July 1943.

Beirut. B.M.E.O. MS. 10/2/2. M.E.S.C. "Preliminary Survey of Egypt." 5 pts. M.E.S.C., Program Division. Cairo, 1945.

Beirut. B.M.E.O. MS. 51/2/2. "Report on Cotton Cultivation and Textile Industries in Egypt" [by J. D. Hynd and H. R. Hill]. N.p., November 1944.

Beirut. B.M.E.O. MS. 13/1/3, no. 3, M.E.S.C. AP 11800/EGY. "Systems of Land Tenure under the Land Reclamation Schemes." M.E.S.C. Cairo, 26 June 1944.

Beirut. B.M.E.O. MS. 54/2/3. "Twenty Mining Reports on Egypt, 1942–1945" [by R. D. Duncan and J. D. Boyd]. N.p.

ERITREA, CYRENAICA, AND TRIPOLITANIA

Beirut. B.M.E.O. M.E.S.C. "Report on Agricultural Possibilities in Eritrea" [by Russell S. Kifer]. M.E.S.C., Food Division. Cairo, 1944.

Beirut. B.M.E.O. M.E.S.C "Report on Visit to Cyrenaica and Tripolitania for Investigation and Discussion Regarding Utilization of Lentiscus Berries" [by Dr. J. Hassid]. M.E.S.C., Food Division. Cairo, 3 August 1944.

Beirut. B.M.E.O. M.E.S.C. "Report on a Visit to Eritrea" [by Lt. Col. R. Quinnell]. M.E.S.C., Transport Division. Cairo, January 1944.

Beirut. B.M.E.O. M.E.S.C. "Report on Visit to Eritrea" [by R. W. Munro]. M.E.S.C., Food Division. Cairo, 3 March 1944.

ETHIOPIA

Beirut. B.M.E.O. M.E.S.C. "Report on Ethiopian Agriculture" [by Lt. Col. F. Joyce]. M.E.S.C., Food Division. Addis Ababa, 1942.

Beirut. B.M.E.O. M.E.S.C. "Notes on Ethiopian Currency Problems." M.E.S.C., Program Division. Cairo, 1943.

Beirut. B.M.E.O. M.E.S.C. "Report on Visit to Ethiopia" [by A. F. Anderson]. M.E.S.C., Transport Division. Cairo, 1944.

IRAQ

Beirut. B.M.E.O. M.E.S.C. "General Economic Position in Iraq." M.E.S.C., Program Division, Territorial Papers Submitted to the Middle East Financial Conference, Cairo, April 1944, no. A-5. Cairo, 1944.

Beirut, B.M.E.O. M.E.S.C. "Loans and Savings in Iraq." M.E.S.C., Program Division, Territorial Papers Submitted to the Middle East Financial Conference, Cairo, April 1944, no. C-5. Cairo, 1944.

Beirut. B.M.E.O. MS. 13/1/3, no. 4. M.E.S.C. AP/11800/IRQ. "Land tenure in Iraq." M.E.S.C. N.p.

Beirut. B.M.E.O. M.E.S.C. "The Monetary Situation in Iraq" [by A. H. Ebtehaj]. M.E.S.C., Program Division, Territorial Papers Submitted to the Middle East Financial Conference, Cairo, April 1944, no. A-8. Cairo, 1944.

Beirut. B.M.E.O. MS. 1.12/4. "Report on Cereal Production in Iraq" [by G. J. Fleming]. N.p., 11 July 1942.

Beirut. B.M.E.O. MS. 8/12/2. "Report on Forests and Forestry in the Northern Liwas of Iraq" [by J. Smith]. N.p., 1944.

Beirut. B.M.E.O. MS. 8/12/3. "Some Comments on Dr. J. Smith's Report on Iraqi Forests" [by E. P. Stebbing]. N.p., 1946.

Beirut. B.M.E.O. MS. 6/12/1. M.E.S.C. "Survey of the Livestock Industry in Iraq" [by I. Gillespie]. M.E.S.C., Food Division, Agricultural Reports, no. 3. Cairo, May 1943.

Beirut. B.M.E.O. MS. 62/12/1. M.E.S.C. "The Staple Exports of Iraq." M.E.S.C., Food Division. Cairo, 16 November 1943.

PALESTINE AND TRANSJORDAN

Beirut. B.M.E.O. MS. 21/5/2. "Agricultural Statistics in Palestine and Transjordan" [by Warder Jenkins]. N.p., 7 November 1944.

Beirut. B.M.E.O. MS. 13/1/3, no. 5. M.E.S.C. AP/11800/PAL. "Finance of Jewish Settlement." M.E.S.C. N.p., 7 June 1943.

Beirut. B.M.E.O. M.E.S.C. "Food Control: Report for Quarter Ending 30th September 1942" [by G. Walsh, Food Controller, Palestine]. M.E.S.C., Food Division. Jerusalem, 1942.

Beirut. B.M.E.O. MS. 55/5/1. "Milling Observations in Palestine, April 20th–23rd, 1944" [by J. H. Shollenberger]. N.p.

Beirut. B.M.E.O. MS. 49/5/1. "Report on an Investigation into Paper and Board Mills of Palestine" [by C. G. Ingamells]. N.p., May 1944.

Beirut. B.M.E.O. M.E.S.C. "Report on Customs Information and Related Matters for Trans-Jordan." M.E.S.C., Program Division. Cairo, 2 October 1943.

Beirut. B.M.E.O. M.E.S.C. "Report on Palestine" [by J. H. Little]. M.E.S.C., Food Division. Cairo, July 1944.

Beirut. B.M.E.O. MS. 54/6/2. M.E.S.C. "Report on Transjordan Mining"
[by R. Duncan]. M.E.S.C. Cairo, May 1945.
Beirut. B.M.E.O. M.E.S.C. "Report on a Visit to Palestine" [by R. H.
Court]. M.E.S.C., Transport Division. N.p., 10 December 1944.
Beirut. B.M.E.O. MS. 11/5/1. "Reports of the Palestine War Supply Board
for the Years 1941 to 1945." N.p.
Beirut. B.M.E.O. MS. 10/5/0. M.E.S.C. "Survey of Palestine." M.E.S.C.
Cairo, [1945].
Beirut. B.M.E.O. MS. 51/5/1. "Textiles in Palestine: Report on a Visit to
Palestine March 1945" [by R. Hill]. N.p.
Beirut. B.M.E.O. MS. 54/6/1. "Transjordan Phosphate Report [by C. G.
Peacock]." N.p., 9 September 1943.

SAUDI ARABIA

Beirut. B.M.E.O. M.E.S.C. "Note on the Food Situation in Central and
North East Saudi Arabia." M.E.S.C., Food Division. Cairo, November
1943.
Beirut. B.M.E.O. MS. 43/13/1. "The Organisation of Transport and Food
in the Kingdom of Saudi Arabia" [by J. F. Coneybear, Wing Comdr.
Dunstan Skilbeck, R.A.F., and Harold E. Myers]." N.p., 1943.
Beirut. B.M.E.O. MS. 10/13/2. "Survey of the Organisation of Agriculture,
Food Supplies and Transport in Saudi Arabia" [by J. F. Coneybear,
Wing Comdr. Dunstan Skilbeck, R.A.F., and Harold E. Myers]. N.p.,
February 1944.

THE SUDAN

Beirut. B.M.E.O. M.E.S.C. "Control of Prices, Distribution, Imports and Ex-
ports: Sudan." M.E.S.C., Program Division, Territorial Papers Submitted
to the Middle East Financial Conference, Cairo, April 1944, no. D-10.
Cairo, 1944.
Beirut. B.M.E.O. M.E.S.C. "Report on Forestry and Soil Conservation in the
Sudan" [by Glen W. Russ]. M.E.S.C., Food Division, Agricultural Re-
ports, no. 8. Khartoum, October 1943.
Beirut. B.M.E.O. MS. 54/3/1. "Report on the Gold-Mining Operations in
the Anglo-Egyptian Sudan" [by J. D. Boyd]. N.p., September 1944.
Beirut. B.M.E.O. M.E.S.C. "Sudanese Timber for Match Manufacture."
M.E.S.C., Materials Division. Cairo, 1943.

SYRIA AND LEBANON

Beirut. B.M.E.O. MS. 6/7/4. "A Scheme to Increase the Poultry Population
of Syria and Lebanon" [by Najib Alam ad-Din]. N.p., 1943.
Beirut. B.M.E.O. MS. 54/7/1. M.E.S.C. "A Short Note on Certain Min-
eral Deposits in Syria and Lebanon" [by John Coulter]. Report for the
Director of Industrial production, M.E.S.C. Johannesburg, January 1945.

Beirut. B.M.E.O. MS. 49/7/1. "A Survey of the Paper and Board Industry of Syria and Lebanon" [by C. G. Ingamells]. N.p., 11 November 1944.

Beirut. B.M.E.O. "Cereal Collection and Price Policy for 1944/45 Crop in Syria and Lebanon, Iraq and Persia" [by Keith A. H. Murray]. N.p., April 1944.

Beirut. B.M.E.O. MS. 55/7/20. Spears Mission. "Chief Industrial Developments in Syria and Lebanon 1941/1943." Spears Mission, Economic Section. N.p.

Beirut. B.M.E.O. MS. 46/7/2. "Control Scheme for Hides, Leather, and Tanning Material in the Levant States" [by J. Strakosh]. N.p., 14 August 1944.

Beirut. B.M.E.O. MS. 15/7/5. "Dehydration in Palestine, Syria, and Lebanon" [by W. H. E. Matthews and B. W. Fleming]. N.p., August 1943.

Beirut. B.M.E.O. MS. 13/11/3, no. 7. M.E.S.C. AP/11800/SYR. "Land Tenure in the Estate of Mesherfe (Homs-Hama Plain)" [by Paul J. Khlat]. M.E.S.C. Cairo, 24 June 1944.

Beirut. B.M.E.O. MS. 13/1/2, no. 2. M.E.S.C. AP/858. "Land Tenure in the Fertile Crescent." M.E.S.C., Food Division. Cairo, 1944.

Beirut. B.M.E.O. Spears Mission. "Memorandum on Rationing in Syria and Lebanon." Spears Mission, Economic Section. Beirut, 3 August 1943.

Beirut. B.M.E.O. MS. 19/7/2. Spears Mission. "Notes on Price Control." Spears Mission, Economic Section. [Beirut], 19 June 1943.

Beirut. B.M.E.O. M.E.S.C. "Report on Customs Information and Related Matters for Syria and the Lebanon" [by J. Harold DeVeau]. M.E.S.C., Program Division. Cairo, 4 November 1943.

Beirut. B.M.E.O. MS. 3/7/2. Spears Mission. "Report on irrigation in Syria and Lebanon" [by H. Addison]. Spears Mission. Beirut, July–August 1942.

Beirut. B.M.E.O. MS. 13/1/3, no. 8. M.E.S.C. AP/11800/SYR. "Report on Land Tenure in the Village of Kfer-Sa'ab (North Lebanon)" [by Paul J. Khlat]. M.E.S.C., Food Division. Cairo, 21 December 1944.

Beirut. B.M.E.O. MS. 54/7/4. "Report on Lignite in the Aitouli Area (Near Djezzine) in Southern Lebanon" [by R. Borchers]. N.p., 28 January 1943.

Beirut. B.M.E.O. MS. 51/7/5. "Report on the Syria and Lebanon Cotton Industry" [by R. T. Moore]. N.p., 11 April 1943.

Beirut. B.M.E.O. MS 21/7/1. "Résultat du recensement de la récolte en céréales panifiables de l'année 1942." N.p.

Beirut. B.M.E.O. MS. 55/7/2. "Some Revised Notes on the Industries of Syria and the Lebanon" [by P. R. Clark]. N.p., 5 February 1943.

Beirut, B.M.E.O. MS. 51/7/3. "Textile industry of Syria and the Lebanon" [by J. D. Hynd]. N.p., March 1944.

Beirut. B.M.E.O. MS. 54/7/2. M.E.S.C. "The Occurrence and Exploitation of

Lignite in the Lebanon" [by John Coulter]. Report for the Director of Industrial Production, M.E.S.C. Johannesburg, June 1944.

MISCELLANEOUS AREA STUDIES

Beirut. B.M.E.O. M.E.S.C. "Agriculture in Turkey" [by Wing Comdr. Dunstan Skilbeck, R.A.F.]. M.E.S.C., Food Division. Cairo, 4 January 1944.

Beirut. B.M.E.O. M.E.S.C. "Cereals Collection in Italy" [by Keith A. H. Murray]. M.E.S.C., Food Division, Agricultural Reports, no. 11. Cairo, July 1944.

Beirut. B.M.E.O. MS. 0/12/2. "Large Scale Production in the Middle Euphrates" [by V. D. Carbutt]. N.p., 1944.

Beirut. B.M.E.O. MS. 3/8/3. "Preliminary Notes on Irrigation Pumps in the Euphrates Valley" [by H. Addison]. N.p., 10 September 1943.

Beirut. B.M.E.O. M.E.S.C. "Report on Forestry and Soil Conservation in Cyprus" [by Glen W. Russ]. M.E.S.C., Food Division, Agricultural Reports, no. 7. Nicosia, June 1943.

Bibliography and Other Sources

Books and Articles

"The Aftermath of the Middle East Supply Centre," *Great Britain and the East* 61 (November 1945): 82–83.

"Agricultural Mission to Saudi Arabia," U.S., Department of State, *Bulletin* 6 (28 March 1942): 261.

Ahoury, Jean. "Les répercussions de la guerre sur l'agriculture Egyptienne," *Egypte Contemporaine* 38 (March–April 1947): 234–235.

Alami, Sami. "Possibilities of Industrialization Within a Customs Union of Iraq, Syria, Lebanon, Palestine, and Transjordan." Master's thesis, American University of Beirut, 1946.

Alderson, Wroe. "Programs Established for Licencing Exports," *Foreign Commerce Weekly* 11 (3 April 1943): 3 ff.

Allen, George V. "American Advisers in Persia," U.S., Department of State, *Bulletin* 11 (23 July 1944): 88–93.

Allen, Harold B. *Rural Education and Welfare in the Middle East.* London: H.M.S.O., 1946.

Altricham, Lord. "Les problèmes du Moyen-Orient," *Politique Etrangère* 12 (July 1947): 261–274.

American Christian Palestine Committee. *The Arab War Effort.* New York, n.d. [1947?]

American Council on Public Affairs. *Regionalism and World Organization.* Washington: American Council on Public Affairs, 1944.

American University of Beirut, Economic Research Institute. *A Selected and Annotated Bibliography of Economic Literature on the Arabic Speaking Countries of the Middle East 1938–1952.* Beirut: 1954.

"American Policy in Iran—Under Secretary of State Acheson Answers Ex-Ambassador Hurley's Charges," U.S., Department of State, *Bulletin* 13 (23 December 1945): 984–986.

American Zionist Emergency Council. *Press Book on Palestine Jewish Contribution to the War against the Axis.* 2d ed. New York: n.d. [1943?]

The Anglo-Palestine Yearbook—1946. London: Anglo-Palestine Publications, 1946.

Anis, Mahmoud. "Value of Agriculture [sic] Products and other Commodities Pertaining to Agriculture for the Years 1937–42," *Egypte Contemporaine* 36 (March 1945): 357–368.

Antonius, George. *The Arab Awakening*. London: Putnam, 1938.
"Appointment of American Director of Economic Operations in the Middle East," U.S., Department of State, *Bulletin* 9 (11 September 1943): 167.
"Appointment of Leo T. Crowley as Foreign Economic Administration and Appointment of Herbert H. Lehman as Special Assistant to the President," U.S., Department of State, *Bulletin* 9 (25 September 1943): 205–206.
Archon, Dion J. J. "The United States and the Eastern Mediterranean." Ph.D. dissertation, Harvard University, 1951.
Arndt, H. W. "British Business Men on Postwar Reconstruction," *International Affairs (Review Supplement)* 18 (June 1942): 437–443.
Aufricht, Hans. *War, Peace and Reconstruction: A Classified Bibliography*. New York: Commission to Study the Organization of Peace, November 1943.
Ausman, L. H. "Civilian Requirements for the Middle East," *Commercial Intelligence Journal*, no. 2095 (25 March 1944): 1–2.
Australian Institute of International Affairs. *The Middle East: Australia's Frontline*. Sydney, January 1941.
Babcock, F. Lawrence. "The Explosive Middle East," *Fortune* 30 (September 1944): 116 ff.
———. "The Much Promised Land," *Fortune* 30 (October 1944): 166–172.
Barr, Robert J. "Iraq Today," *Foreign Commerce Weekly* 10 (20 February 1943): 6.
———. "Palestine's Economy," *Foreign Commerce Weekly* 8 (12 September 1942): 3 ff.
———. "Palestine's New Economic Controls," *Foreign Commerce Weekly* 10 (13 February 1943): 11 ff.
———. "Postwar Trade Prospects in Egypt, Iraq, Palestine," *Foreign Commerce Weekly* 19 (30 June 1945): 6–10.
Barrell, Lawrence L. "The Middle European Blueprint." Ph.D. dissertation, New York University, 1957.
Barton, James L. *The Story of Near East Relief*. New York: Macmillan Co., 1930.
Bee, John M. "Egypt After the War," *Great Britain and the East* 58 (7 February 1942): 9.
———. "A Glimpse of War-Time Egypt," *Great Britain and the East* 59 (25 July 1942): 16–17.
———. "Self Sufficiency in the Middle East," *Great Britain and the East* 58 (13 June 1942): 9–10.
———. "The United Kingdom Commercial Corporation," *Great Britain and the East* 58 (4 February 1942): 10–11.
Beeley, Harold. "The Middle East in 1939 and in 1944," *Royal Central Asian Journal* 32 (January 1945): 8–23.

"Behind the British Victory in North Africa: The Story of Supply," (by "a British Officer"), *Foreign Affairs* 22 (January 1944): 318–325.

Bevilecque, Domenico. "L'infiltrazione Americana nei paeci arabi," *Oriente Moderno* 22 (October 1942): 409–410.

Biddle, Eric H. *Manpower: A Summary of the British Experience.* Chicago: Public Administration Service, 1942.

Boardman, Francis. "Civilian Requirements from War to Peace: The Middle East Supply Center," U.S., Department of State, *Bulletin* 13 (23 December 1945): 994–999.

Bonné, Alfred. "Aspects of Economic Reconstruction in West and East," *International Affairs* 22 (October 1946): 521–532.

———. *The Economic Development of the Middle East.* New York: Oxford University Press, 1945.

———. *State and Economics in the Middle East.* 2nd ed. rev. London: Routledge & Kegan, Paul, 1955.

Bourdillon, Sir Bernard H. "Colonial Development and Welfare," *International Affairs* 20 (July 1944): 369–380.

"Britain in the World," *Economist* 145 (4 September 1943): 300–302.

British Chamber of Commerce of Egypt. *Report on Postwar Trade.* Cairo, August 1944.

Brookings Institution, International Studies Group. *Anglo-American Economic Relations: A Problem Paper.* Washington D.C.: 1950.

Brown, Cecil B. *Suez to Singapore.* New York: Random House, 1942.

Brown, Courtney C. "The Combined Boards," U.S., Department of State, *Bulletin* 13 (1 July 1945): 17–20.

Bryant, Sir Arthur. *The Turn of the Tide, 1939–1943; A study based on the diaries and autobiographical notes of Field Marshal the Viscount Alanbrooke.* London: William Collins Sons & Co., 1957.

Budd, Charlotte R. "Iraq's Cigarette Trade and Industry Booming," *Foreign Commerce Weekly* 15 (1 April 1944): 13 ff.

Bullard, Sir Reader W. *Britain and the Middle East.* London: Hutchinson's University Library, 1951.

Butler, Harold. "The American Approach to Reconstruction," *Agenda* 1 (April 1942): 97–107.

Cahill, Kathleen F. "The Economic Importance of Egypt," *Foreign Commerce Weekly* 6 (14 March 1942): 3 ff.

Calhoun, John A. "Iran in 1943," *Foreign Commerce Weekly* 15 (1 April 1944): 8 ff.

Carleton, Alford. "The Syrian Coup d'Etat of 1949," *Middle East Journal* 4 (Winter 1949): 1–11.

Carmichael, Joel. "Notes on Arab Unity," *Foreign Affairs* 21 (October 1943): 148–153.

Caroe, Olaf. *Wells of Power: The Oilfields of South-Western Asia.* London: Macmillan & Co., 1951.

Centre D'Etudes de Politique Etrangère. *Industrialisation de l'Afrique du Nord*. Paris: A. Colin, 1952.

"Il Centro per i Rifornimenti del Medio Oriente," *Oriente Moderno* 22 (11 December 1942): 506.

Chalmers, Henry. "Current Trends in Foreign-Trade Policies, Review of 1944. Part I. Steps Toward Relaxation of Wartime Export Controls," *Foreign Commerce Weekly* 18 (17 February 1945): 10 ff.

————. "Current Trends in Foreign-Trade Policies, Review of 1944. Part II," *Foreign Commerce Weekly* 18 (24 February 1945): 6 ff.

————. "Economic Pooling and Lend-Lease Operations among the Belligerent Allies," *Foreign Commerce Weekly* 10 (13 March 1943): 3 ff.

"Changes in Procedure for Petroleum, Petroleum Products, and Related Products Under Middle East Program Licence," Current Export Bulletin no. 132, *Foreign Commerce Weekly* 13 (20 November 1943): 36.

Chejne, Anwar G. "Egyptian Attitudes Toward Pan-Arabism," *Middle East Journal* 11 (Summer 1957): 253–268.

Churchill, Winston S. *Closing the Ring*. Boston: Houghton Mifflin Co., 1951.

————. *The Grand Alliance*. Boston: Houghton Mifflin Co., 1950.

————. *The Hinge of Fate*. Boston: Houghton Mifflin Co., 1950.

————. *Their Finest Hour*. Boston: Houghton Mifflin Co., 1949.

Clapp, Gordon R. "An Approach to Economic Development: A Summary of the United Nations Economic Survey Mission for the Middle East," *International Conciliation* no. 460 (April 1950): 203–217.

Clarke, R. W. B. *The Economic Effort of War*. London: Allen & Unwin, 1940.

Collins, R. J. *Lord Wavell (1883–1941)*. London: Stoughton, 1947.

"Combined British-American Raw Materials, Munitions and Shipping Boards," U.S., Department of State, *Bulletin* 6 (31 January 1942): 87–88.

"Commonwealth or Empire," *Economist* 145 (4 September 1943): 318–321.

"Controls of Exports from the U.S. of Munitions Materials and Machinery Essential to National Defense," U.S., Department of State, *Bulletin* 3 (6 July 1940): 11–12.

Cooke, Hedley V. *Challenge and Response in the Middle East: The Quest for Prosperity, 1919–1951*. New York: Harper & Brothers, 1952.

Coon, Carleton S. *Caravan: The Story of the Middle East*. New York: Henry Holt Co., 1951.

"Co-ordination of British and American Economic Warfare Procedures," U.S., Department of State, *Bulletin* 6 (14 February 1942): 153.

Court, William H. B. *Coal*. London: H.M.S.O., 1951.

Craig-Martin, Paul F. "Cotton and the Middle East," *Middle East Journal* 6 (Summer 1952): 299–314.

Crowley, Leo T. "The Foreign Economic Administration," *Foreign Commerce Weekly* 14 (5 February 1944): 5.

————. "The United States Commercial Company," *Foreign Commerce Weekly* 15 (24 June 1944): 3 ff.

Dajani, Burhan. "The Economic Significance of a Unity Between Iraq, Syria, Lebanon, Transjordan, and Palestine." Master's thesis, American University of Beirut, 1944.

Dawson, V. H. "Iraq in 1946," *Royal Central Asian Journal* 33 (July–October 1946): 271–280.

Deighton, H. S. "Les relations anglo-égyptiennes," *Politique Etrangère* 12 (March 1947): 23–50.

DeNovo, John A. *American Interests and Policies in the Middle East, 1900–1939.* Minneapolis, Minn.: University of Minnesota Press, 1964.

"The Development of Egyptian Agriculture during the War," *Palnews Economic Journal* 15 (Mid–August 1946): 11.

"Development of the Arab League," U.S., Department of State, *Bulletin* 16 (18 May 1947): 963–970.

"Dissolution of the Middle East Supply Center—Joint Statement by Governments of United States and United Kingdom," U.S., Department of State, *Bulletin* 13 (30 September 1945): 493–494.

"Distribution of Lend-Lease Material," U.S., Department of State, *Bulletin* 10 (18 March 1944): 256.

Dodd, Norris E. "A Survey of Activities in the Food and Agriculture Organization in the Middle East," *Middle East Journal* 4 (July 1950): 352–355.

Dorra, Albert J. "L'industrie égyptienne et ses possibilités de développement," *Egypte Contemporaine* 34 (November 1943): 409–482.

East, W. Gordon. "The Mediterranean: Pivot of Peace and War," *Foreign Affairs* 31 (July 1953): 619–633.

"The Economic Development of the British Colonial Empire," *Bulletin of International News* 20 (20 February 1943): 139–145.

"Economic Reorganization in North African Territories under Allied Military Occupation," *International Labour Review* 47 (May 1943): 628–629.

Eddy, William A. *F.D.R. Meets Ibn Saud.* New York: American Friends of the Middle East, 1954.

"Eden Memorandum. Memorandum of British Government on Distribution of Lend-Lease Material, September 10, 1941," U.S., Department of State, *Bulletin* 5 (13 September 1941): 204–205.

"Egypt: Largest Market in the Near East," *Foreign Commerce Weekly* 3 (19 April 1941): 99 ff.

Elliott, William Yandell. *The British Commonwealth at War.* New York: Alfred A. Knopf, 1943.

Erickson, Ephraim Gordon. "Protest Society: Social Irrationality in the Extra-Territorial One-Sex Company Town." Ph.D. dissertation, University of Chicago, 1947.

Esco Foundation for Palestine. *Palestine, A Study of Jewish, Arab and British Policies.* 2 vol. New Haven: Yale University Press, 1947.

Essaleh, Salah. "L'état actuel de l'économie Syrienne." Doctoral dissertation, Université de Paris, 1943.

Evans, Laurence. *United States Policy and the Partition of Turkey, 1914–1924*. Baltimore, Md.: Johns Hopkins Press, 1965.

Ezekiel, Mordecai, ed. *Towards World Prosperity*. New York: Harper and Brothers, 1947.

Fabian Colonial Bureau. *International Action and the Colonies*. London: Fabian Publications, 1943.

Falaki, Mahmoud Saleh el-. "Pour une politique permanente du blé en Egypte," *Egypte Contemporaine* 34 (December 1943): 597–605.

Farra, Adnan. *L'industrialisation en Syrie*. Geneva: P. E. Grinet, 1950.

"F.E.A. Cites Record of Export-Control Relaxations During 1944," *Foreign Commerce Weekly* 15 (11 April 1944): 36–37.

"F.E.A. Licensing Policy for Shipments to the Middle East," (Current Export Bulletin no. 242) *Foreign Commerce Weekly* 19 (12 May 1945): 54.

Fernan, Friedrich Wilhelm. *Moslems on the March*. New York: Alfred A. Knopf, 1954.

Francis, Eric V. *The Battle for Supplies*. London: J. Cape, 1942.

Francis, René. *Egypt and Industry*. Cairo: N.p., 1949.

Franck, Dorothea S. and Peter G. "The Middle East Economy in 1948," *Middle East Journal* 3 (April 1949): 201–210.

———. "The Middle East Economy in 1949," *Middle East Journal* 4 (April 1950): 221–243.

Frechtling, Louis E. "Allied Strategy in the Near East," *Foreign Policy Reports* 17 (1 February 1942): 274–283.

———. "War in the Eastern Mediterranean," *Foreign Policy Reports* 16 (1 February 1941): 270–280.

"Functional Collaboration in World Affairs," *Nature* 152 (11 December 1943): 671–673.

Gervasi, Frank. *War Has Seven Faces*. Garden City, N.Y.: Doubleday, Doran & Co., 1942.

Ghatit, Muhammad Ali al-. "L'agriculture en Egypte et l'après-guerre," *Egypte Contemporaine* 35 (January–February 1944): 59.

Gibb, H. A. R. "Middle Eastern Perplexity," *International Affairs* 20 (October 1944): 458–482.

Godard, Jean. "Etude statistique de la situation économique en Syrie et au Liban," *Egypt Contemporaine* 34 (March–April 1943): 369–400.

———. "Le problème du blé en Syrie et au Liban pendant la guerre," *Egypte Contemporaine* 35 (March–April 1944): 309–344.

Godard, Jean. "L'oeuvre politique, économique et sociale de la France Combattante en Syrie et au Liban." Doctorat en droit dissertation, Faculté de Droit et des Sciences Economiques, Université Saint-Joseph, Beirut, Lebanon, 1942.

Goldmann, Nahum. "An Eye-Witness Report on Jewish Palestine," *Free World* 9 (January 1945): 47.

Goldberg, Samuel. "Economic Position of Iraq," *Foreign Commerce Weekly* 1 (19 October 1940): 141 ff.

————. "Iran's Trade Position Difficult. Lend-Lease Aid Timely," *Foreign Commerce Weekly* 7 (13 June 1942): 9 ff.

————. "Syria Before the Clash," *Foreign Commerce Weekly* 3 (28 June 1941): 531–532.

————. "Trade Agreement Between Iran and the United States," *Foreign Commerce Weekly* 11 (24 April 1943): 14 ff.

Gross, Feliks. *Crossroads of Two Continents.* New York: Columbia University Press, 1945.

————. "Peace Planning for Central and Eastern Europe," *Annals of American Academy of Political and Social Science* 232 (March 1944): 169–176.

"Growth of the UKCC," *Economist* 145 (13 November 1943): 651–652.

Haberler, Gottfried. "The Political Economy of Regional or Continental Blocs," in Seymour E. Harris, ed., *Postwar Economic Problems.* Cambridge: Harvard University Press, 1943.

Hailey, Lord. "Colonial Policy and Some of the Postwar Problems," *Agenda* 1 (April 1942): 107–118.

Hall, H. Duncan. *North American Supplies.* London: H.M.S.O., 1955.

Hall, H. Duncan, and Wrigley, C. C. *Studies of Overseas Supply.* London: H.M.S.O., 1956.

Hancock, W. K., and Gowing, M. M. *British War Economy.* London: H.M.S.O., 1949.

Hansen, Alvin. "World Institutions for Stability and Expansion," *Foreign Affairs* 22 (January 1944): 248–255.

"Harbors of the Mediterranean," *Egyptian Gazette,* 10 April 1939.

Hargreaves, E. L., and Gowing, M. M. *Civil Industry and Trade.* London: H.M.S.O., 1952.

Harris, Sir Douglas G. "The War Supply Board," *Palnews* (10 March 1941): 1–2.

Harris, C. R. S. "Some Thoughts in Reconstruction," *Agenda* 1 (July 1942): 205–214.

Harris, Seymour E. *Foreign Economic Policy for the United States.* Cambridge: Harvard University Press, 1948.

————. *International and Interregional Economics.* New York: McGraw-Hill Book Co., 1957.

————, ed. *Postwar Economic Problems.* New York: McGraw-Hill Book Co., 1943.

Harvey, Heather J. *Consultation and Co-operation in the Commonwealth.* London: Oxford University Press, 1952.

Hashem, Mohamed Zaki. "The Theory of Economic Development of Underdeveloped Countries with a Study of the Development of the Egyptian Economy: 1927–1947." Ph.D. dissertation, Harvard University, 1950.

Heatherington, Donald F. "Great Britain's Wartime Exports," *Foreign Commerce Weekly* 17 (16 December 1944): 3 ff.

————. "Sterling Balance and Britain's External Debt. Part I," *Foreign Commerce Weekly* 17 (28 October 1944): 7 ff.

————. "Sterling Balance and Britain's External Debt. Part II," *Foreign Commerce Weekly* 17 (4 November 1944): 13 ff.

————. "The United Kingdom Commercial Corporation," *Foreign Commerce Weekly* 15 (22 June 1944): 6 ff.

Henderson, K. D. D. *The Making of the Modern Sudan.* London: Faber & Faber, 1953.

Himadeh, Said B., ed. *Economic Organization of Palestine.* Beirut: American University of Beirut, 1938.

————. *Economic Organization of Syria.* Beirut: American University of Beirut, 1936.

————. *Al-Nizam al-Iqtisadi fi al-Iraq* [Economic Organization of Iraq]. Beirut: American University of Beirut, 1938.

Hodgkin, T. *Nationalism in Colonial Africa.* London: F. Muller, 1956.

Hogg, E. G. "Iraq," *Royal Central Asian Journal* 27 (April 1940): 179–191.

Holborn, Louise W., ed. *War and Peace Aims of the United Nations.* 2 vols. Boston: World Peace Foundation, 1943–48.

Hoselitz, Bert F. "Socialist Planning and International Economic Relations," *American Economic Review* 33 (December 1943): 839–852.

Hoskins, Halford L. *The Middle East.* New York: Macmillan Co., 1954.

————. "The Guardianship of the Suez Canal," *Middle East Journal* 4 (April 1950): 148.

Hourani, A. H. *Syria and Lebanon: A Political Essay.* London: Oxford University Press, 1946.

Howard, H. N. "Middle Eastern Regional Organization: Problems and Prospects," *Proceedings of the Academy of Political Science* 24 (January 1952): 101–111.

Hull, Cordell. *The Memoirs of Cordell Hull.* 2 vols. New York: Macmillan Co., 1948.

Hunter, Guy. "Britain in the Middle East," *Great Britain and the East* 62 (April 1946): 49.

————. "Economic Problems: The Middle East Supply Centre," in George Kirk, *The Middle East in the War.* London: Oxford University Press, 1952.

Hurewitz, J. C. *Middle East Dilemmas: The Background of United States Policy.* New York: Harper & Brothers for Council on Foreign Relations, 1953.

————. *The Struggle for Palestine.* New York: W. W. Norton & Co., 1950.

Hyamson, Albert M. *Palestine Under the Mandate, 1920–1948.* London: Methuen, 1950.

Ibrahim, Nihad N. "Foreign Trade and Economic Development of Syria." Ph.D. dissertation, Columbia University, 1951.

Ingrams, Harold and Doreen. "The Hadhramaut in Times of War," *Geographical Journal* 105 (January–February 1945): 1–25.

"An International Example," *Economist* 145 (4 September 1943): 314–318.
International Labour Office. *The Exploitation of Foreign Labour by Germany*. Studies and Reports, Series C, no. 25. Montreal: 1945.
"International Programming of the Distribution of Resources: a Symposium," *American Statistical Association Journal* 39 (September 1944): 281–296.
Ireland, Philip W. "The Near East and the European War," *Foreign Policy Reports* 16 (15 March 1940): 2–16.
Issawi, Charles. *Egypt: An Economic and Social Analysis*. London: Oxford University Press, 1947.
Izzeddin, Nejla. *The Arab World*. Chicago: Henry Regnery Co., 1953.
Jackson, R. G. A. "Some Aspects of the War and its Aftermath in the Middle East," *Royal Central Asian Journal* 32 (July–October 1945): 258–268.
Janeway, Eliot. *The Struggle for Survival: A Chronicle of Economic Mobilization in World War II*. New Haven: Yale University Press, 1951.
Jewish Agency for Palestine. *The Economic War Effort of Jewish Palestine*. Jerusalem: 1946.
Jordan, Henry P., ed. *Problems of Postwar Reconstruction*. Washington: American Council for Public Affairs, 1942.
Kadi, Mustafa al-. "Iraq's Contribution to the War Effort," *Arab World* 1 (June 1944): 54.
Kahrl, Faith Jessup. "September Incident in Lebanon," *Arab World* 1 (Summer 1944): 51.
Kassardji, L. "Middle East Supply Centre," *Commercial Intelligence Journal* no. 1977 (20 December 1941): 717.
Keen, Bernard A. *The Agricultural Development of the Middle East*. London: H.M.S.O., 1946.
Kettaneh, F. H. "From Chariots to Tanks," *Rotarian* 60 (May 1942): 16–20.
Khadduri, Majid. "Towards an Arab Union: The League of Arab States," *American Political Science Review* 40 (February 1946): 90–100.
Khlat, Paul J. "War Economic Policy in Syria and Lebanon." Master's thesis, American University of Beirut, 1944.
Kiernan, R. H. *Wavell*. London: George G. Harrap & Co., 1945.
Kirk, George. *The Middle East in the War*. Survey of International Affairs, 1939–1946, Royal Institute of International Affairs. London: Oxford University Press, 1952.
Kitchen, Helen A. "*Al-Ahram:* The *Times* of the Arab World," *Middle East Journal* 4 (April 1950): 155–169.
Lackany, S. "From the Middle East Monetary Conference to Bretton Woods," *Egypte Contemporaine* 35 (1944): 95–109.
Landis, James M. "Anglo-American Co-operation in the Middle East," *The Annals of the American Academy of Political and Social Science* 240 (July 1945): 64–72.
———. "Economic Relationships Between the United States and Egypt," *Egypte Contemporaine* 36 (March 1945): 217–227.

————. "Middle East Challenge," *Fortune* 32 (September 1945): 160–164.
Langer, William L., and Gleason, S. Everett. *The Undeclared War, 1940–1941.* New York: Harper & Brothers for Council on Foreign Relations, 1953.
Lawrence, T. E. *Seven Pillars of Wisdom.* Garden City, N.Y.: Doubleday, Doran & Co., 1926.
League of Nations. Economic Intelligence Service. *Wartime Rationing and Consumption.* Geneva: 1942.
Lebanon, Republic of. *The Economic Development of Lebanon.* Report by Sir Alexander Gibb and Partners to the Government of Lebanon. London: 1948.
Leduc, Gaston. "L'évolution économique du Moyen-Orient," *Politique Etrangère* 12 (July 1947): 284–300.
Leighton, Richard M. "Allied Unity of Command in the Second World War: A Study in Regional Organization," *Political Science Quarterly* 67 (September 1952): 399–425.
Leighton, R. M., and Coakley, R. W. *Global Logistics and Strategy, 1940–1943.* U.S., Department of the Army. Washington, D.C.: G.P.O., 1955.
Lenczowski, George. *The Middle East in World Affairs.* Ithaca: Cornell University Press, 1952.
————. *Russia and the West in Iran, 1918–1948: A Study in Big Power Rivalry,* Ithaca: Cornell University Press, 1949.
"Lend-Lease Aid: Iraq and Iran," U.S., Department of State, *Bulletin* 6 (2 May 1942): 383.
"Lend-Lease Operations: Procedure for Handling Problems Arising in Connection with the British White Papers of September 10, 1941," U.S., Department of State, *Bulletin* 6 (24 January 1942): 81–82.
Levi, I. "Réflexions sur certains de nos problèmes économiques et sociaux," *Egypte Contemporaine* 34 (December 1943): 535–548.
Liddell Hart, Capt. B. H. *The Tanks: The History of the Royal Tank Regiment.* 2 vols. New York: Frederick A. Praeger, 1959.
Lloyd, E. M. H. *Food and Inflation in the Middle East, 1940–1945,* Studies on Food, Agriculture, and World War II, Food Research Institute. Stanford: Stanford University Press, 1956.
Lohbeck, Don. *Patrick J. Hurley, an American.* Chicago: Henry Regnery Co., 1956.
Lotz, J. D. "Problems and Proposals: The Iranian Seven Year Plan," *Middle East Journal* 4 (Winter 1950): 102–105.
McClellan, Grant S. "Palestine and America's Role in the Middle East," *Foreign Policy Reports* 21 (1 July 1945): 98–107.
McNeill, William H. *America, Britain and Russia, Their Cooperation and Conflict, 1941–1946.* Survey of International Affairs, 1939–1946, Royal Institute of International Affairs. London: Oxford University Press, 1953.
Magnes, Judah L. "Toward Peace in Palestine," *Foreign Affairs* 21 (January 1943): 239–249.

Mallakh, R. el-. "The Effects of the Second World War on the Economic Development of Egypt." Ph.D. dissertation, Rutgers University, 1954.

Mance, Sir Oliver. "The Future of British Trade with Turkey," *Royal Central Asian Journal* 27 (January 1943): 17.

Manuel, Frank E. *The Realities of American-Palestine Relations.* Washington, D.C.: Public Affairs Press, 1949.

Matloff, Maurice, and Snell, Edwin M. *Strategic Planning for Coalition Warfare, 1941–1942.* Washington: G.P.O., 1953.

Medlicott, W. N. *The Economic Blockade.* Vol. I. London: H.M.S.O., 1952.

"Merchanting Under Exchange Control," *Economist* 145 (4 September 1943): 330–333.

Messiqua, M. "Agriculture et industrie: Aspect international du Problème," *Egypte Contemporaine* 35 (January–February 1944): 3–15.

———. "Problèmes économiques égyptiens d'après-guerre," *Egypte Contemporaine* 35 (March–April 1944): 231–237.

Michaelis, Alfred. "Trade Relations Between the Countries of the Near East in 1938," *Palnews Economic Annual for Palestine* 8 (1939): 118 ff.

"The Middle East I: Food and Politics," *Economist* 144 (20 February 1943): 230.

"Middle East Conference on Agricultural Development," *International Labour Review* 49 (April–May 1944): 480–490.

"Middle East Supply Centre," *Economist* 141 (15 November 1941): 604.

"The Middle East Supply Centre," *International Labour Review* 47 (January 1943): 67–68.

"Middle East Supply Center Restrictions Eased," *Foreign Commerce Weekly* 18 (6 January 1945): 20 ff.

Mikesell, Raymond F., and Chenery, Hollis B. *Arabian Oil: America's Stake in the Middle East.* Chapel Hill: University of North Carolina Press, 1949.

Motter, T. H. Vail. *The Persian Corridor and Aid to Russia.* Washington, D.C.: G.P.O., 1953.

Murray, Keith A. H. "Feeding the Middle East in War-Time," *Royal Central Asian Journal* 32 (July–October 1945): 233–247.

———. "Some Regional Economic Problems of the Middle East," *International Affairs* 23 (January 1947): 11–19.

"The Mutual Security Program: A Program for Peace," *Department of State Bulletin* 26 (17 March 1952): 403–415.

Nassif, E. "Entités nationales et commerce international," *Egypte Contemporaine* 34 (April–May 1943): 335–354.

National Bank of Egypt. *Reports of Ordinary General Meetings.* Cairo, 1940–1945.

"New Trade Waters Chartered," *Business Week* no. 744 (4 December 1943): 47–48.

Oxford Institute of Statistics. *Studies in War Economics.* Oxford, 1947.

Palestine. Office of the High Commissioner. *Catalogue of the Palestine*

Government Industrial Exhibition, Cairo, 1941. Jerusalem: Government Printer, 1941.

——. *The Palestine War Supply Board.* Jerusalem: Government Printer, 1942.

——. Department of Statistics. *Statistical Abstract of Palestine 1944–1945.* Jerusalem: Government Printer, 1946.

——. Palestine War Supply Board. Files, 1941–1945. Deposited in State Archives, Hakirya, Israel.

"Palestine's Potentialities," *Great Britain and the East* 56 (27 February, 1941): 172.

"Palestine Under War Conditions," *Bulletin of International News* 18 (22 March 1941): 324–328.

"Palestine War Supplies Board," *Great Britain and the East* 56 (8 May 1941): 343.

Parr, Grant, and Janssen, G. E. "War Meets Peace in Egypt," *National Geographic Magazine* 81 (April 1942): 503–526.

Pasvolsky, Leo. "The Problem of Economic Peace After the War," U.S., Department of State, *Bulletin* 6 (7 March 1942): 210–219.

Polk, William R., and Butler, W. Jack. *What the Arabs Think,* Headline Series, Foreign Policy Association, no. 96 (New York: November–December 1952).

"Post-War Export Policy," *Economist* 144 (19 June 1943): 780–782.

Prest, Alan R. *War Economics of Primary Producing Countries.* Cambridge: Cambridge University Press, 1948.

"The Principles of Trade," *Economist* 146 (1 January to 19 February 1944): 4 ff.

"Program License Authorizing Exportations to the Middle East," *Foreign Commerce Weekly* 12 (16 September 1943): 36 ff.

Rennell of Rodd, Lord. *British Military Administration of Occupied Territories in Africa* (during 1941–47). London: H.M.S.O., 1948.

Roosevelt, Elliott. *As He Saw It.* New York: Duell, Sloan and Pierce, 1946.

Rosen, S. McKee. *The Combined Boards of the Second World War—An Experiment in International Administration.* New York: Columbia University Press, 1951.

Rosensky, Joseph C. "Armed Forces Provide Stimuli for Post-War Export Sales," *Foreign Commerce Weekly* 14 (25 March 1944): 17 ff.

Rosenstein-Rodan, P. N. "The International Development of Economically Backward Areas," *International Affairs* 20 (April 1944): 158–165.

Rossi, Ettore. "Il Vicino e Medio Oriente di fronte al conflitto Europeo," *Oriente Moderno* 20 (March 1940): 157–176.

Rowan-Robinson, Henry. *Wavell in the Middle East.* New York: Hutchinson & Co., 1942.

"Refugee Centers in the Middle East," U.S., Department of State, *Bulletin* 10 (10 June 1944): 533–534.

"Regional Meeting for the Near and Middle East of the International Labour Organization, Istanbul, Nov. 1947," *International Labour Review* 58 (July 1948): 1–17.

"Relaxation of Import Controls for the Middle East," U.S., Department of State, *Bulletin* 11 (31 December 1944): 846–847.

"Review of the Work of the Middle East Supply Center," U.S., Department of State, *Bulletin* 12 (30 September 1945): 493.

Royal Institute of International Affairs. *Documents on Regional Organisation Outside Western Europe, 1940–1949*. London: Oxford University Press, 1950.

———. *The Middle East: A Political and Economic Survey*. London: Royal Institute of International Affairs, 1950.

———. *The World in March 1939*. Survey of International Affairs, 1939–1946. London, 1952.

Samuel, Edwin. "The Government of Israel and Its Problems," *Middle East Journal* 3 (January 1949): 10.

Sarc, Ömer Celâl. "Economic Policy of the New Turkey," *Middle East Journal* 2 (October 1948): 440.

Sayegh, Fayez A. *Arab Unity*. New York: Devin-Adair Co., 1958.

———. "Recent Trends Toward Arab Unity," *Lands East* 3 (April 1958): 8–13.

Sayers, R. S. *Financial Policy, 1939–45*. London: H.M.S.O., 1956.

Sayre, Joel. *Persian Gulf Command*. New York: Random House, 1945.

Schatz, Jean. "La guerre et ses conséquences sur le commerce extérieur," *Egypte Contemporaine* 31 (December 1940): 547 ff.

———. "La Syrie et ses relations commerciales avec l'Egypte," *Egypte Contemporaine* 30 (February–March 1939): 215–246.

———. "Le Commerce Extérieur de l'Egypte pendant les deux guerres mondiales," *Egypte Contemporaine* 36 (November–December 1945): 763–845.

Schellenbacher, E. E. "Government Influence on Foreign Trade," *Foreign Commerce Weekly* 18 (3 February 1945): 3.

Schueller, Richard. "New Methods of Trade Policy," in Henry R. Jordan, ed., *Problems of Postwar Reconstruction*. Washington: American Council of Public Affairs, 1942.

Shaffer, Robert. *Tents and Towers of Arabia*. New York: Dodd, Mead & Co., 1952.

Sherwood, Robert E. *Roosevelt and Hopkins*. rev. ed. New York: Harper & Brothers, 1950.

Shwadran, Benjamin. *The Middle East, Oil, and the Great Powers*. New York: Frederick A. Praeger, 1955.

Simpich, Frederick. "Mediterranean Checkerboard," *National Geographic Magazine* 81 (April 1942): 527–550.

Simpich, Frederick, and Moore, W. Robert. "Bombs over Bible Lands," *National Geographic Magazine* 80 (August 1941): 141–180.

Smith, Kingsbury. "The American Plan for a Reorganized World," *American Mercury* 55 (November 1942): 536–547.

Soule, George M. "The United States and Britain's Economic Policy," *Annals of American Academy of Political and Social Science* 240 (July 1945): 55–63.

Speiser, E. A. *The United States and the Near East.* Cambridge: Harvard University Press, 1950.

Staley, Eugene. "The Economic Implication of Lend Lease," *American Economic Review* 33 (March 1943): 362–376.

Stettinius, Edward R., Jr. *Lend-Lease: Weapon for Victory.* New York: Macmillan Co., 1944.

Stoddard, Lothrop. *The New World of Islam.* New York: Charles Scribner's Sons, 1922.

Straight, Michael. *Make this the Last War: The Future of the United Nations.* New York: Harcourt, Brace & Co., 1943.

Sulzberger, Cyrus L. "German Preparations in the Middle East," *Foreign Affairs* 20 (July 1942): 663–678.

"Syria and Lebanon, Economic Conditions," *Foreign Commerce Weekly* 15 (29 April 1944): 17 ff.

Taft, Charles B. "An Integrated Post-War Economic Program," U.S., Department of State, *Bulletin* 11 (November 1944): 610–613.

Tannous, Afif I. "War-Time Food Situation in the Middle East," *Foreign Agriculture* 11 (March 1945): 34–45.

Thomas, Lewis V., and Frye, Richard N. *The United States and Turkey and Iran.* Cambridge: Harvard University Press, 1951.

Toynbee, Arnold and Veronica, eds. *The Realignment of Europe.* Survey of International Affairs, 1939–1946, Royal Institute of International Affairs. London: Oxford University Press, 1955.

————. *The War and the Neutral.* Survey of International Affairs, 1939–1946, Royal Institute of International Affairs. London: Oxford University Press, 1956.

U.K., Board of Trade. *Aims and Plan of Work of the Export Council.* London: H.M.S.O., 1940.

————. *Board of Trade Journal 1940–45.* London: H.M.S.O.

————. *Overseas Economic Surveys: Egypt, May 1945.* London: H.M.S.O., 1945.

————. *Overseas Economic Surveys: Iran, April 1948.* London: H.M.S.O., 1948.

————. *Overseas Economic Surveys: Iraq, February 1945.* London: H.M.S.O., 1946.

————. *Overseas Economic Surveys: Iraq, June 1949.* London: H.M.S.O., 1949.

————. *Overseas Economic Surveys: Palestine, February 1945.* London: H.M.S.O., 1945.

————. *Overseas Economic Surveys: Turkey, September 1947.* London: H.M.S.O., 1948.

————. *Report of the British Goodwill Trade Mission to Egypt, Nov.–Dec. 1945.* London: H.M.S.O., 1946.

U.K., British Information Services. *Britain and Middle East Development.* New York: 1951.
———. *The British Colonial Development and Welfare Acts.* ID-892 Rev. New York: February 1953.
———. *The British Middle East Office.* New York: January 1952.
———. *50 Facts about the Middle East.* New York: 1944.
———. His Excellency the Viceroy's Speech at the Opening of the Eastern Group Conference at Delhi on Friday the 25th October 1940. Mimeographed. New York: 1940.
———. *The Organization of the British Foreign Service.* New York: September 1949.
———. *Paiforce, the Official Story of the Persia and Iraq Command, 1941–46.* London: H.M.S.O., 1948.
———. *West Indian Federation.* New York: August 1953.
U.K., Central Office of Information. *International Economic Organisation. The Transition from War to Peace.* London: H.M.S.O., 1947.
U.K., Colonial Office. *Annual Report on Aden and Aden Protectorate, 1946.* London: H.M.S.O., 1948.
———. *Report of West Indian Royal Commission.* London: H.M.S.O., 1945.
U.K., Eastern Supply Group Council. Eastern Group List: Engineering Stores. Mimeographed. Simla, 1943.
U.K., Foreign Office. British Embassy, Washington. Release on British Supply Mission, Middle East. Mimeographed. Washington, D.C., 30 October 1945.
U.K., House of Commons. Official Reports. *Parliamentary Debates.* London: H.M.S.O.
U.K., Mesopotamia Commission. *Report of the Commission Appointed by Act of Parliament to Enquire into the Operation of War in Mesopotamia.* London: H.M.S.O., 1917.
U.K., Ministry of Information. Broadcast on Middle East Supply Centre. Press Release. London: 30 October 1942.
———. "British Army Brings Development to the Middle East." Overseas Publicity Telegram, no. 143. London: 3 December 1942.
———. *The Work of the Middle East Supply Centre during the European War.* Cairo: Nile Press, 1945.
U.K., Ministry of Supply. British Ministry of Supply Mission. United Kingdom Commercial Corp., Mission, New York. "The Flow of Civilian Requirements to the Middle East-Persian Gulf Areas." Mimeographed. New York: 30 April 1943
U.K., War Office. Commander in Chief, The Middle East Forces (General Sir Bernard Paget). "Middle East Review, 1944." Mimeographed. Cairo: 1945.
U.N., Conciliation Commission for Palestine. *Final Report of the United Nations Economic Survey Mission for the Middle East, Part I and II,* Lake Success: 1949.

————. Definitions of the Term "Middle East." Research Memorandum no. 10, Doc. 51–38164, February 1951.

U.N., Economic and Social Council, Official Records. Ninth Session, *Report of the Adhoc Committee for the Middle East,* Supplement no. 4, (E/1360–E/AC.26/16), New York: 1949.

U.N., Food and Agriculture Organization of the United Nations. *Report of the Near East Pre-Conference Regional Meeting. Beirut, Sept. 12–17, 1949.* Doc. C 49/I and II/6. Washington, D.C.: 21 November 1949.

U.N., Secretariat, Department of Economic Affairs. *Review of Economic Conditions in the Middle East.* New York, 1951.

"Unrest in the Levant," *Economist* 145 (3 July 1943): 2–4.

U.S., Bureau of the Budget. Special Mission at U.S. Embassy, London. "Regional Organization in the Middle East," 2 vols. London: 28 May 1944.

————. *Foreign Trade of the United States, 1936–48.* Washington, D.C.: G.P.O., 1951.

————. *International Transactions of the U.S. During the War, 1940–1945.* Washington, D.C.: G.P.O., 1948.

U.S., 76th Congress. *Lend-Lease,* 7th Quarterly Report to Congress. Washington, D.C.: G.P.O., December 1942.

U.S., Department of Agriculture, Plant Pest Control Branch. "Senn Pest," *Cooperative Economic Insect Report,* vol. 7, no. 5 (1 February 1957): 88.

————. "The Senn Pest," PA-582 (Washington, D.C.: G.P.O., August 1963).

U.S., Department of Commerce, Bureau of Foreign and Domestic Commerce. Memorandum to Regional and District Offices, "The Commodity Index as used by the Middle East Supply Centre in Middle East Import Control." Washington, D.C.: 24 July 1944.

————. *Foreign Aid by the United States Government, 1940–51.* Washington, D.C.: G.P.O., 1952.

U.S., Department of State. *Foreign Relations of the United States: Diplomatic Papers, 1933, 1940, 1941, 1942, 1943, 1944, 1945.* Washington, D.C.: G.P.O., 1948–1969.

————. *Mandate for Palestine.* Washington, D.C.: G.P.O., 1931.

————. "Official History of Lend-Lease—Middle East, Part 2: Civilian Lend-Lease" [by Letitia Lewis]. Washington, n.d.

————. *Postwar Foreign Policy Preparation 1939–1945* by Klaus Knorr, Publication no. 3580, General Foreign Policy Series 15. Washington, D.C.: G.P.O., 1949.

————. *Regional Organizations,* Publication no. 4944. Washington, D.C.: G.P.O., April 1953.

————. *Toward World Economic and Social Advance,* Publication no. 2811. Washington, D.C.: G.P.O., 1947.

U.S., Department of War. U.S. Army Forces in the Middle East

Headquarters, Economic Division. "British Financial Policy in the Middle East." Mimeographed. Cairo: 10 February 1944.

———. U.S. Army Forces in the Middle East (USAFIME) Headquarters, Economic Division. "Exchange Rates in the Middle East." Mimeographed. Cairo: 29 January 1944.

———. United States Army, Persian Gulf Command, Office of the Fiscal Adviser. "Irrigation in Iran." Mimeographed. Teheran: March 1944.

———. United States Army, Persian Gulf Command, Office of the Fiscal Director. "The Sterling Bloc in the Middle East." Mimeographed. 10 February 1944.

U.S., Foreign Economic Administration. *Report to Congress on Operations, September 25, 1944.* Washington, D.C.: G.P.O., 1944.

———, Special Areas Branch. The Combined Food Board, The Combined Raw Materials Board, The Combined Production and Resources Board and their Recommendations pertaining to the Middle East, As of June 1944. Mimeographed. Washington, D.C.: July 1944.

———. Lend-Lease Procedure in the Middle East. Mimeographed. Washington, D.C.: October 1944.

———. The Middle East Supply Center. Mimeographed. Washington, D.C.: May 1944.

———. Professional and Administrative Personnel of Special Areas Branch. Mimeographed. Washington, D.C.: 26 May 1944.

———, United States Commercial Company. The United Kingdom Commercial Corporation, Middle East Board of Direction (Its Organization, Functions and Operating Relationship with the MESC), by Charles Breasted. Mimeographed. Cairo: August 1943.

U.S., General Services Administration. National Archives and Records Service. *Federal Records of World War II, Vol. I: Civilian Agencies; Vol. II: Military Agencies.* Washington, D.C., G.P.O., 1950–1951.

U.S., International Development Advisory Board. *Partners in Progress, Report to the President of the United States.* Washington, D.C.: G.P.O., March 1951.

U.S., Office of War Information. *American Handbook.* Washington, D.C.: Public Affairs Press, 1945

———. "The Middle East Supply Center," *Foreign Commerce Weekly* 11 (5 June 1943): 8 ff.

"U.S. Supply Arrangements for the Middle East," U.S., Department of State, *Bulletin* 13 (4 November 1945): 727.

Walton, Francis. *Miracle of World War II.* New York: Macmillan & Co., 1956.

Ward, Barbara. *The West at Bay.* New York: W. W. Norton & Co., 1948.

Wardlow, Chester. *The Transportation Corps: Responsibilities, Organization, and Operations.* Washington, D.C.: G.P.O., 1951.

Warriner, Doreen. *Land and Poverty in the Middle East.* London: Royal Institute of International Affairs, 1948.

"Wartime Commercial and Industrial Developments in the Middle East (The Middle East Supply Center)," *International Labour Review* 47 (January 1943): 66–69, 47 (June 1943): 751–753, 48 (July 1943): 81–82.

"War-time Economy of Transjordan during the Years 1939/1944," *Middle East Economic and Statistical Bulletin* no. 27 (July 1945): 17–18.

Weinryb, Bernard D. "Industrial Development of the Middle East," *Quarterly Journal of Economics* 61 (May 1947): 471–499.

Wild, Paysan S., Jr. "Machinery of Collaboration between the United Nations," *Foreign Policy Reports* 18 (1 July 1942): 94–107.

Wilmington, Martin W. "The Middle East Supply Center: A Reappraisal," *Middle East Journal* 6 (Spring 1952): 144–166.

Winant, Frederick G. "The Combined Middle East Supply Program," U.S., Department of State, *Bulletin* 10 (26 February 1944): 199–203.

———, and Dawson, John P. "The Middle East Supply Program," *Foreign Commerce Weekly,* 15 (April 1, 1944), 3 ff.

Winterton, Earl. "Imperial Strategic Reserves," *Royal Central Asian Journal* 29 (January 1942): 30–34.

———. "The Mobilization of the British Commonwealth," *Quarterly Review* no. 278 (April 1941): 157–170.

Witherow, Grace A. "U.S. Cash Foreign Trade (Final 1942 figures)," *Foreign Commerce Weekly* 11 (3 April 1943): 4 ff.

Woodbridge, George. *UNRRA, the History of the United Nations Relief and Rehabilitation Administration.* 3 vols. New York: Columbia University Press, 1950.

Woodward, Sir Llewellyn. *British Foreign Policy in the Second World War.* London: H.M.S.O., 1962.

Worthington, E. B. *Middle East Science: A Survey of Subjects Other Than Agriculture.* London: H.M.S.O., 1946.

Wu Yuan-Li. *Economic Warfare.* New York: Prentice-Hall, 1952.

Young, Philip. "F.E.A. Functions in the Export Field," *Foreign Commerce Weekly* 15 (15 April 1944): 8.

Zionist Organization of America. *The Palestine Yearbook, Vol. 2: 5705 (1945–46).* New York: 1946.

Unpublished Private Papers

(* Indicates wartime position of correspondent.)

William S. Culbertson,* Ambassador, Chairman of United States Special Economic Mission to North Africa and Middle East (1944–45). Private records pertaining to Mission.

Marshall Macduffie,* Director of Material Supplies, Middle East Supply Centre, 1942–45. Private records pertaining to functions at M.E.S.C.

Letters

Armitage, Flora A., British Information Service. 15 December 1953.
Biaggi, Paulette. Paris, 15 August 1952.
Crawford, F. W., Director, Development Division, British Middle East Office, Beirut. Cairo, 18 September 1951.
Dawson, John P., * Executive Director, Combined Agency for Middle East Supplies, Washington (1943–1944). Ann Arbor, Mich., 18 October 1951.
Jackson, R. G. A. London, 17 October 1951.
———. London, 15 August 1952.
———. London, 20 June 1952.
Landis, James M., * Minister, Director of American Economic Operations in the Middle East, 1943–1946. N.p., 12 July 1951.
Loomis, Capt. F. Kent, U.S.N., Assistant Director of Naval History, U.S., Department of the Navy. Washington, D.C., 9 July 1959.
Nicholson, E. M., * U.K., Ministry of War Transport. N.p., 16 September 1952.
Shimoni, Yaakov, Counsellor, Embassy of Israel, Washington. Memorandum, "Israeli Opinion of the M.E.S.C.," Washington, D.C., 1 September 1953.
Shurcliff, Alice W., Director of Division for Foreign Labor Conditions, U.S. Department of Labor. Washington, D.C., 13 October 1952.
Taft, Charles P., * Director, Office of Wartime Economic Affairs, U.S. Department of State. Cincinnati, Ohio, 14 September 1952.

Other Letters

Dawson, John P., * Executive Director, Combined Agency for Middle East Supplies, Washington, D.C. (1943–1944). To Norman S. Mangouni, Director, State University of New York Press. Cambridge, Mass., 30 December 1970.
Diamond, William, * Near Eastern Affairs Division, U.S. Department of State. To Harvey H. Hall, Editor, *Middle East Journal*. Washington, D.C., 27 February 1952.
Kitchen, Jeffrey C., Near Eastern Affairs Division, U.S. Department of State. To Harvey H. Hall, Editor, *Middle East Journal*. Washington, D.C., 4 March 1952.

Interviews

Alexandrian, Nigoghos, Businessman, Baghdad. Bois de Boulogne, Lebanon, 5 August 1970.
Amin, Mustafa, Co-Publisher, *Akhbar El-Yom,* Cairo. 25 July 1954, Cairo.
Anderson, Rex A., Chief of Administration, Management Staff, U.S., Department of Commerce. Washington, 14 July 1951.
Apelian, George A., * Owner, Apelian Tire Co., Aleppo, Syria. Bois de Boulogne, Lebanon, 5 August 1970.

Aziz, Hassan Abdul,* Leather Merchant, Cairo. Cairo, 31 August 1954.

Azmi, Kamil, Assistant Secretary General, Federation of Egyptian Industries, Cairo. Cairo, 15 July 1954.

Badeau, Dr. John S., * Regional Chief for the Middle East, U.S. Office of War Information. New York, 10 February 1956.

Bailey, E. E., * Deputy Director General, Middle East Supply Centre (1942–1945), * Director General (1945). London, 7 September 1954.

Bailey, Ronald W., * Press Secretary, British Embassy, Cairo. Washington, D.C., 27 August 1952.

Barnea, Joseph, * Economic Research Institute, Jewish Agency of Palestine, Jerusalem. United Nations, N.Y., 15 February 1955.

Biddle, Eric H., * Head of Special Mission of Budget Bureau, London. United Nations, N.Y., 14 January 1953.

Boardman, Francis, Near Eastern Affairs Division, U.S., Department of State, Washington, D.C., 21 August 1952.

Bonné, Alfred, * Director of Economic Research Bureau of Jewish Agency for Palestine, Jerusalem. New York, 15 May 1951; 7 April 1954.

Brown, Winthrop, * Executive Officer, U.S. Mission for Economic Affairs, London, 1942–1945. London, 5 September 1954.

Bullard, Sir Reader,* British Minister and Ambassador in Teheran (1939–1946). New York, 15 January 1953.

Burns, Norman, Principal Economic Officer, Office of Near Eastern Affairs, U.S., Department of State. Washington, D.C., 10 July 1952.

Coneybear, John F., * Assistant Director of Transport, M.E.S.C. (1943); * Chief Representative, M.E.S.C., Jidda, Saudi Arabia (1944). New York, 12 December 1952.

Coombs, Earl, * U.S. Treasury Delegation, Cairo. New York, 15 September 1952.

Crawford, F. W., Director, Development Division, British Middle East Office. Beirut, 6 July 1954.

Cristelow, Allan, * U.K. Member of Executive Committee of Combined Agency for Middle East Supplies (C.A.M.E.S.), Washington, 1943–1944. Washington, D.C., 19 August 1952, 20 August 1952, 28 August 1952.

Culbertson, William S., * Chairman of the U.S. Special Economic Mission to North Africa and the Middle East (1944–45). Washington, D.C., 15 August 1952.

Cumberbatch, A. Noel, * British Commercial Attaché, Teheran, 1940–1945. London, 10 September 1954.

Diab, Georges N., Member of Editorial Staff, *Commerce du Levant* (Beirut). Beirut, 9 July 1954.

Djabri, Tarek, * Landowner in Aleppo, Syria. New York, 28 July 1953.

Eagleton, Clyde, Professor of International Law, New York University. New York, 15 November 1951.

Eborall, C. H., * Psychological Warfare Officer in charge of Balkan Propaganda, G.H.Q., British Middle East Command. New York, 15 October 1952.

Eisinger, L., * Assistant Director of Materials Supplies, M.E.S.C. London, 13 September 1954.

Ekserdjian, N. M., * Military Liaison Officer, M.E.S.C., at General Headquarters, British Forces, Middle East, Cairo. London, 12 September 1954.

Empson, Charles E., * Commercial Counsellor, British Embassy, Cairo, 1940–1944. New York, 15 November 1956.

Ezrachi, Ettan, Economist, Israeli delegation to the United Nations. New York, 6 February 1953.

Frechtling, Louis E., Near Eastern Affairs Division, U.S. Department of State. Washington, D.C., 15 July 1951.

Gordon, William A., * Transportation Division, M.E.S.C. New York, 5 December 1952.

Gunter, John W.,* U.S. Treasury representative, Cairo (1944–1945). Washington, D.C., 2 August 1952.

Hamdy, A. H., Vice President, North East Africa Trading Co., Cairo. Cairo, 10 July 1954.

Higgins, Thomas J., * Traffic Manager, W. D. Blood & Co., Exporters and Importers, New York. New York, 31 May 1956.

Hyde, Henry Van Zile, * Chief of Medical Requirements Division, M.E.S.C. Washington, D.C., 15 August 1951.

Iliff, William A. B., * United Kingdom Treasury Representative, Cairo. Washington, D.C., 18 August 1952.

Jackson, Robert G. A., * Director General, M.E.S.C. New York, 1 June 1954.

Jones, G. Lewis, * U.S. Commercial Attache, Cairo, May 1942. Washington, D.C., 15 August 1951.

Kekhia, Hassan S., * Local Collection Officer, Office des Céréales Panifiables, Syria. New York, 27 August 1953.

Kettaneh, Francis H., * President, Kettaneh Brothers (New York, London, Cairo). New York, 6 February 1953.

Khadduri, Majid, Johns Hopkins University, School of Advanced Studies. Washington, D.C., 1 August 1952.

Kofsky, Bernard W., * Staff of the U.S. War Manpower Commission. United Nations, N.Y., 16 June 1953.

Lackany, S., Bey, Vice President, Zilkha Bank, Cairo. Cairo, 10 July 1954.

Landis, James M., * Director of American Economic Operations in the Middle East, 1943–1945. New York, 9 February 1953.

Lardicos, N., * Commercial Assistant, American Embassy, Cairo. Cairo, 19 July 1954.

Levison, George A., * Special Assistant (and deputy) to Director of American Economic Mission to the Middle East (1944–1945). New York, 2 December 1953.

Lewis, Letitia, Historical Policy Research Division, U.S. Department of State. Washington, D.C., 25 July 1952.

Macduffie, Marshall, * Director of Material Supplies, m.e.s.c. New York: August 14, 1952; 20 January 1953.

Majidian, Ahmad, New York representative of Bank Melli (National Bank of Iran). New York, 18 May 1953.

Malinowski, Dr. Wladyslaw R., Chief, Regional Commissions Section, Department of Economic Affairs, United Nations. United Nations, N.Y., 16 June 1953.

Mavromichalis, B., * Drug importer and distributor in Jerusalem. New York, 12 January 1953.

Maxwell, Russell L., * Commanding General, U.S. Forces in the Middle East, Cairo. New York, 2 October 1952.

McCloud, John, * u.k.c.c. representative in Turkey and Kenya. New York, 25 December 1954.

Michaelis, Alfred,* Editor of *Palnews Economic Journal*, Tel Aviv (1940–1946). New York, 13 February 1953, 14 April 1953.

Mikesell, Raymond F., * United States Treasury Representative, Middle East (1944–1945). Washington, D.C., 30 October 1953.

Mills, Arthur, * Regional Director, Office des Céréales Panifiables, Beirut (1942–1945). Beirut, 13 July 1954.

Mizrachi, M., * Publisher, *Commerce du Levant*. Beirut, 12 July 1954.

Moffat, Douglas M., * Principal United States Representative *per interim*, Executive Committee, M.E.S.C. (1943). New York, 24 October 1952.

Orchard, John E., * Director, General Areas Branch, U.S. Foreign Economic Administration (1943–1944). New York, 16 April 1953.

Pansera, Filippo, M.D., * Resident Physician, Italian Hospital, Cairo. Cairo, 18 July 1954.

Phares, Georges, Director, Bureau des documentations Syriennes et Arabes, Damascus. Damascus, 7 July 1954.

Polk, Judd, Chief, British Commonwealth and Middle East Division, Office of International Finance, U.S. Treasury Department. Washington, D.C., 20 August 1952.

Prior, Sir Geoffrey, * British Political Resident, Persian Gulf Area, 1939–1946. New York, 28 March 1953.

Raymond, E. R., * Agricultural Attache, U.S. Legation, Cairo. Washington, D.C., 15 August 1951.

Riddleberger, James W., * U.S. member of Middle East Supplies Committee, London. Washington, D.C., 22 August 1952.

Rifaat, Mohammed A., * Director, Import Permit Office, Egypt, 1943; * Member of Joint U.S.-U.K.-Egyptian Control of Imports Committee (1942–1945). Cairo, 20 July 1954.

Robinson, C. K., Executive Secretary for Agricultural Economics, Caribbean Commission, United Kingdom Section. United Nations, N.Y., 16 June 1953.

Sanua, Victor D., * Staff member of printing concern in Cairo. New York, N.Y., 5 June 1957.

Saunders, Dero A., * Assistant Chief, Middle East Division, Special Areas Branch, Foreign Economic Administration, 1944; * Director of American Economic Mission to the Middle East (1945). New York, 20 September 1951.

Sayegh, Fayez A., * Officer in Charge of Prosecution in Departments of Food and Price Control, Palestine (1942–1943). United Nations, N.Y., 23 June 1953.

Schulte, Arthur D., * Representative of United States Commercial Corporation in the Middle East, 1944. New York, 20 March 1956.

Seroussi, N., President, N. Seroussi Co., Khartoum. Khartoum, 10 August 1954.

Shalom, Nessim, * Secretary of Anglo-Egyptian Supplies Committee; * First Secretary, Egyptian Federation of Industries (March 1942–December 1944). United Nations, N.Y., 14 September 1953.

Short, Livingston, L., * Member of Executive Committee of M.E.S.C., 1944–1945. New York, 21 September 1951.

Simpson, K. J., Levant Department, U.K., Foreign Office. London, 10 September 1954.

Tanamly, Abdel Monem el-, Assistant Director, Financial and Economic Affairs Department, Ministry of Finance. New York, 27 November 1952.

Tannous, Afif I., Office of Foreign Agricultural Relations, U.S. Department of Agriculture. Washington, D.C., 10 July 1951.

Thompson, R. C., * Member of U.S. Special Economic Mission to the Middle East (1944–1945). New York, 12 January 1953.

Umari, Nathir Akram, Iraq Delegation to the United Nations. New York, 15 February 1954.

Winant, Frederick G., * Chairman of Executive Committee, M.E.S.C. (1942–1943). Washington, D.C., 15 July 1951, 22 August 1952, 28 August 1952, 29 August 1952.

Witcon, E., * Deputy Controller of Supply, Government of Palestine, 1942–1944. Tel Aviv, 3 September 1954.

Woodbridge, George, * Deputy Director General, M.E.S.C. (1945); * Director of Programming, M.E.S.C. (1944). Washington, D.C., 18 August 1952.

Wordsworth, M. E., * District Commissioner, Sudan Government, 1931–1946. Beirut, 13 July 1954.

Worthington, E. B., * Member of the Scientific Advisory Mission to the Middle East Supply Centre, 1943–1944. New York, 23 March 1953.

Newspapers and Periodicals

Agenda (London).
Ahram, al- (Cairo).
American Mercury (New York).
Arab World (New York: Arab Information Office).

Bourse Egyptienne (Cairo).
Bulletin (Washington, D.C.: U.S., Department of State).
Bulletin de la Chambre de Commerce française du Caire (Cairo).
Bulletin of the Economic Research Institute of the Jewish Agency for Palestine (Jerusalem).
Commerce du Levant (Beirut).
Cyprus Post (Nicosia).
Economist, The (London).
Egypte Contemporaine (Cairo: Société Fuad I d'Economie, de Statistique et de Législation).
Egyptian Gazette (Cairo).
Egyptian Mail (Cairo).
Financial Times (London).
Foreign Affairs (New York: Council on Foreign Relations).
Foreign Commerce Weekly (Washington, D.C.: U.S., Department of Commerce).
Foreign Policy Bulletin (New York: Foreign Policy Association).
Foreign Policy Reports (New York: Foreign Policy Association).
Fortune (New York).
Great Britain and the East (London).
International Affairs (London: Royal Institute of International Affairs).
International Labour Review (Geneva: International Labour Office).
Journal of Political Economy (Chicago).
Journal de Teheran (Teheran).
Lands East (Washington, D.C.: Middle East Institute).
Messagero, Il (Rome).
Middle East Journal (Washington, D.C.: Middle East Institute).
Middle Eastern Affairs (New York: Council for Middle Eastern Affairs).
Monthly Labor Review (Washington, D.C.: U.S., Department of Labor).
Moyen-Orient (Paris).
Nabard-i Imruz (Teheran)
New York Times, The (New York).
Oriente Moderno (Rome: Instituto per l'Oriente).
Palestine Gazette (Jerusalem).
Palestine Post (now Jerusalem Post).
Palnews (Tel Aviv: Palestine News Service).
Political Science Quarterly (New York).
Politique étrangère (Paris: Centre d'etudes de Politique Etrangère).
Revue d'Egypte Economique et Financiere (Cairo).
Revue Egyptienne de Droit International (Cairo).
Royal Central Asian Journal (London: Royal Central Asian Society).
Times, The (London).
World Affairs (London: Royal Institute of International Affairs).

Index

Abi Chahla, Hassan Bey, 150
Aden, 3-4, 24, 28
Afghanistan, 2
Afrika Korps, 15, 49, 55, 116
Allen, Dr. H. B., 156
Algeria, 155
Allied Maritime Transport Council, 35
American Economic Mission to the Middle East (A.E.M.M.E.), 65
American University in Cairo, The, 66
American University of Beirut, 120
Anglo-American Combined Boards, 95, 101
Anglo-American Coordinating Committee, 181
Anti-Inflation Conference, 146
Anti-Locust Research Centre, 123
Arabian Peninsula, xvii, 123
Arab League (see League of Arab States)
Arab Sheikhdoms, xvii, 4, 25
"Arcadia" (conference), 54
Armenians, 24
Atlantic Charter, 55, 78
Auchinleck, Gen. Sir Claude, 37-39, 185
Azerbaijan, 23
Aziz, Hassan Abdul, 104 ff.

Bahrein, 133
Bailey, E. E., 156

Baliol-Scott, N., 47-48
Bank Melli (see National Bank of Iran)
Basra, 16, 62-63, 130
Benghazi, 100, 105
Bernadotte, Count Folke, xi
Bonné, Alfred, 152
British East Africa, 24, 90, 123, 125, 170
British Middle East Command, 6, 15, 19, 30-32, 35, 40, 47, 49, 53, 75, 81-82, 109, 140
British Military Mission in the Levant (Spears Mission), 81, 121, 190, 192
British Somaliland, xviii, 3-4, 127
British Supply Council, 52
British White Paper of 1939, 26
Brooke, Gen. Sir Alan Francis (Viscount Alanbrooke), 38
Brown, F. J., 188-189
Brown, Winthrop J., 188
"bulk indent," 90, 138, 193
Bullitt, William C., 65

Casey, Richard G., 45-46, 82
cereals, 18, 42, 76, 114-119, 121-123
Ceylon, 127
Churchill, Winston S., 3, 13-14, 31, 33, 37-39, 178
colonialism, 28

Combined Agency for Middle East Supplies (CAMES), 70-74, 82, 87, 89, 94-97, 101, 188-189, 193
Coneybear, John F., 66
Cristelow, Allan, 188-189
crops, xv, 18, 25, 40, 58, 77, 115, 119
Culbertson Mission, 164 ff., 206
Culbertson, William S., xviii, 164-165
currency, 146, 199
Cyprus, xviii, 3-4, 18, 22, 28, 116-117, 125-127
Cyrenaica, xvii, 4, 105, 121, 124, 181, 213

Dawson, John P., 67, 156
Donovan, Gen. William B., 62
Dill, Gen. Sir John, 37, 140

East African Supply Centre, 169-170
East African Governors' Conference, 170
Eastern Group Supply Conference, 12, 31
Eastern Group Supply Council (E.G.S.C.), 31, 37, 173, 180
economic regionalism, x, xvii, 1, 7, 151 ff., 167
economic warfare, 22-23, 178
Economist, The (London), 5, 61
Eden, Anthony, 6, 37, 43, 140
Egypt, xvii, 2-4, 12, 17-18, 21-25, 27, 30, 33-34, 37, 46, 49, 52, 54, 56, 59-60, 73, 76, 106-107, 115, 117-118, 124-127, 149-150, 166, 197, 213
Eighth Army, xvii, 55, 60, 63, 122, 176
El Alamein, ix, xiv, 5, 8, 16, 48-49, 62, 68, 122-123, 185, 187
Elliott, Harold, 129
Empson, Charles, 33
Eritrea, xviii, 3-4, 124-125, 150, 213

Eritrea Base Command, 60
Ethiopia, xviii, 3-4, 21-22, 37, 39, 124-125, 199, 213-214
Export Control Office, 51

Faruq I, King of Egypt, 26, 79
Food and Agriculture Organization of the United Nations, xiii-xiv
food rationing, 119
Foreign Economic Administration (F.E.A.), 67, 71, 94-96, 188
France, 2, 10-12, 23, 160
French Army of the Levant, 21, 23
fuels, 18, 34, 76

gold, 146-147
Gold Coast, 59
Graziani, Marshal Rodolfo, 15
Greece, 15, 26, 32-33, 37, 39-40, 117, 127
Greeks, 24

Hadhramaut, 22, 127
Haifa, 16, 107
Haining, Gen. Sir Robert, 38, 179-180
Hankey, Lord, 32-33
Harman, Avraham, xviii
Harriman, W. Averell, 62, 188
Hauser, John M., 4
health, public, 135-139
Hebrew University of Jerusalem, The, 7, 43
Hopkins, Harry, 190-191
Hoskins, Harold B., 67, 187
Hull, Cordell, 58, 164, 202
Hurley, Maj. Gen. Patrick J., 65, 78, 203
Hutchinson, Brig. B. A., 32, 36
Hyde, Dr. Henry Van Zile, 66, 135

Ibn Saud, King of Saudi Arabia, 43, 56, 125, 183
Iliff, William A. B., 144

Imperial Defense Conference of 1937, 9, 11
India, xviii, 9, 11, 14, 24, 123-125
Indian Ocean, 15, 59
inflation, 29, 109, 140 ff., 198-199
Iran, xiii, xviii, 4, 14-15, 17, 21-23, 25-27, 56, 60, 63, 67, 107, 115-116, 121, 125-127, 142, 150, 156, 167, 173, 175, 199, 203
Iran, United States Military Mission to, 63
Iraq, xiii, xvii, 2-4, 6, 14-17, 21, 23, 25-27, 30, 63, 81, 107, 121, 125, 131, 150, 152, 173, 175, 189, 197, 214
Italy, 127
Italian Somaliland, xviii, 3-4

Jackson, Comdr. Robert G. A., ix-xv, xviii, 41-47, 64, 68, 74, 81-83, 153-157, 161
Jews, x-xi, 24, 26, 77, 107, 198-199
Joint Anglo-Egyptian Supplies Committee, 115
Jones, Jesse, 187
Jordan (see Transjordan)

Kahn, R. F., 144, 149, 200
Keen, Dr. Bernard A., 156
Kenya, 124
Keown-Boyd, Sir Alexander, 36, 40-41, 43
Keynes, Lord, 200
Khorramshahr, 22, 130, 137
Kifer, Russell S., 64
Killearn, Lord (see Sir Miles Lampson)
Kirk, Alexander, 52, 54, 64
Kut-al-Imara, 11-12
Kuwait, 127

Lampson, Sir Miles (Lord Killearn), 33-34

Landis, James M., 4, 65-67, 78-79, 152, 155-157, 161, 164, 186-187
League of Arab States, x, 7, 139, 163, 167, 200-201
Leahy, Adm. William D., 164
Lean, O. B., 124
Lebanon, xiii, xvii, 4, 21-23, 27, 29, 40, 60, 76-77, 117, 121-122, 124-127, 142, 145, 150, 152, 165-166, 190, 215-216
Leduc, Gaston, 198
lend-lease, 49, 53, 56-57, 59, 62-63, 66, 71, 73-76, 95, 112, 131, 145, 164, 193, 199, 203
Lend-Lease Act of 1941, 56-57, 62
Lend-Lease Administration, Office of, 52, 60
Levant Service Command, 60
Libya, 15, 25-26, 37, 125, 150, 176
Lindsell, Gen. Sir Wilfred, 81
Litani River, xiii
Lloyd, E. M. H., 115-118, 126-127, 144, 149, 156
locusts, xiii, 21, 25, 76, 123-125
Lyttleton, Capt. Oliver, 3, 38-39, 41-42, 44-45, 82-83

Macduffie, Marshall, xviii, 57, 64, 69, 84, 111, 156
Magnes, Judah L., 7
malaria, 25
Malta, 3-4, 33
manpower, 21, 23-24
Maria Theresa Thalers, 199
Massaua, 22, 59
Maxwell, Maj. Gen. Russell L., 52-54, 63-64
Messagero, Il (Rome), 48
"Middle East," defined, xvii-xviii, 2
Middle East Anti-Locust Unit, 40, 100, 124
Middle East Economic Advisory Committee, 40

Middle East Financial Conference, 140 ff.

Middle East Intelligence Centre, 40

Middle East Medical Advisory Committee (M.E.M.A.C.), 136-137

Middle East Provisions Office, 37-39, 41, 49, 180

Middle East Service Command, 60

Middle East Supply Centre, established, 36; dissolved, 163

Middle East Agricultural Development Conference (1944), 79, 151, 154-155

Middle East Relief and Refugee Administration (MERRA), 40, 155

Middle East Supplies Committee, 70, 73, 88

Middle East War Council, 39, 43, 64, 140

Millspaugh, Dr. Arthur C., 60

minorities, discrimination against, 24

mobilization, in India, 9; in Turkey, 24; in the U.K., 9-11; in the U.S., 80

Moffat, Douglas M., 64, 69

Montgomery, Gen. Sir Bernard Law, 8, 60

Morocco, 155

Mouvement interne du Ravitaillement (M.I.R.A.), 121

Moyne, Lord, 198

Murray, Dr. Keith A. H. (Lord Murray), xiii, xvii, 115, 156-157

Murray, Wallace, 202

Murphy, Robert D., 4

Nahhas, Mustafa al-, Pasha, 27

National Bank of Egypt, 12

National Bank of Iran (Bank Melli), 198

nationalism, Arab, 2, 28, 75

"navycert," 20

Near East Animal Health Institute, xiii

Netherlands, The, 127

neutralism, 25

Neutrality Act of 1939, 62

Ninth Air Force, 54

Nicholson, E. Max, 34-36, 81, 88, 156

North Africa, U.S. Military Mission to, 52, 63

North African Economic Board, 4, 174

Nuri al-Said, 6

Office des Céréales Panifiables (O.C.P.), 121-122

oil, Middle East supplies, 14, 22, 114, 128, 133-134; U.S. interests, 68, 165-166

Owen Falls, xviii

Parliament, 11, 31

Palestine, xvii, 3-4, 7, 12, 18, 21-22, 26, 28, 33, 49, 76-77, 106-107, 117-118, 120-121, 124-127, 149-150, 152, 167, 190, 197, 199, 214-215

Palestine War Supply Board, 12, 91-92

Pearl Harbor, 49, 53

Persia (see Iran)

Persia and Iraq Command (Paiforce), 63

Persian Corridor, 59, 109, 130

Persian Gulf, xiv, xvii, 15, 25, 123-124

Persian Gulf Service Command (U.S.), 60, 63, 81

Pétain, Marshal Henri Philippe, 12

Political and Economic Planning Committee, 34

Princess Margarethe, S.S., 97

prisoners of war, 19

railroads, in Egypt, 27, 34, 114; in Iran, 127

Rajputana Desert, 123
Rashid Ali al-Kaylani, 26, 48, 189
Red Sea, xiv, 15-16, 173
Riddleberger, James W., 188
Rommel, Gen. Erwin, 24, 37, 48, 63, 109, 116
Roosevelt, Franklin D., 62, 78, 183, 186, 202
Rountree, William A., 57, 64
reverse lend-lease, 74, 193
Royal Air Force (R.A.F.), 81, 108, 125, 137
Royal Navy, 20, 81

Salter, Sir Arthur, 35
Saudi Arabia, 4, 6, 22, 26, 43, 56, 60, 66, 125-126, 165-166, 199, 203, 215
Saunders, Dero A., 67
Sayegh, Fayez, 152
Schwarzkopf, Col. H. Norman, 60
Senn pest (*Eurygaster integriceps* Puton), 21, 25, 119, 174-175
Seroussi, N., 103 ff.
shipping controls, 20, 34, 51-53, 70-72, 75-77, 87-88, 182
Short, Livingston L., 66
silver bullion, 199
Skilbeck, Dr. Dunstan, xiii
Somervell, Gen. Brehon B., 81
Spears, Maj. Gen. Sir Edward, 190
Spears Mission (see British Military Mission in the Levant)
Stalingrad, 8
Stettinius, Edward R., Jr., 203
Stimson, Henry L., 65, 69
submarines, 10, 13, 15, 53, 75, 153
Sudan, the, xvii, xviii, 3-4, 28, 76, 103, 120-121, 124-125, 149-150, 215
Suez Canal, 14, 16-17, 166-167
Swinton, Lord, 4
Syria, xvii, 2, 4, 21-23, 27, 29, 40, 46, 60, 77, 105, 117-118, 121-122, 124-125, 145, 150, 152, 165-166, 190, 215-216

Thibodeaux, Ben, 57, 64
tires, 18, 61, 127-128, 131-132
Tobruk, 55, 116
trade regulations, 30, 57, 102, 197
Trans-Iranian Railway, 22
Transjordan, xvii, 3-4, 26, 28, 151-152, 214-215
transportation, 127-135, 196-197
Tripolitania, xvii, 4, 124, 181, 213
Truman Committee, 60, 191, 203
Truman, Harry S, 166
Tunis, 60
Turkey, xviii, 2, 4, 16-17, 22-25, 33, 40, 58, 106-107, 116-118, 125, 150, 170, 185

United Kingdom Commercial Corporation (U.K.C.C.), 34, 40, 58, 106-107, 116-118, 125, 150, 170, 185
United Kingdom, Board of Trade, 48, 88; Colonial Office, 88, 98, 180; Foreign Office, 58, 88, 180; India Office, 88; Ministry of Economic Warfare, 32, 88; Ministry of Food, 32, 48, 88, 99, 117; Ministry of Shipping, 32, 34-35, 38; Ministry of Supply, 48, 88; Ministry of War Transport, 38, 40, 42, 48, 51-52, 75, 82, 88, 93, 98-99; Supply Section for the Middle East (S.S.M.E.), 88-89; Treasury, 88; War Office, 88, 117
United Nations, xii, xvii, 2, 44, 79, 163-164, 167
United Nations Conference on Food and Agriculture, 154
United Nations Development Programme, xiii-xiv
United Nations Relief and Reconstruction Agency (UNRRA), xi, 44, 127, 155
United Nations Economic and Social Office in Beirut (U.N.E.S.O.B.), xii-xiii

United States Commercial Corporation (U.S.C.C.), 111, 195
United States Armed Forces in the Middle East (U.S.A.F.I.M.E.), 63
United States, Board of Economic Warfare, 57; Board of War Communications, 60; Bureau of the Budget, 60; Department of Agriculture, 57, 60, 95; Department of State, xv, 51, 57, 67, 71, 73, 166; Mission for Economic Affairs, 88; Typhus Commission, 137; War Food Administration, 60, 71, 95; War Production Board, 71, 95-96; War Shipping Administration, 60, 71, 95-96, 99
Union of Soviet Socialist Republics (U.S.S.R.), xiv, 3, 12, 14, 125-126, 160
Uvarov, Dr. B. P., 123-125

varlık vergisi, 24
Vulcan Foundries, 107

vehicles, 197

Wadsworth, George, 166-167
Wafd Party, 27
Ward, Barbara, 5
Wavell, Gen. Sir Archibald, 2, 14, 19, 32-34, 37-38, 161, 178
West African Supply Centre, 169
Wheeler, Gen. Raymond A., 63
Willkie, Wendell, 78
Winant, Frederick G., 51-55, 57, 59, 61, 64-65, 68-69, 71, 73, 83, 156
Winterton, Earl, 11, 31
Woodbridge, George, xviii, 66, 156
Worthington, Dr. E. Barton, xiii, 156
World War I, 2, 8, 11, 18, 35, 139
Wright, Sir Norman, xiii

Yemen, 3-4
Yugoslavia, 39, 117

Zhukov, Marshal Georgi K., 8